BANKS AND BANKING DEVELOPMENTS

COMMUNITY BANKS AND CREDIT UNIONS

EFFECT OF REGULATIONS AND COMPLIANCE BURDENS

BANKS AND BANKING DEVELOPMENTS

Additional books and e-books in this series can be found
on Nova's website under the Series tab.

BANKS AND BANKING DEVELOPMENTS

COMMUNITY BANKS AND CREDIT UNIONS

EFFECT OF REGULATIONS AND COMPLIANCE BURDENS

RICHARD L. MIZELLE
EDITOR

Copyright © 2019 by Nova Science Publishers, Inc.

All rights reserved. No part of this book may be reproduced, stored in a retrieval system or transmitted in any form or by any means: electronic, electrostatic, magnetic, tape, mechanical photocopying, recording or otherwise without the written permission of the Publisher.

We have partnered with Copyright Clearance Center to make it easy for you to obtain permissions to reuse content from this publication. Simply navigate to this publication's page on Nova's website and locate the "Get Permission" button below the title description. This button is linked directly to the title's permission page on copyright.com. Alternatively, you can visit copyright.com and search by title, ISBN, or ISSN.

For further questions about using the service on copyright.com, please contact:
Copyright Clearance Center
Phone: +1-(978) 750-8400　　　Fax: +1-(978) 750-4470　　　E-mail: info@copyright.com.

NOTICE TO THE READER

The Publisher has taken reasonable care in the preparation of this book, but makes no expressed or implied warranty of any kind and assumes no responsibility for any errors or omissions. No liability is assumed for incidental or consequential damages in connection with or arising out of information contained in this book. The Publisher shall not be liable for any special, consequential, or exemplary damages resulting, in whole or in part, from the readers' use of, or reliance upon, this material. Any parts of this book based on government reports are so indicated and copyright is claimed for those parts to the extent applicable to compilations of such works.

Independent verification should be sought for any data, advice or recommendations contained in this book. In addition, no responsibility is assumed by the Publisher for any injury and/or damage to persons or property arising from any methods, products, instructions, ideas or otherwise contained in this publication.

This publication is designed to provide accurate and authoritative information with regard to the subject matter covered herein. It is sold with the clear understanding that the Publisher is not engaged in rendering legal or any other professional services. If legal or any other expert assistance is required, the services of a competent person should be sought. FROM A DECLARATION OF PARTICIPANTS JOINTLY ADOPTED BY A COMMITTEE OF THE AMERICAN BAR ASSOCIATION AND A COMMITTEE OF PUBLISHERS.

Additional color graphics may be available in the e-book version of this book.

Library of Congress Cataloging-in-Publication Data

ISBN: 978-1-53616-066-6

Published by Nova Science Publishers, Inc. † New York

CONTENTS

Preface		vii
Chapter 1	Community Banks: Effect of Regulations on Small Business Lending and Institutions Appears Modest, but Lending Data Could Be Improved *United States Government Accountability Office*	1
Chapter 2	Community Banks and Credit Unions: Regulators Could Take Additional Steps to Address Compliance Burdens *United States Government Accountability Office*	177
Index		257
Related Nova Publications		265

PREFACE

Community banks—generally small and locally focused institutions—are important sources of credit to small businesses. Since the 2007–2009 financial crisis, regulators have made significant changes to the regulatory environment. Chapter 1 examines the data regulators use to measure small business lending, as well as the extent of any regulatory effects on the amount of community banks' small business lending and their lending processes, changes in bank populations, and financial performance.

Chapter 2 examines (1) the regulations community banks and credit unions viewed as most burdensome and why, and (2) efforts by depository institution regulators to reduce any regulatory burden. GAO analyzed regulations and interviewed more than 60 community banks and credit unions (selected based on asset size and financial activities), regulators, and industry associations and consumer groups.

Chapter 1 - Community banks—generally small and locally focused institutions—are important sources of credit to small businesses. Since the 2007–2009 financial crisis, regulators have made significant changes to the regulatory environment. While intended to increase institution soundness and better protect consumers, regulations and supervision can also have effects that Congress or regulators may not have intended. In particular, questions arose as to whether regulatory changes reduced community banks' ability to make small business loans. GAO was asked to assess the effect of regulatory changes since 2010 on community banks and small business lending. GAO examined the data regulators use to measure small business lending, as well as the extent of any regulatory effects on the amount of community banks' small business lending and their lending processes, changes in bank populations, and financial performance. GAO analyzed community bank lending and financial data from 2001 through 2017, built econometric models using these and other data, and surveyed a nationally representative sample of over 450 community banks. GAO also interviewed staff from community banks (selected to ensure a range of sizes and geographic regions), small business advisers, banking and consumer advocacy groups, and financial regulators.

Chapter 2 - In recent decades, many new regulations intended to strengthen financial soundness, improve consumer protections, and aid anti-money laundering efforts were implemented for financial institutions. Smaller community banks and credit unions must comply with some of the regulations, but compliance can be more challenging and costly for these institutions. GAO examined (1) the regulations community banks and credit unions viewed as most burdensome and why, and (2) efforts by depository institution regulators to reduce any regulatory burden. GAO analyzed regulations and interviewed more than 60 community banks and credit unions (selected based on asset size and financial activities), regulators, and industry associations and consumer groups. GAO also analyzed letters and transcripts commenting on regulatory burden that regulators prepared responding to the comments.

In: Community Banks and Credit Unions ISBN: 978-1-53616-066-6
Editor: Richard L. Mizelle © 2019 Nova Science Publishers, Inc.

Chapter 1

COMMUNITY BANKS: EFFECT OF REGULATIONS ON SMALL BUSINESS LENDING AND INSTITUTIONS APPEARS MODEST, BUT LENDING DATA COULD BE IMPROVED[*]

United States Government Accountability Office

ABBREVIATIONS

Federal Reserve	Board of Governors of the Federal Reserve System
BCFP	Bureau of Consumer Financial Protection
Call Report	Consolidated Reports of Condition and Income

---

[*] This is an edited, reformatted and augmented version of United States Government Accountability Office; Report to the Chairman, Committee on Small Business, House of Representatives, Publication No. GAO-18-312, dated August 2018.

Dodd-Frank Act	Dodd-Frank Wall Street Reform and Consumer Protection Act
FDIC	Federal Deposit Insurance Corporation
FDIC Improvement Act	Federal Deposit Insurance Corporation Improvement Act of 1991
FinCEN	Financial Crimes Enforcement Network
MSA	metropolitan statistical area
NCUA	National Credit Union Administration
OCC	Office of the Comptroller of the Currency
SBA	Small Business Administration

WHY GAO DID THIS STUDY

Community banks—generally small and locally focused institutions—are important sources of credit to small businesses. Since the 2007–2009 financial crisis, regulators have made significant changes to the regulatory environment. While intended to increase institution soundness and better protect consumers, regulations and supervision can also have effects that Congress or regulators may not have intended. In particular, questions arose as to whether regulatory changes reduced community banks' ability to make small business loans.

GAO was asked to assess the effect of regulatory changes since 2010 on community banks and small business lending. GAO examined the data regulators use to measure small business lending, as well as the extent of any regulatory effects on the amount of community banks' small business lending and their lending processes, changes in bank populations, and financial performance. GAO analyzed community bank lending and financial data from 2001 through 2017, built econometric models using these and other data, and surveyed a nationally representative sample of over 450 community banks. GAO also interviewed staff from community banks (selected to ensure a range of sizes and geographic regions), small business advisers, banking and consumer advocacy groups, and financial regulators.

WHAT GAO RECOMMENDS

GAO makes three recommendations to banking regulators to reevaluate and modify, as needed, the data they collect to measure small business lending. They agreed to the recommendations.

WHAT GAO FOUND

The data that banks report to regulators have characteristics that make determining how community banks' small business lending changed since 2010 difficult. However, GAO's analysis found that the regulatory environment likely had a generally modest effect on various aspects of community banks and their small business lending.

Regulators Data on Small Business Lending

The data community banks report to regulators do not accurately capture lending to small businesses because the data exclude some loans to small businesses. Specifically, the definition of small business loans used for banks' reporting excludes loans greater than $1 million and has not been adjusted for inflation since 1992. In addition, the data capture loans by their size rather than the size of the borrowing entity, and therefore could include small loans to large businesses. These limitations hamper regulators' and policymakers' ability to assess actual changes in banks' small business lending, including any effect of regulation.

Amount of Lending

GAO's analysis used alternative measures of small business lending and found that community banks' lending likely declined following the financial crisis but then increased from 2013 through 2017. After adjusting regulators' data to account for community bank mergers and other exits, remaining banks' small business lending increased by 5 percent from 2013 through 2017, and total business lending by all community banks grew to exceed 2010 levels. GAO's econometric models also found that community banks' small business lending since 2010 can be explained largely by macroeconomic, local market, and bank characteristics, and that the potential effect of regulatory changes was likely modest.

Lending Processes

Based on our nationally representative survey of community banks, GAO estimates that most community banks made changes to their small business lending processes since 2010. Most banks cited the regulatory environment as the primary reason for these changes, which included seeking more documentation from borrowers and taking longer to make loans. Representatives of entities that assist small businesses were mixed on whether these changes affected small businesses' ability to obtain loans.

Number of Community Banks

From 2010 through 2017, the population of community banks decreased by about 24 percent, largely due to mergers among community banks and a decline in the rate of new bank formations. However, GAO's econometric model found that macroeconomic, local market, and bank characteristics explained the majority of these trends, but changes in the regulatory environment and other factors may have also played a small role.

Community Bank Financial Performance

Although many institutions reported increasing or reallocating staff and other resources to assist with regulatory compliance since 2010, GAO's analysis suggests that the effect of these changes on profitability and customer service were likely modest. As regulatory changes do not occur in isolation and their cumulative effect cannot be easily quantified, these results should be interpreted with caution.

RECOMMENDATIONS FOR EXECUTIVE ACTION

We are making a total of three recommendations, one each to the Federal Reserve, FDIC, and OCC.

- The Chairman of the Board of Governors of the Federal Reserve System should collaborate with FDIC and OCC to reevaluate, and modify as needed, the requirements for the data banks report in the Consolidated Reports of Condition and Incomes to better reflect lending to small businesses. (Recommendation 1)
- The Chairman of the Federal Deposit Insurance Corporation should collaborate with the Federal Reserve and OCC to reevaluate, and modify as needed, the requirements for the data banks report in the Consolidated Reports of Condition and Incomes to better reflect lending to small businesses. (Recommendation 2)
- The Comptroller of the Currency should collaborate with the Federal Reserve and FDIC to reevaluate, and modify as needed, the requirements for the data banks report in the Consolidated Reports of Condition and Incomes to better reflect lending to small businesses. (Recommendation 3)

INTRODUCTION

August 6, 2018

Dear Mr. Chairman:
Financial regulators have implemented many new regulations in the aftermath of the 2007–2009 financial crisis. The Dodd-Frank Wall Street

Reform and Consumer Protection Act (Dodd-Frank Act) of 2010 included numerous reforms to strengthen practices and oversight of financial institutions.[1] Although community banks and credit unions were exempt from several provisions of this act, they have had to respond to additional regulatory requirements as a result of it and other regulatory efforts. These institutions have historically played an important role in serving their local customers, including providing credit to small businesses. Because small businesses are important to the economic well-being of the United States, questions have been raised about the effect of regulations on their ability to access credit from smaller depository institutions. According to Census Bureau data, businesses with less than 500 employees accounted for about 48 percent of U.S. total employment in 2015. A 2017 Small Business Administration (SBA) report indicated that small businesses annually contribute almost 40 percent of the U.S. private nonfarm output, but noted that these businesses typically faced challenges accessing credit, a key element of small business survival and growth.[2]

You asked us to examine the effects of changes in the regulatory environment on community banks and credit unions and their ability to meet the needs of small businesses. Changes in the regulatory environment encompass changes to specific laws and regulations as well as changes in how existing requirements are implemented and enforced. This chapter examines, for the period 2010 through 2017, the effect of the regulatory environment on community banks and credit unions, including (1) the data regulators use to measure the volume of small business lending and how and why small business lending volumes changed, (2) how and why small business lending processes changed among these institutions, and (3) how and why the number of institutions and their financial performance changed, as well as (4) actions regulators took to identify and mitigate the effects of changes in the regulatory environment on these institutions and their small business customers.[3] In response to your request, we also provided you with a report in February 2018 that addressed which

---

[1] Pub. L. No. 111-203, 124 Stat. 1376 (2010).
[2] Small Business Administration, Office of Advocacy, *Small Business Lending in the United States, 2014-2015* (Washington, D.C.: June 2017).
[3] Throughout this report, data we report for 2017 are as of June 2017 unless otherwise noted.

regulations institutions viewed as most burdensome and what actions financial regulators had been taking to reduce this burden.[4]

To identify how and why community banks' and credit unions' small business lending, number of institutions, and financial performance changed, we took the following steps:

- Analyzing available data. We analyzed bank and credit union regulatory data on the level of small business lending; mergers, failures, and new institution formation; and the market shares, resource costs, profitability, and operational efficiency of these institutions from 2001 through 2017.[5] Because of limitations with regulators' data, we also used two alternative measures—(1) business loans of $1 million or less made by survivor community banks (that is, community banks that did not become or merge with a large bank, voluntarily exit the market, or fail during the period we examined) and (2) community banks' total business loans—as proxy measures of small business lending. We believe that these measures, identified through our internal analyses and our conversations with bank regulators, were suitable as alternative measures of small business lending.

---

[4] GAO, *Community Banks and Credit Unions: Regulators Could Take Additional Steps to Address Compliance Burdens*, GAO-18-213 (Washington, D.C.: Feb. 13, 2018).

[5] In this report, we define community banks using FDIC's definition, which takes into account institutions' assets, foreign interests, specializations, and geographic characteristics. Community banks include banks with up to $39.5 billion in assets in 2017. We considered all banks that were not community banks to be large banks. In addition, our analysis excluded the largest credit unions with total assets above an annual threshold (equal to $201 million in 2001 and $994 million in 2017). The remaining credit unions included in our population represented approximately 95 percent of all credit unions as of June 2017. For purposes of our review, all loans for business activities made by credit unions are considered small business loans. NCUA terms these loans "member business loans" and they include any loan, line of credit, or letter of credit where the proceeds will be used for a commercial, industrial, agricultural, or professional purpose and the net balance is $50,000 or greater. Data we report on banks and credit unions are as of June 2017 and all dollar figures in the report are in 2016 dollars. Finally, excepting some trends reported for business loans of $1 million or less, we analyzed community bank and credit union data as reported for each period without further adjustments for mergers, consolidations, or other changes in the community bank or credit union population that may occur from period to period.

- Econometric modeling. We developed econometric models to better understand how many of the changes in community bank trends (such as small business lending, mergers, and new bank formations) could potentially be attributable to changes in the regulatory environment since 2010. Because measuring the cumulative effect of changes in the regulatory environment is difficult, we used a two-stage approach that did not involve estimating regulatory effects directly. First, we developed models that used data on macroeconomic, local market, and bank characteristics (factors represented by variables we could measure) from 2003 through 2009 to forecast community bank trends from 2010 through 2016. Second, by comparing the observed trends that actually occurred during the period to the trends forecasted by the models, we drew conclusions about the influence of "other factors," which could include the influence of changes in the regulatory environment since 2010, changes in demand for small business loans, technological advancements, and incentives for banks to achieve economies of scale, among other things. However, because we cannot distinguish the components of the "other factors" category from one another, we cannot know with certainty the effect of changes in the regulatory environment on community bank trends.
- Surveying community banks and credit unions. We surveyed generalizable samples of more than 450 community banks and 450 credit unions (selected to represent urban and rural areas, geographic regions, and a range of size categories) to identify why they may have made changes to their operations from January 2010 through August 2017.[6]
- Interviewing key stakeholders. We interviewed 18 banks and credit unions, selected to represent a range of asset sizes and geographic

---

[6] We administered our surveys from July 10, 2017 through August 25, 2017 (for community banks) and from July 17, 2017 through August 25, 2017 (for credit unions). In our surveys, we asked community bank and credit union chief executive officers to consider changes to their lending and management decisions since January 2010. In this report, we refer to the period of our survey as covering January 2010 through August 2017.

regions; consumer groups and financial services advocacy groups chosen because of their familiarity with community banks and credit unions and changes in the regulatory environment; and entities that advocate on business issues or that provide advice to businesses on lending issues.

To determine how regulators identified the effects of regulatory changes, we interviewed staff from the Board of Governors of the Federal Reserve System (Federal Reserve), the Bureau of Consumer Financial Protection (BCFP), the Federal Deposit Insurance Corporation (FDIC), the National Credit Union Administration (NCUA), and the Office of the Comptroller of the Currency (OCC).[7] We also analyzed studies by these entities and other researchers and academics on trends in banking and lending. In addition, we interviewed staff from SBA. Appendix I provides more detail on our scope and methodology, and appendix II provides the structure and specifications of the econometric modeling and the data we used as inputs.

We conducted this performance audit from November 2016 to August 2018 in accordance with generally accepted government auditing standards. Those standards require that we plan and perform the audit to obtain sufficient, appropriate evidence to provide a reasonable basis for our findings and conclusions based on our audit objectives. We believe that the evidence obtained provides a reasonable basis for our findings and conclusions based on our audit objectives.

BACKGROUND

Community banks are generally smaller banks that provide relationship banking services to local communities and have management and board members who reside in the communities they serve. Regulators

---

[7] BCFP has been commonly known as the Consumer Financial Protection Bureau or CFPB. According to BCFP officials, the agency is discontinuing use of CFPB and now uses the agency's statutory name.

and others have observed that community banks tend to differ from larger banks in their relationships with customers. Large banks are more likely to engage in transactional banking, which focuses on highly standardized products that require little human input and are underwritten using statistical information. In contrast, community banks are more likely to engage in what is known as relationship banking, in which banks consider not only data and statistics but also nonquantifiable information acquired primarily by working with the banking customer over time. Using this banking model, community banks may be able to extend credit to customers, such as small business owners, who might not be considered for a loan from a larger bank that engages in transactional banking.

Small business lending is a significant activity by community banks. As of June 2017, community banks had over $292 billion outstanding in business loans with original principal balances under $1 million (which is how small business loans are defined in regulatory reports), which represented about 19 percent of these institutions' total lending. In that same month, large banks held about $390 billion outstanding in business loans with original principal balances under $1 million, representing 5 percent of their total lending.

Credit unions are nonprofit, member-owned institutions that take deposits and make loans. Unlike banks, credit unions are subject to limits on their membership because members must share a "common bond"—for example, working for the same employer or living in the same community. In addition to providing consumer products to their members, credit unions are also allowed to make loans for business activities subject to certain restrictions. These "member business loans" are defined as a loan, line of credit, or letter of credit that a credit union extends to a borrower for a commercial, industrial, agricultural, or professional purpose.[8]

---

[8] See 12 U.S.C. § 1757a(c)(1)(A); 12 C.F.R § 723.2. The statutory cap on outstanding member business loans does not apply in the case of an insured credit union that is chartered for the purpose of making, or that has a history of primarily making, member business loans to its members; that serves predominantly low-income members; or that is a community development financial institution as defined by the Community Development Banking and Financial Institutions Act of 1994. 12 U.S.C. § 1757a(b).

Regulators Overseeing Community Banks and Credit Unions

The regulator responsible for overseeing a community bank or credit union varies depending on how the institution has been chartered and whether it is federally insured (see Table 1). Federal depository institution regulators are responsible for ensuring the safety and soundness of the institutions they oversee, protecting federal deposit insurance funds, promoting stability in financial markets, and enforcing compliance with applicable consumer protection laws. All depository institutions that are covered by federal deposit insurance have a federal prudential regulator that oversees the safety and soundness of the institution and may issue regulations and take enforcement actions against institutions within its jurisdiction.

Other federal agencies also impose regulatory requirements on banks and credit unions. These include rules issued by BCFP, which was created by the Dodd-Frank Act and implements and, where applicable, enforces federal consumer financial laws.[9] BCFP has supervisory and enforcement authority for federal consumer financial laws for insured depository institutions with more than $10 billion in assets and their affiliates. The federal depository institution regulators— FDIC, the Federal Reserve, OCC, and NCUA—examine how federally insured institutions with $10 billion or less in assets comply with consumer protection requirements. Although community banks and credit unions with less than $10 billion in assets would not typically be subject to examinations by BCFP, they are generally required to comply with the rules related to consumer protection issued by this agency.

---

[9] The Dodd-Frank Act defines "Federal consumer financial law" in the Consumer Financial Protection Act of 2010 (Title X of the Dodd-Frank Act) and a number of other consumer laws and implementing regulations. See 12 U.S.C. § 5481(14). For example, federal consumer financial laws include the Equal Credit Opportunity Act, the Truth in Lending Act, the Fair Debt Collection Practices Act, and the Fair Credit Reporting Act. See 12 U.S.C. § 5481(12).

Table 1. Federal Depository Institution Regulators and Their Functions

Agency	Basic function
Board of Governors of the Federal Reserve System (Federal Reserve)	Supervises state-chartered banks that opt to be members of the Federal Reserve System, bank holding companies, savings and loan holding companies and the nondepository institution subsidiaries of those organizations, and nonbank financial companies designated for Federal Reserve supervision by the Financial Stability Oversight Council.
Federal Deposit Insurance Corporation (FDIC)	Insures the deposits of all banks and thrifts approved for federal deposit insurance; supervises insured state-chartered banks that are not members of the Federal Reserve System, as well as insured state savings associations and insured state-chartered branches of foreign banks; resolves all failed insured banks and thrifts; and may be appointed to resolve large bank holding companies and nonbank financial companies supervised by the Federal Reserve. Also, has backup supervisory responsibility for all federally insured depository institutions.
National Credit Union Administration (NCUA)	Charters and supervises federally chartered credit unions and insures deposits in federally chartered and the majority of state-chartered credit unions.
Office of the Comptroller of the Currency (OCC)	Charters and supervises national banks, federal savings associations, and federally chartered branches and agencies of foreign banks.

Source: GAO. # GAO-18-312.

In addition, the Financial Crimes Enforcement Network (FinCEN) issues regulations that financial institutions, including banks and credit unions, must follow. FinCEN is a component of the Department of the Treasury's Office of Terrorism and Financial Intelligence, and it supports government agencies by collecting, analyzing, and disseminating financial intelligence information to combat money laundering. It is responsible for administering the Bank Secrecy Act, which, with its implementing regulations, generally requires banks, credit unions, and other financial institutions, among others, to collect and retain various records of customer transactions, verify customers' identities in certain situations, maintain anti-money laundering programs, and report suspicious and large cash transactions.[10] FinCEN relies on financial regulators and other entities to conduct examinations of U.S. financial institutions across a variety of financial sectors to determine compliance with these regulations.

Impact of the 2007–2009 Financial Crisis

Assessing the effect of changes in the regulatory environment in the period following the 2007–2009 crisis is complicated by the severity of the crisis's economic impact on the United States. In a January 2013 report, we reviewed academic and other sources and found that the 2007–2009 financial crisis, like past financial crises, was associated with a steep decline in output and the most severe economic downturn since the Great Depression of the 1930s.[11] The U.S. economy entered a recession in December 2007 that lasted until June 2009, with U.S. real gross domestic product falling by nearly 5 percent and not regaining its pre-recession level until the third quarter of 2011. Some studies noted that the impacts of the crisis could persist beyond 2018 or be permanent.

The 2007–2009 crisis was also associated with large declines in employment, household wealth, and other economic indicators that could have affected the rate of new business formations and demand for small business loans. The monthly unemployment rate peaked at around 10 percent in October 2009 and remained above 8 percent for over 3 years, the longest such stretch since the Great Depression. Between 2005 and 2011, households collectively lost about $9.1 trillion (in constant 2011 dollars) in national home equity in part because of the decline in home prices. The Federal Reserve's Survey of Consumer Finances found that median household net worth fell by $49,100 per family, nearly 39 percent, from 2007 through 2010. Such dramatic declines in net worth, combined with an

---

[10] Pub. L. No. 91-508, tits. I and II, 84 Stat. 1114 (1970) (codified as amended at 12 U.S.C. §§ 1829b, 1951-1959; 18 U.S.C. §§ 1956-1957 and 1960; and 31 U.S.C. §§ 5311-5314 and 5316-5332). The Bank Secrecy Act is the commonly used term for the Currency and Foreign Transactions Reporting Act, its amendments, and the other statutes relating to the subject matter of that act. 31 C.F.R. § 1010.100(e).

[11] See GAO, *Financial Regulatory Reform: Financial Crisis Losses and Potential Impacts of the Dodd-Frank Act*, GAO-13-180 (Washington, D.C.: Jan. 16, 2013).

uncertain economic outlook and reduced job security, can cause consumers to reduce spending, and lower the financial health of businesses and their willingness to seek credit. Reduced consumption, all else being equal, further reduces aggregate demand and real gross domestic product. However, our 2013 report noted that analyzing the peak-to-trough changes in certain measures, such as home prices, can overstate the impacts associated with the crisis, as valuations before the crisis may have been inflated and unsustainable.[12]

Changes to Financial Regulations since 2010

In response to the 2007–2009 financial crisis, Congress passed the Dodd-Frank Act, which became law on July 21, 2010. The act included numerous reforms to strengthen oversight of financial services firms, including consolidating consumer protection responsibilities within BCFP, which the act created. The Dodd-Frank Act also directed or granted authority to federal financial regulatory agencies to issue hundreds of regulations to implement the act's reforms. Many of the act's provisions target the largest and most complex financial institutions, and regulators have noted that much of the act is not meant to apply to community banks or credit unions.

Although the Dodd-Frank Act exempts small institutions, such as community banks and credit unions, from several of its provisions and authorizes federal regulators to provide small institutions with relief from certain regulations, it also contains provisions that impose additional restrictions and compliance costs on these institutions. As we reported in 2012, federal regulators, state regulatory associations, and industry associations collectively identified provisions within 7 of the act's 16 titles that they expected to affect community banks and credit unions.[13]

---

[12] GAO-13-180.
[13] For example, see GAO, *Community Banks and Credit Unions: Impact of the Dodd-Frank Act Depends Largely on Future Rule Making*, GAO-12-881 (Washington, D.C.: Sept. 13, 2012).

In addition to regulations resulting from the Dodd-Frank Act, other regulations have created potential burdens for community banks. For example, depository institution regulators also revised the capital requirements applicable to banking organizations, including community banks. These requirements were to implement the Basel III framework, a comprehensive set of reforms to strengthen global capital and liquidity standards issued by an international body consisting of representatives of various countries' central banks and regulators. These new requirements significantly changed the risk-based capital standards for banks and bank holding companies and introduced new leverage and liquidity standards. As we reported in November 2014, officials interviewed from community banks did not anticipate any difficulties in meeting the new U.S. capital requirements but expected to incur additional compliance costs.[14]

Although a number of provisions may ultimately affect lending by smaller institutions, we noted in our 2012 report that officials from federal agencies, state regulatory associations, and industry associations identified only one provision in the Dodd-Frank Act that was directly related to small business lending.[15] This provision was section 1071 of the Dodd-Frank Act, which amended the Equal Credit Opportunity Act to require financial institutions to compile, maintain, and report information concerning credit applications made by women-owned, minority-owned, and small businesses in accordance with regulations issued by BCFP. The purpose of the provision was to facilitate the enforcement of fair lending laws and enable communities, governmental entities, and creditors to identify the business and community development needs and opportunities of women-owned, minority-owned, and small businesses. In May 2017, BCFP issued a request for information to seek public comments to inform its efforts to implement this additional reporting.[16]

However, some Dodd-Frank Act provisions have also likely resulted in reduced costs for community banks. For example, revisions to how deposit

---

[14] GAO, *Bank Capital Reforms: Initial Effects of Basel III on Capital, Credit, and International Competitiveness*, GAO-15-67 (Washington, D.C.: Nov. 20, 2014).
[15] GAO-12-881.
[16] See Request for Information Regarding Small Business Lending Market, 82 Fed. Reg. 22318 (May 15, 2017).

insurance premiums are calculated reduced premiums by 33 percent for banks with less than $10 billion in assets between the first and second quarters of 2011. Another change reduced the audit-related costs that some banks were incurring in complying with provisions of the Sarbanes-Oxley Act.

Potential Benefits of Financial Regulation

Financial regulations can also provide significant benefits. For example, a primary objective of banking regulations is to promote the safety and soundness of banks and the banking system.[17] Effective regulation and supervision can safeguard against future financial crises and provide an important source of confidence to the market about the general health and resiliency of the banking sector. Past banking-related crises have demonstrated the need for federal banking regulators to respond proactively to problems developing in the banking system. In February 2018, we reported that staff of federal regulators and consumer groups noted various benefits of regulations related to mortgage activities and requirements to report suspicious banking activities.[18] For example, they said that collecting data on a mortgage applicant's demographic characteristics (such as an applicant's race, ethnicity, and sex) has helped address discriminatory lending practices and are essential for the enforcement of fair lending laws and regulations.[19] Similarly, regulators have reported that requirements for institutions to report large cash deposits help ensure that the U.S. financial sector is not used to aid illicit

---

[17] GAO, *Bank Regulation: Lessons Learned and a Framework for Monitoring Emerging Risks and Regulatory Response*, GAO-15-365 (Washington, D.C.: June 25, 2015).

[18] GAO-18-213.

[19] Under the Home Mortgage Disclosure Act of 1975, depository institutions with more than $45 million in assets that do not meet regulatory exemptions must collect, record, and report data about their applicable mortgage lending activity. See 12 U.S.C. § 2803 and 12 C.F.R. 1003 supp.I.

activity, including the sale of illegal narcotics, terrorism, and human trafficking.[20]

MAJOR FINDINGS

Small Business Lending Data Have Substantial Limitations, but the Effect of the Regulatory Environment on Lending Volumes Appears Modest

Limitations in the data banks report to bank regulators make it difficult to determine how small business lending by community banks changed after 2010. However, alternative proxies that partially address these limitations suggest that such lending has increased since the financial crisis. In addition, our econometric analysis indicates that changes in the regulatory environment likely had a modest effect on community banks' small business lending volumes from 2010 through 2016.[21] Further, small business lending by credit unions, which accounts for a small share of total small business lending, increased considerably from 2010 through 2017.[22]

---

[20] The Currency and Foreign Transactions Reporting Act, commonly known as the Bank Secrecy Act, as amended by the Uniting and Strengthening America by Providing Appropriate Tools Required to Intercept and Obstruct Terrorism Act of 2001 (USA PATRIOT Act), establishes reporting, recordkeeping, and other anti-money laundering requirements for financial institutions, including a customer identification program and performance of customer due diligence or enhanced due diligence in certain situations, unless they are exempted by regulation. Pub. L. No. 91-508, tits. I and II, 84 Stat. 1114 (1970) (codified as amended at 12 U.S.C. §§ 1829b, 1951-1959; 18 U.S.C. §§ 1956-1957 and 1960; and 31 U.S.C. §§ 5311-5314 and 5316-5332); Pub. L. No. 107-506, § 352, 115 Stat. 272, 322 (codified at 31 U.S.C. § 5318(h)). Additionally, during examinations related to these requirements, regulators evaluate institutions' programs for identifying and reporting transactions that involve sanctioned countries and persons to ensure they comply with the economic sanctions administered and enforced by the Office of Foreign Assets Control.

[21] In this report, we define community banks using FDIC's definition, which takes into account institutions' assets, foreign interests, specializations, and geographic characteristics. Community banks include banks with up to $39.5 billion in assets in 2017.

[22] Our analysis considered only small and medium credit unions, which accounted for about 95 percent of all credit unions in June 2017. In this report, we define small and medium credit unions as credit unions with total assets less than a maximum threshold. The maximum threshold increases each year based on a compound annual growth rate and was $994 million in 2017. Credit unions make loans for business activities subject to certain

Measuring Small Business Lending Using Call Report Data Poses Challenges

The data banks report to bank regulators on their lending do not provide a fully accurate measure of loans to small businesses. Specifically, in Consolidated Reports of Condition and Income (Call Reports)—financial reports that banks provide to regulators—banks are required to report any loans they make to businesses with original principal balances of $1 million or less.[23] These data, which bank regulators use as a proxy to measure small business lending, appear to show that community bank lending to small businesses declined after the financial crisis. Specifically, community banks' total business loans with original principal balances of $1 million or less decreased by 16 percent from 2010 through 2017, from $347 billion in outstanding loans to $292 billion.

However, using business loans with original principal balances of $1 million or less is not an accurate measure of small business lending for two reasons:[24]

- The measure is based on loan size rather than size of the business obtaining the loan. As a result, a loan for more than $1 million obtained by a small company is not reported as a small business loan. In November 2017, FDIC presented preliminary results of a survey indicating that banks with less than $1 billion in total assets

---

restrictions. As defined by NCUA, business loans include any loan, line of credit, or letter of credit where the proceeds will be used for a commercial, industrial, agricultural, or professional purpose and the net balance is $50,000 or greater. For the purpose of our review, all loans for business activities made by credit unions are considered small business loans. Because loans less than $50,000 are not included in this definition of business loans, this approach likely underestimates small business lending by credit unions. Data we report for 2017 are as of June 2017.

[23] Call Reports are quarterly financial reports prepared by insured depository institutions for federal banking regulators. The reports include detailed information on the operating condition of the institutions, such as income and asset levels. Regulators use the reports to gauge the individual and collective health of banks and thrifts. The Call Report data on small business lending we present here include farm loans of $500,000 or less and 2017 data are as of June 2017. For additional information about our methodology, see appendix I.

[24] The Call Report data on business loans, including small business loans, do not include loans made to borrowers using residential property as collateral. According to FDIC officials, by not including these loans, the Call Report data may be undercounting business lending.

(a population that includes most community banks) made about $93 million in commercial and industrial loans— one type of business loan included in the Call Report data on small business lending—as of December 31, 2015, that were not counted under this measure because the loans to small businesses exceeded the $1 million threshold.[25] In addition, banks would also report as part of this measure loans obtained by a large company for less than $1 million, which further distorts its use as a measure of lending to small businesses.

- Inflation distorts the accuracy of the measure over time. The loan thresholds for Call Report data on small business lending —$1 million for businesses and $500,000 for loans to farms— are not adjusted for inflation and have not changed since 1992. As a result, the number of loans that fall under these thresholds decreases over time due to inflation alone, which averaged about 2 percent annually from 1992 through 2017.[26] Therefore, the data this measure captures have likely significantly underestimated banks' lending to small businesses since 1992. As shown in Figure 1, if the measure's $1 million threshold had been indexed to inflation, banks would have reported loans with original principal balances under around $1.6 million as small business loans in 2017. A $1 million loan in 2017 was equivalent to a loan of about $625,000 in 1992 terms.

---

[25] Federal Deposit Insurance Corporation, Community Bank Advisory Committee, Preview: FDIC Small Business Lending Survey (Washington, D.C.: Nov. 1, 2017). According to FDIC officials, they anticipate issuing the final report in 2018. The Call Report data on small business lending include unsecured commercial and industrial and commercial real estate loans of $1 million or less and farm loans of $500,000 or less. The FDIC study focused mainly on the commercial and industrial portion of these data but also found that small business loans collaterized by residential property are also excluded from the Call Report data on small business lending. The findings of this study suggest that the measure used to report data on small business lending could result in an undercount of loans to small businesses. However, these findings cannot be viewed as conclusive evidence of an undercount of small business lending because the study relied on one quarter of data and one type of loan. Nevertheless, it is indicative of inaccuracies that may emerge when using loan amount to proxy small business lending.

[26] In this report, we adjusted for inflation using the Bureau of Economic Analysis' Gross Domestic Product Implicit Price Deflator.

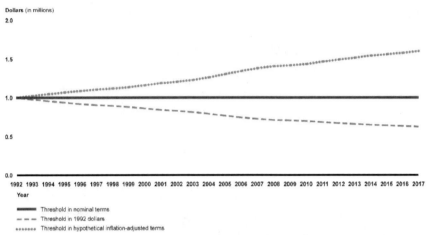

Source: GAO analysis of Bureau of Economic Analysis data. | GAO-18-312.

Notes: These lines represent how the $1 million small business loan threshold would have changed if it had been indexed to inflation when it was established in 1992 (dotted line) and what the $1 million small business loan threshold represents in 1992 terms because it was not indexed to inflation when it was established (dashed line). Data we report for 2017 are as of June 2017.

Figure 1. Effect of Inflation on Bank Regulators' $1 Million Threshold for Small Business Lending, 1992–2017.

Another factor affecting the use of these data for assessing community banks' lending to small businesses is that the population of these banks changes over time. Thus, the amount of lending captured by the data can decline as a result of banks exiting the population, rather than as a result of banks decreasing their lending. A bank exits the population of community banks when the bank:

- no longer meets the definition of a community bank (for example, by merging or growing to become a large bank),
- voluntarily exits (for example, by becoming a credit union), or

- fails without being acquired by another community bank.[27]

As a result, these exits can overstate the extent to which small business lending as captured in the Call Report data appear to decrease over time.

Alternative Measures Addressing Some Small Business Lending Data Limitations Suggest That Lending May Have Increased in Recent Years

To address some of the limitations of the Call Report data on small business lending, we examined two alternative measures of community bank small business lending. These alternative measures suggest that community banks' small business lending likely increased from 2013 through 2017 after decreasing from 2010 through 2012 following the financial crisis. Our first alternative measure adjusted the Call Report data to account for exits by banks leaving the population of community banks. To account for the effect of these departures, we identified as "survivor" community banks those community banks that existed or formed since 2001 and remained in existence through 2017, and we excluded banks that exited the population of community banks at any time from 2001 through 2017.[28]

---

[27] Failures are the closing of banks or credit unions by a federal or state regulator and generally occur when an institution is unable to meet its obligations to depositors and others. Mergers are generally a means by which banks or credit unions can expand their size and geographic reach by merging with or acquiring other institutions operating under separate ownership. Growth can cause community banks to become large banks (that is, banks that are not community banks), leading to exits from the population of community banks.

[28] Survivor community banks include community banks that merged with another community bank such that the resulting bank remained a community bank. Analyzing survivor community banks allowed us to focus on community banks by excluding institutions that later became large banks or credit unions or otherwise ceased operating as community banks. Because the number of community banks in existence declined over the period we analyzed, survivor community banks represented about 79 percent of the full community bank population in 2001, and their proportion of the full population increased each year until reaching 100 percent in June 2017.

Analyzing the lending by these survivor community banks allowed us to capture changes in bank lending levels rather than changes resulting from banks leaving the population of community banks.

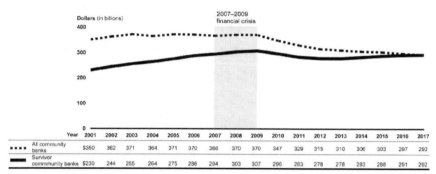

Source: GAO analysis of Federal Deposit Insurance Corporation (FDIC) data. | GAO-18-312.

Notes: We defined community banks using FDIC's definition, which takes into account institutions' assets, foreign interests, specializations, and geographic characteristics. Community banks include banks with up to $39.5 billion in assets in 2017. Survivor community banks (those that continued operating as community banks from 2001 through 2017) represented about 79 percent of the full community bank population in 2001, and their proportion of the full population increased each year until reaching 100 percent in 2017. All dollar amounts are in constant 2016 dollars, and data we report for 2017 are as of June 2017.

Figure 2. Volume of Community Banks' Outstanding Business Loans with Original Principal Balances of $1 Million or Less, 2001–2017, by Bank Population.

When we adjusted the Call Report data on small business lending to account for exits from the community bank population, we found that survivor community banks' volume of loans outstanding decreased by 6 percent from 2010 through 2012, but increased by 5 percent from 2013 through 2017 (see Figure 2).[29] This analysis suggests that exits explain some portion of the 16 percent decline shown by the Call Report data on small business lending from 2010 through 2017.

---

[29] Data we report for 2017 are as of June 2017.

Adjusting the Call Report data for exits from the community bank population does not address all the limitations of these data discussed above. Specifically, examining Call Report data for survivor community banks also does not capture small business loans larger than $1 million, and they may include loans under $1 million made to large businesses. In addition, this analysis does not overcome the limitation of the $1 million small business loan threshold not being adjusted for inflation. Finally, restricting the population of banks for analysis may also introduce some bias by excluding information on changes in small business lending by the institutions that exited.

A second alternative measure we used to try to overcome the limitations of the Call Report data on small business lending was to examine community banks' total loans to businesses, which banks also report to regulators and includes business loans of all sizes. Because data on total business lending includes loans of any size, inflation does not cause a growing proportion of small business loans to be excluded from the data over time. FDIC officials said they typically use the Call Report total business lending measure as a proxy measure for community banks' small business lending activity. FDIC officials noted that the preliminary results of their recent small business lending survey confirm that many community bank business loans are small business loans. According to this survey, 86 percent of banks with assets less than $250 million and 77 percent of banks with assets between $250 million and $1 billion said that "largely all" of their commercial and industrial lending is to small businesses.[30] However, measuring community banks' small business lending using data on these institutions' total business lending overestimates these institutions' small business lending by including loans to large businesses.

---

[30] Federal Deposit Insurance Corporation, Community Bank Advisory Committee, Preview: FDIC Small Business Lending Survey (Washington, D.C.: Nov. 1, 2017). According to FDIC, as of September 2017, approximately 98 percent of banks with assets less than $1 billion met FDIC's definition of a community bank.

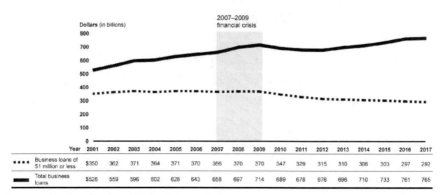

Source: GAO analysis of Federal Deposit Insurance Corporation (FDIC) data. | GAO-18-312.

Notes: We defined community banks using FDIC's definition, which takes into account institutions' assets, foreign interests, specializations, and geographic characteristics. Community banks include banks with up to $39.5 billion in assets in 2017. All dollar amounts are in constant 2016 dollars, and data we report for 2017 are as of June 2017.

Figure 3. Volume of Community Banks' Outstanding Business Loans with Original Principal Balances of $1 Million or Less and Total Business Loans, 2001–2017.

We found that community banks' total business lending increased from 2010 through 2017 (see Figure 3).[31] Specifically, we found that community banks' total business lending dipped slightly after the financial crisis, but exceeded precrisis levels by 2017 (similar to lending by survivor community banks, which also began to increase in the years following the financial crisis). Without accounting for exits from the community bank population, community banks' total business loans outstanding increased from about $689 billion 2010 to about $765 billion in 2017, or approximately 11 percent.[32] When we accounted for exits from the community bank population, the increase was even larger. Specifically,

---

[31] These figures include some small business loans guaranteed by SBA, which are made to small businesses as defined by SBA, may exceed $1 million, and increased significantly from 2010 through June 2017. According to SBA data, the amount of small business lending by banks guaranteed each year through SBA's 7(a) loan program—SBA's primary lending program—increased by 65 percent during this period—from about $18 billion worth of loans guaranteed in 2010 to about $24.5 billion worth of loans guaranteed in 2017. (These dollar amounts are in constant 2016 dollars).

[32] The 2010–2017 increase in total business lending was even greater for large banks, whose dollar amount of total business lending increased by 42 percent during this period.

survivor community banks' total business lending increased by about 36 percent, from $563 billion in outstanding loans in 2010 to $765 billion in 2017. These results again suggest that some portion of the decline shown by the Call Report data on small business lending for the full population of community banks from 2010 through 2017 is likely due to the limitations of that measure rather than actual changes in banks' lending activities.

Regulators Have Not Taken Steps to Address the Limitations in the Call Report Measure of Small Business Lending

As previously discussed, the data that banks report to regulators do not reflect the full range of their lending to small businesses because they are based on loan rather than firm size and have not been adjusted for inflation. The use of Call Report data on business loans with original principal balances of $1 million or less as a measure of small business lending was established as a result of the Federal Deposit Insurance Corporation Improvement Act of 1991 (FDIC Improvement Act). The act requires FDIC, the Federal Reserve, and OCC to collect information from insured depository institutions that is sufficient to assess the availability of credit to small businesses and small farms.[33]

FDIC officials said they recognize that the data they use for community banks' small business lending have some flaws, but they define small business loans as they do to minimize the reporting burden for banks. When establishing the reporting requirements in 1992, bank regulators considered categorizing loans as small business loans based on the total sales volume of borrowing businesses and farms. However, they did not adopt that definition after receiving a large number of comments that it would be burdensome to implement.[34] FDIC officials also said that banks would likely find continually adjusting the loan threshold in their reporting

---

[33] See Pub. L. No. 102-242, § 122, 105 Stat. 2236, 2251 (codified at 12 U.S.C. § 1817 note). Regulators collect data on "loans to small businesses and small farms" on the Call Reports.

[34] See Reporting of Information on Small Business and Small Farm Lending by Insured Banks, Thrifts, and U.S. Branches of Foreign Banks, 57 Fed. Reg. 54235 (Nov. 17, 1992).

systems for inflation to be difficult and potentially burdensome. In addition, Federal Reserve officials told us that bankers and other stakeholders often express concerns about the burden of collecting data on small business lending, noting that community banks often use basic systems and sometimes rely on paper record keeping.[35]

Officials from FDIC, the Federal Reserve, and OCC told us their agencies have not reevaluated the reporting requirements since they were established in 1992, except for mandated reviews in which bank regulators must determine whether each Call Report item should remain in place.[36] FDIC and OCC officials also said they were not aware of their agencies making or considering any formal proposals to alter the requirements, but officials from the Federal Reserve said they have proposed changing the definition so that it is based on the size of the borrowing firm. When bank regulators established the existing requirements for reporting on small business loans, they cited a 1989 survey that found a correlation between business size and loan size, but bank regulators told us they have not reexamined this correlation because they have no reason to believe it does not still hold true. Some evidence suggests that basing the reporting requirements for small business lending on firm size and adjusting them for inflation may not be as burdensome as bank regulators and others once thought. For example, a 2016 survey found that community banks already use a borrowing firm's total revenue as the top factor in defining small business loans.[37] In addition, technological changes since 1992 may facilitate

---

[35] In response to a 2016 request for comments on updates to the Call Reports, a small number of commentators (5 of the approximately 1100 respondents) stated that reporting data on business loans of $1 million or less was particularly burdensome. According to regulators, concerns about the potential burden from reporting small business lending activities were also raised during banker outreach meetings and as part of the Economic Growth and Regulatory Paperwork Reduction Act of 1996 reviews. (This act directs the Federal Reserve, FDIC, and OCC to review at least every 10 years all of their regulations and through public comments identify areas of the regulations that are outdated, unnecessary, or unduly burdensome. See 12 U.S.C. § 3311).

[36] Every 5 years, bank regulators must review the information they require banks to report in Call Reports. See 12 U.S.C. § 1817(a)(11)(a). Bank regulators must also reduce or eliminate any items they conclude are no longer necessary or appropriate. See 12 U.S.C. § 1817(a)(11)(b).

[37] Board of Governors of the Federal Reserve System and Conference of State Bank Supervisors, Community Banking in the 21st Century 2016 (St. Louis, Mo.: September 2016). The results are based on a web survey developed by Conference of State Bank Supervisors staff in concert with individuals from the Federal Reserve, academia, and Cornell University's

banks' ability to collect these data without creating additional undue burden on banks.

Because the reporting requirements for small business loans likely exclude a significant portion of loans to small businesses, bank regulators are hindered in their ability to assess the availability of credit to small businesses and small farms, as required by the FDIC Improvement Act. Moreover, the Federal Reserve recently began a new survey on small business lending because, officials told us, existing data are not sufficient for understanding and addressing related policy issues, which further underscores the limitations of available data.[38] Federal internal control standards also state that entities should obtain relevant data from reliable internal and external sources to achieve their objectives.[39] Without reporting requirements that better reflect banks' lending to small businesses, bank regulators and policymakers may be limited in their ability to assess the effects of regulation and other factors on the availability of credit to these firms.

Macroeconomic, Local Market, and Bank Characteristics Largely Explain Community Bank Small Business Lending Since 2010, but the Regulatory Environment Also May Have Played a Small Role

Our econometric analysis suggests that the effect of changes in the regulatory environment on small business lending, if any, was relatively small from 2010 through 2016. To examine influences on community banks' small business lending from 2010 through 2016, we developed

---

Survey Research Institute and distributed in April 2016 to community banks (defined as commercial banks and savings and loan associations with less than $10 billion in assets). In all, 557 community banks participated, down from 1,008 in 2014 and 974 in 2015. The sampling strategy and response rate are not reported, but a comparison to similar banks did not reveal notable differences along key characteristics such as asset size and geographic diversification.

[38] In February 2018, the Federal Reserve began collecting quarterly survey data on the availability and cost of small business commercial and industrial loans made to U.S. nonfarm small businesses (defined as nonfarm businesses in the United States with no more than $5 million in total annual revenues) through the Small Business Lending Survey (FR 2028D).

[39] GAO, *Standards for Internal Control in the Federal Government*, GAO-14-704G (Washington, D.C.: September 2014).

econometric models of each of our two alternative measures of small business lending—survivor community banks' business loans of $1 million or less and all community banks' total business lending. Because measuring the cumulative effect of changes in the regulatory environment is difficult, each model attempts to determine the extent to which macroeconomic, local market, and bank characteristics—factors we can measure—explained community banks' small business lending compared to all other factors:[40]

- Macroeconomic, local market, and bank characteristics. Macroeconomic conditions include growth in gross state product and interest rates. Local market demographics and competition include unemployment rates, population density and growth, changes in house prices, and the extent of market competition among all banks and credit unions. Bank characteristics include bank size, whether a bank is geographically diversified, the extent of performing and nonperforming loans, and the level of equity capital.
- Other factors. This category includes all factors that may have affected small business lending volumes other than those listed above. We did not include data for these factors directly in our model. These factors may include changes in the regulatory environment after 2010, changes in demand for small business loans, technological changes, and lending by nonbank competitors, among others.[41]

---

[40] Developing quantitative measures for changes in the regulatory environment is difficult because such changes involve not only changes in laws and regulations but also how they are implemented and enforced. In addition, regulatory changes can vary in their effect, meaning that the total number of new regulations that became effective in a given period could, for example, be a misleading way to measure the extent of change in the regulatory environment during that period.

[41] Lending by nonbank competitors includes, for example, lending by individuals or institutions, such as hedge funds, that primarily use online platforms to lend to consumers and small businesses. Because some of the variables we included in our model, especially those related to local market competition and bank characteristics, could be affected by changes in the regulatory environment, we conducted additional analysis of each of our models excluding these variables. These models had similar results.

To examine the cumulative effect of the regulatory environment on small business lending, we estimated each model using data on macroeconomic, local market, and bank characteristics from 2003 through 2009. We then used these results to forecast the small business lending trends that would have occurred from 2010 through 2016 given the macroeconomic, local market, and bank characteristics that prevailed during this later period.[42] We then compared the lending levels our model forecasted to those that actually occurred. To the extent these differed, a greater difference between actual and forecasted lending indicates a greater influence by the set of factors that includes the regulatory environment.[43]

Our models found that macroeconomic, local market, and bank characteristics explained the majority of community banks' outstanding small business lending from 2010 through 2016, leaving a relatively small portion of lending volumes that could potentially be explained by changes in the regulatory environment.[44] Because macroeconomic, local market, and bank characteristics forecasted small business lending trends that closely resembled the actual trends, we were able to conclude that the influence of other factors, such as changes in the regulatory environment after 2010 and changes in demand for small business loans, was likely relatively small. Because the extent to which any of these other factors

---

[42] Specifically, we extrapolated the 2003–2009 relationships between small business lending and macroeconomic, local market, and bank characteristics to the 2010–2016 period in order to develop our forecast. Because the period from 2003 through 2009 preceded post-2010 changes in the regulatory environment, using 2003–2009 data to construct our model allowed us to assess the effect of macroeconomic, local market, and bank characteristics independent of the influence of changes in the regulatory environment after 2010. Using the estimated coefficients from the regression model (including the constant term) and values for macroeconomic, local market, and bank characteristics from 2010 through 2016, we forecasted the effects of these factors absent the presence of any "other factors," including changes in the regulatory environment, after 2010.

[43] In addition, we compared the difference between the actual levels of lending and what our model predicted from 2003 through 2009. The relatively small differences between the actual and predicted lending indicates that our model was a reasonable fit for the data.

[44] Actual amounts of community bank small business lending were within the 95 percent confidence intervals for the forecasted lending amounts. This suggests that the net effect on community banks' small business lending from factors we included in our model (macroeconomic, local market, and bank characteristics) may not have fundamentally changed between the two periods we analyzed (2003 through 2009 and 2010 through 2016) and that the effect of other factors we did not include in our model were likely small from 2010 through 2016.

actually influenced lending levels is unknown, our analysis does not provide definitive conclusions about the effect of changes in the regulatory environment on small business lending. Rather, it provides reasonable information on the potential role of regulation (see app. II for a more complete discussion of our model's approach and limitations).

Specifically, as shown in Figure 4, we found the following:

- Survivor community banks' business loans of $1 million or less. Our model of survivor community banks' outstanding business loans with original principal balances of $1 million or less found that the actual volume of these loans was on average 2 percent less than forecasted from 2010 through 2016, based on the macroeconomic, local market, and bank characteristics in place during this period.[45] Although the difference between the forecasted and actual volume of business loans with original principal balances of $1 million or less these banks made was relatively small throughout the period, this difference peaked a few years after the financial crisis (our model forecasted that the volume of outstanding business loans with original principal balances of $1 million or less would be 11 percent higher in 2013 than it actually was) before returning to a difference of 3 percent or less in 2014.
- All community banks' total loans to businesses. Our model of community banks' total outstanding business loans found that the actual volume of these loans was on average 16 percent more than our model forecasted from 2010 through 2016 given the macroeconomic, local market, and bank characteristics that prevailed during that period. Specifically, actual lending levels consistently exceeded the levels our model forecasted each year during this period, with actual loan balances ranging from 6

---

[45] As noted previously, survivor community banks are those that formed prior to or since 2001 and remained in existence through 2017. By analyzing survivor community banks, we help ensure that data illustrate changes in lending levels rather than changes in the population of community banks.

percent to 23 percent higher than forecasted from 2010 through 2016.

Although our models found that the influence of factors other than macroeconomic, local market, and bank characteristics on small business lending was small, the direction of this influence (i.e., the extent to which these other factors contributed to actual lending that was higher or lower than what our models forecasted) varied.[46]

Specifically, our model of survivor community banks' business loans of $1 million or less found that the actual volume of outstanding lending was lower in some years than our model forecasted. This difference in small business lending volumes was attributable to factors we did not include directly in our model, which may include the effect of post-2010 regulatory changes. However, lower-than-forecasted lending could also have been the result of changes in the demand for small business loans, or it could have been affected by some other factor for which we did not include data in our model.

In contrast, our model of community banks' total loans to businesses found that the actual volume of outstanding business loans was consistently higher than what our model forecasted given the macroeconomic, local market, and bank characteristics in place from 2010 through 2016. This difference may be the result of increasing demand for loans over $1 million (which were excluded from the Call Report data on small business lending) as compared to demand for loans under that amount. However, because the data banks report on their lending do not include information on specific loans or average loan amounts, the extent to which increased demand for larger loans affected our results is unknown.

---

[46] To test whether the differences between the results of the survivor loans model and the results of the total loans model were due to these models using data for different community bank populations, we conducted an additional analysis of our total business lending model using data for survivor community banks only. The results of this model were similar to the results of our total business lending model that used data for the full population of community banks, which allowed us to conclude that using data for different community bank populations was not the primary reason for differences in the results for these two models.

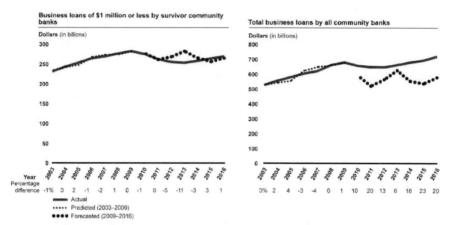

Source: GAO analysis of data from the Federal Deposit Insurance Corporation (FDIC). Board of Governors of the Federal Reserve System, Bureau of Economic Analysis, Bureau of Labor Statistics, Census Bureau, Federal Housing Finance Agency, and National Credit Union Administration. | GAO-18-312.

Notes: We defined community banks using FDIC's definition, which takes into account institutions' assets, foreign interests, specializations, and geographic characteristics. Community banks include banks with up to $39.5 billion in assets in 2017. Survivor community banks are those that continued operating as community banks from 2001 through 2017. The data we used represented 70 percent of community banks for the model of survivor community banks' business loans of $1 million or less and 80 percent of community banks for the model of all community banks' total business loans. From 2003 through 2009, the difference between the actual and predicted lines represents the extent to which our model was a reasonable fit for the data; a smaller difference indicates a better fit. From 2010 through 2016, the difference between the actual and forecasted lines represents the combined influence of "other factors" we were unable to include directly in our econometric model. These other factors may include changes in the regulatory environment, changes in demand for small business loans, technological changes, and lending by nonbank competitors, among other things. Because the individual influence of each of these other factors is unknown, our ability to determine the effect of changes in the regulatory environment on community bank small business lending is limited. Actual amounts of community bank small business lending were within the 95 percent confidence intervals for the forecasted lending amount. All dollar amounts are in constant 2016 dollars.

Figure 4. Actual Outstanding Amounts of Survivor Community Banks' Business Loans with Original Principal Balances of $1 Million or Less and All Community Banks' Total Business Loans Compared to Amounts Expected Based on Macroeconomic, Local Market, and Bank Characteristics, 2003–2016.

Credit Unions Have Increased Small Business Lending since 2010

Although credit unions account for a small share of total bank and credit union small business lending, their lending to small businesses increased considerably from 2010 through 2017.[47] Our analysis of NCUA data found the following:

- Dollar amount of small business lending. Small business lending by credit unions increased by 109 percent from 2010 through 2017, from $12 billion in outstanding loans in 2010 to $25 billion in 2017.
- Number of small business loans. The number of small business loans by credit unions increased by about 85 percent, from about 79,000 outstanding loans in 2010 to about 146,000 outstanding loans in 2017.

As shown in Figure 5, small business lending by credit unions increased each year from 2002 through 2017, indicating sustained growth. However, we cannot conclude that changes in the regulatory environment had no effect on credit union small business lending, because we do not know how credit union small business lending would have trended in the absence of such changes.[48]

---

[47] As noted previously, our analysis considered only small and medium credit unions, which accounted for about 95 percent of all credit unions in June 2017. NCUA, the credit union regulator, defines small business loans differently than bank regulators. Specifically, as defined by NCUA, business loans include any loan, line of credit, or letter of credit where the proceeds will be used for a commercial, industrial, agricultural, or professional purpose and the net balance is $50,000 or greater. For the purpose of our review, all loans for business activities made by credit unions are considered small business loans. Because loans less than $50,000 are not included in this definition of business loans, this approach likely underestimates small business lending by credit unions. Data we report for 2017 are as of June 2017.

[48] We did not conduct econometric modeling of credit unions' small business lending for a variety of reasons, including the unique characteristics of credit unions and the small share of total small business lending accounted for by credit unions.

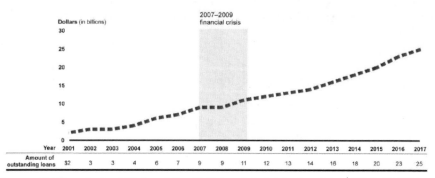

Source: GAO analysis of National Credit Union Administration data. | GAO-18-312.

Note: Our analysis considered only small and medium credit unions, which accounted for about 95 percent of all credit unions in June 2017. We excluded large credit unions with total assets above an annual threshold (equal to $201 million in 2001 and $994 million in 2017). Amounts of credit union small business lending are in constant 2016 dollars, and data we report for 2017 are as of June 2017.

Figure 5. Dollar Amount of Credit Union Small Business Loans Outstanding, 2001–2017.

COMMUNITY BANKS REPORTED THAT THE REGULATORY ENVIRONMENT WAS A PRIMARY REASON FOR CHANGING LENDING PROCESSES

We found, based on our generalizable survey, that the majority of community banks changed their small business lending processes from January 2010 through August 2017, including increasing documentation requirements and processing time, and most cited the regulatory environment as the primary reason for these changes. A smaller proportion of credit unions also changed their small business lending processes, and the regulatory environment was the reason they cited most frequently.

Community Banks

We estimated, based on our survey results, that 79 percent of community banks increased documentation requirements for small business borrowers from January 2010 through August 2017.[49] As shown in Figure 6, the regulatory environment was the top factor community bank representatives cited as the reason for this increase. Specifically, according to our survey, an estimated 97 percent of the community banks that reported increasing the amount of documentation they required borrowers to provide as part of obtaining a loan cited the regulatory environment as a factor that affected the increase to a moderate or great extent.[50] However, we estimated that about 50 percent of the community banks that increased documentation requirements also indicated that economic conditions affected this increase to a moderate or great extent.[51]

To obtain perspectives on the potential effect of changes to bank lending processes, we interviewed a judgmentally selected sample of small business advisers from six states' Small Business Development Centers as well as representatives of six small business advocacy groups.[52] A few of these small business advisers agreed that the amount of required documentation for obtaining loans had increased after the financial crisis, but the types of additional documentation sought by banks varied. One adviser said banks sought documentation they had not previously required, such as student loan information, appraisals, and personal asset verification. Representatives of one community bank also said they had introduced additional documentation requirements for small business loans beyond what was required by regulation—such as additional years of financial statements—to preempt any questions from bank examiners about borrowers' creditworthiness.

---

[49] To obtain community bank representatives' perspectives on the extent to which the regulatory environment may have affected small business lending and other issues, we conducted a generalizable survey of the chief executive officers of 466 community banks. For more information about our survey methodology and our complete survey results for community banks, see appendixes I and III, respectively. The 95 percent confidence interval for this estimate is (75, 84).
[50] The 95 percent confidence interval for this estimate is (94, 99).
[51] The 95 percent confidence interval for this estimate is (44, 57).
[52] Small business advisers are staff from Small Business Development Centers who provide coaching and other assistance to aspiring and existing small business owners throughout the country.

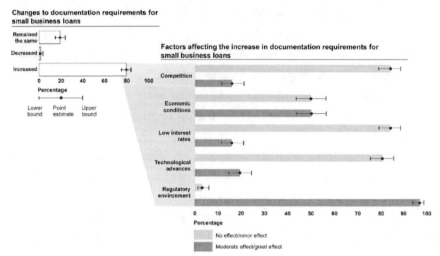

Source: GAO analysis of Community bank survey data. | GAO-18-312.

Notes: We defined community banks using the Federal Deposit Insurance Corporation's definition, which takes into account institutions' assets, foreign interests, specializations, and geographic characteristics. Community banks include banks with up to $39.5 billion in assets in 2017. We conducted a survey of the chief executive officers of 466 community banks from July 10, 2017 through August 25, 2017. Survey results are generalizable to the population of community banks. The lower and upper bounds of the 95 percent confidence intervals for our survey estimates are given on the left and right ends, respectively, of each whisker. Bars do not sum to 100 percent because respondents could select multiple factors as having affected the increase in documentation requirements for small business loans.

Figure 6. Survey Estimates of Factors Affecting the Increase in Documentation Required for Community Bank Small Business Loans, January 2010–August 2017.

We also estimated, based on our survey results, that 69 percent of community banks increased the time they took to process small business loans from January 2010 through August 2017.[53] As shown in Figure 7, almost all community banks that reported an increase in processing time attributed the increase to changes in the regulatory environment, among other factors. Community banks we interviewed also discussed reasons that processing time had increased.

---

[53] The 95 percent confidence interval for this estimate is (64, 74).

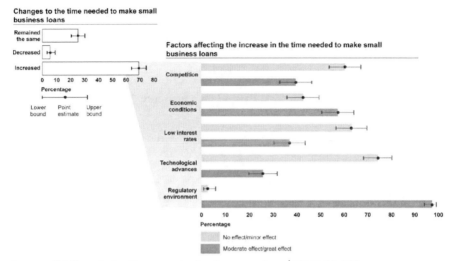

Source; GAO analysis of community bank survey data. | GAO-18-312.

Notes: We defined community banks using FDIC's definition, which takes into account institutions' assets, foreign interests, specializations, and geographic characteristics. Community banks include banks with up to $39.5 billion in assets in 2017. We conducted a survey of the chief executive officers of 466 community banks from July 10, 2017 through August 25, 2017. Survey results are generalizable to the population of community banks. The lower and upper bounds of the 95 percent confidence intervals for our survey estimates are given on the left and right ends, respectively, of each whisker. Bars do not sum to 100 percent because respondents could select multiple factors as having affected the increase in the time needed to make small business loans.

Figure 7. Survey Estimates of Factors Affecting the Increase in Time Needed to Make Community Bank Small Business Loans, January 2010–August 2017.

For example, one community bank said that the TILARESPA Integrated Disclosure, a requirement related to residential mortgage lending, increased the time needed to close loans that use residential real estate as collateral, which may include small business loans.[54] Although, according to FDIC officials, the TILA-RESPA Integrated Disclosure rule

---

[54] The combined TILA-RESPA Integrated Disclosure requires mortgage lenders to disclose certain mortgage terms, conditions, and fees to loan applicants during the origination process for certain mortgage loans. The requirement includes exemptions for certain activities, including the extension of credit primarily for a business, commercial, or agricultural purpose, such as a small business loan. See 12 C.F.R. § 1026.3(a).

would likely not apply to these loans, as we have previously reported some compliance burdens arose from misunderstandings of the requirements.[55]

Table 2. Survey Estimates of Factors Affecting Changes to Community Bank Small Business Lending Processes, January 2010–August 2017

Changes community banks made to small business lending processes	Percentage that made the change		Percentage that said their decision to make the change was affected to a moderate or great extent by:				
			Competition	Economic conditions	Low interest rates	Technological advances	Regulatory environment
Increased minimum credit criteria	Estimate	45	25	68	32	26	89
	Confidence interval	39, 50	18, 33	60, 76	24, 40	18, 33	82, 94
Increased product or service fees	Estimate	38	35	40	52	31	77
	Confidence interval	33, 44	26, 44	31, 49	42, 61	22, 39	68, 85
Decreased availability of loans to atypical borrowers	Estimate	26	21	51	17	13	97
	Confidence interval	21, 31	12, 31	39, 62	10, 28	6, 23	91, 99
Decreased products or services offered	Estimate	8	—	—	—	—	96
	Confidence interval	5, 11	—	—	—	—	82, 100

Legend: — = margin of error was greater than +/- 15 percentage points at the 95 percent level of confidence and deemed insufficiently reliable for this chapter.

Source: GAO analysis of community bank survey data. | GAO-18-312.

Notes: We defined community banks using the Federal Deposit Insurance Corporation's definition, which takes into account institutions' assets, foreign interests, specializations, and geographic characteristics. Community banks include banks with up to $39.5 billion in assets in 2017. We conducted a survey of the chief executive officers of 466 community banks from July 10, 2017 through August 25, 2017. Survey results are generalizable to the population of community banks. Confidence intervals are given at the 95 percent level of confidence.

---

[55] GAO, *Community Banks and Credit Unions: Regulators Could Take Additional Steps to Address Compliance Burdens*, GAO-18-213 (Washington, D.C.: Feb. 13, 2018).

Our survey also found that community banks changed their lending processes in other ways, including increasing fees, raising minimum credit criteria, or making other changes, and a majority of banks attributed these actions to changes in the regulatory environment (see Table 2). However, as previously discussed, we found that the effect of the regulatory environment on the volume of community banks' small business lending appeared to be relatively modest, which suggests that changes to community banks' lending processes may not have significantly affected small business' ability to obtain loans.

Representatives of some community banks told us that they perceived a generally stricter regulatory environment, which could explain the decisions to make changes to their lending processes. A few community bank representatives we spoke with said their small business lending processes were affected by increased scrutiny of their lending activities during examinations, and several community bank representatives said they changed their processes in anticipation of increased scrutiny. For example, representatives of one community bank reported testing all potential commercial customers—including small businesses—to assess how they would react to different financial situations, although no regulation requires them to do so. In addition, some institutions could perceive a stricter regulatory environment because of fines imposed for regulatory infractions. Although not specifically related to small business lending, since 2010 federal agencies have collected billions of dollars in settlement payments and penalties from financial institutions for alleged violations of regulations related to mortgage loan origination and servicing and Bank Secrecy Act/anti-money laundering activities.[56]

Small business advisers had mixed views on the extent to which changes to banks' lending processes affected small businesses' ability to obtain loans. According to several advisers we interviewed, tightened credit standards since 2010 have made obtaining small business loans more difficult, and a few advisers said that meeting documentation requirements

---

[56] GAO, *Financial Institutions: Penalty and Settlement Payments for Mortgage-Related Violations in Selected Cases*, GAO-17-11R (Washington, D.C.: Nov. 10, 2016) and *Financial Institutions: Fines, Penalties, and Forfeitures for Violations of Financial Crimes and Sanctions Requirements*, GAO-16-297 (Washington, D.C.: Mar. 22, 2016).

and higher credit standards was harder for newer small businesses. As a result, some advisers said small businesses were increasingly turning to alternative lenders for their credit needs. In contrast, other advisers said they did not think changes to lending processes affected the availability of credit for small businesses. For example, one small business adviser said he did not think increased fees would discourage small businesses from applying for loans.

Although few of the regulatory changes that have taken effect since 2010 directly relate to small business lending, community banks' small business lending processes may have been affected by regulatory changes in other areas. For example, a few community bank representatives we interviewed said that increased regulation related to residential mortgage lending had spillover effects into their small business lending activities, such as when a customer seeking a business loan used personal real estate as collateral.[57]

However, regulatory changes since 2010 may have also benefited community banks' small business lending and consumers. For example, FDIC officials told us that because regulatory changes have required community banks to hold more capital their safety and soundness has improved. In addition, some changes community banks made to their documentation requirements may have improved bank institution's safety and soundness. For example, as we reported in August 2010, origination features such as low or no documentation of income or assets may be associated with an increased likelihood of default.[58] Similarly, a few community bank representatives we interviewed said regulatory changes have helped community banks return to good business practices, and representatives from one small business advocacy group stated that regulatory changes have helped protect consumers.

---

[57] In February 2018, we reported that community banks identified new requirements related to disclosing home mortgage loans and costs to consumers and changes to required reports on home mortgage loan characteristics as especially burdensome, see GAO-18-213.

[58] GAO, *Nonprime Mortgages: Analysis of Loan Performance, Factors Associated with Defaults, and Data Sources*, GAO-10-805 (Washington, D.C.: Aug. 24, 2010).

Credit Unions

Table 3. Survey Estimates of Factors Affecting Changes to Credit Union Small Business Lending Processes, January 2010 – August 2017

Changes credit unions made to small business lending processes	Percentage that made the change		Percentage that said their decision to make the change was affected to a moderate or great extent by:				
			Competition	Economic conditions	Low interest rates	Technological advances	Regulatory environment
Increased documentation requirements	Estimate	66	18	41	25	24	96
	Confidence interval	57,74	10,28	31,52	16,36	15,34	89, 99
Increased time needed to make loans	Estimate	47	39	59	53	33	96
	Confidence interval	38,55	27,50	48,71	42,65	22,45	88, 99
Increased minimum credit criteria	Estimate	31	—	58	57	—	84
	Confidence interval	24,39	—	44,72	43,70	—	72, 93
Decreased availability of loans to atypical borrowers	Estimate	28	—	—	—	—	97
	Confidence interval	20,37	—	—	—	—	83, 100
Increased product or service fees	Estimate	24	—	—	—	—	—
	Confidence interval	17,33	—	—	—	—	—
Decreased products or services offered	Estimate	22	—	—	—	—	—
	Confidence interval	15,31	—	—	—	—	—

Legend: — = margin of error was greater than +/- 15 percentage points at the 95 percent level of confidence and deemed insufficiently reliable for this chapter.
Source: GAO analysis of credit union survey data. | GAO-18-312.
Notes: We conducted a generalizable survey of 470 credit union chief executive officers of credit unions from July 17, 2017 through August 25, 2017. Our analysis considered only small and medium credit unions, which accounted for about 95 percent of all credit unions as of June 2017. We excluded large credit unions with total assets above an annual threshold (equal to $201 million in 2001 and $994 million in 2017). Confidence intervals are given at the 95 percent confidence level.

Our survey found that the majority of credit unions increased documentation requirements for small business loans from January 2010 through August 2017, and some credit unions also made other changes to their small business lending processes (see Table 3).[59] Representatives of credit unions that changed their lending processes often cited changes in the regulatory environment as the reason, although few of the regulatory changes since 2010 directly relate to small business lending by credit unions.[60] In written comments provided in response to our survey, some credit union representatives cited increased regulatory scrutiny of their lending decisions, including examiners' requests for additional documentation of lending decisions, as affecting their small business lending.

FACTORS OTHER THAN REGULATORY ENVIRONMENT EXPLAIN MOST CHANGES IN THE NUMBER AND FINANCIAL PERFORMANCE OF COMMUNITY BANKS

Long-term community bank trends and macroeconomic, local market, and bank characteristics—rather than changes in the regulatory environment—appeared to explain most changes in the number of community banks and their market shares since 2010. In addition, although many institutions reported in our survey that they increased or reallocated staff and other resources to assist with regulatory compliance from 2010 through 2017, our analysis suggests that the effect of these changes on community banks' financial performance, if any, was minimal.

---

[59] To obtain credit union representatives' perspectives on the extent to which the regulatory environment may have affected small business lending and other issues, we conducted a generalizable survey of 470 credit union chief executive officers. Because we surveyed only small and medium credit unions, our survey results apply only to credit unions that fit these size categories. For more information about our survey methodology and our complete survey results for credit unions, see appendixes I and IV, respectively.

[60] One recent regulatory change that directly related to small business lending by credit unions is a rule that took effect in January 2017. See 12 C.F.R. pt. 723. However, rather than introducing additional requirements or other burdens, this rule gave credit unions more flexibility to make small business loans.

Regulatory Environment Likely Had a Relatively Small Effect on the Decline in Community Bank Numbers

The number of community banks declined by about 24 percent from 2010 through 2017, from about 7,000 to about 5,300.[61] Similarly, the number of credit unions declined by 22 percent during this period. However, these declines are similar to those that occurred prior to 2010: from 2001 through 2009, the number of community banks declined by 16 percent, while the number of credit unions declined 24 percent.

The decline in the total number of community banks since 2010 has been most pronounced among small community banks—those with less than $300 million in assets in 2016 dollars—which declined by 31 percent from 2010 through 2017 (see Figure 9). These banks made up the majority—approximately 74 percent (about 5,200 banks)—of all community banks in 2010, but by 2017 their proportion of the total community bank population had declined to 67 percent. Conversely, the number of larger community banks—those with $1 billion or more in assets in 2016 dollars—increased by 6 percent during this period.[62]

Our analysis indicates that from 2010 through 2017, approximately 1,800 community banks exited the population by merging, consolidating, or failing (see Table 4):[63]

---

[61] Data we report for 2017 are as of June 2017.

[62] FDIC's community bank definition used an asset-size cutoff of about $1.5 billion in 2017. However, it also allows banks that exceed the asset-size cutoff to be considered community banks if they meet certain other characteristics—see appendix I for the complete FDIC community bank definition. In 2017, the largest community bank had about $39.5 billion in assets.

[63] Mergers are generally a means by which banks can expand their size and geographic reach by combining with or acquiring other banks that previously had different owners. According to FDIC, approximately 3 percent of mergers were government assisted. Consolidations occur when an existing bank holding company combines related institutions holding separate charters. Banks generally fail when their financial conditions have deteriorated to the point that they are unable to meet their obligations to depositors and others and they are closed by a federal or state banking regulator.

- Mergers. The majority of the exits from the community bank population—approximately 64 percent (1,181)—resulted from mergers and about 72 percent of these mergers were between community banks. A similar portion of exits—about 66 percent—resulted from mergers from 2001 through 2009, the period before and during the financial crisis. The majority of credit union exits from 2010 through 2017 were also due to mergers.
- Consolidations. Consolidations of related banks under one charter accounted for about 14 percent of community bank exits from 2010 through 2017.[64]

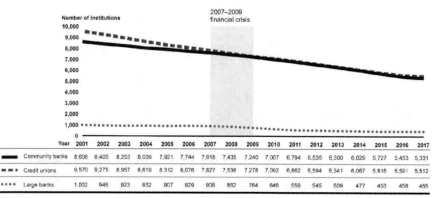

Source: GAO analysis of data from the Federal Deposit Insurance Corporation (FDIC) and National Credit Union Administration. | GAO-18-312.

Notes: We defined community banks using FDIC's definition, which takes into account institutions' assets, foreign interests, specializations, and geographic characteristics. Community banks include banks with up to $39.5 billion in assets in 2017. Large banks are all banks that are not considered community banks. We excluded large credit unions with total assets above an annual threshold (equal to $201 million in 2001 and $994 million in 2017). Data we report for 2017 are as of June 2017.

Figure 8. Number of Community Banks, Credit Unions, and Large Banks, 2001–2017.

- Failures. Failures represented about 18 percent of community bank exits from 2010 through 2017.[65] Over two-thirds of these failures

---

[64] This is in contrast to the period prior to the crisis from 2001 through 2009, when consolidations accounted for about 25 percent of exits.

were in 2010 and 2011, the 2 years immediately after the 2007–2009 financial crisis.

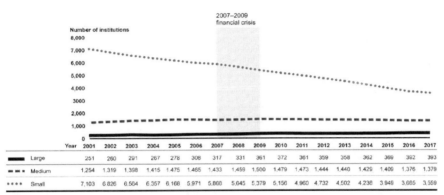

Source: GAO analysis of data from the Federal Deposit Insurance Corporation (FDIC). | GAO-18-312.

Notes: We defined community banks using FDIC's definition, which takes into account institutions' assets, foreign interests, specializations, and geographic characteristics. We define small community banks as having less than $300 million in assets, medium community banks as having between $300 million and less than $1 billion in assets, and large community banks as all banks designated as community banks by FDIC that have $1 billion or more in assets (which included some banks with up to $39.5 billion in assets in 2017). Dollar amounts are in constant 2016 dollars, and 2017 data are as of June 2017.

Figure 9. Number of Community Banks, 2001–2017, by Community Bank Size Category.

Our econometric model estimated that macroeconomic, local market, and bank characteristics explained the majority of community bank mergers from 2010 through 2016. However, other factors—which could include changes in the regulatory environment, the availability of banks for mergers, and incentives to achieve economies of scale, among other things—likely had some effect.[66]

---

[65] This is in contrast to the period prior to the crisis from 2001 through 2009, when failures accounted for about 7 percent of exits.

[66] To determine the extent to which various factors explained community bank mergers, we constructed a model using macroeconomic, local market, and bank characteristics. To help control for potential differences in institutions' size between the banks that merged and those that did not, we randomly selected community banks that were not acquired through a

Table 4. Number and Percentage of Community Bank and Credit Union Exits, 2010–2017, by Type of Exit

Type of exit	Community banks		Credit unions	
	Number of exits	Percentage of total exits	Number of exits	Percentage of total exits
Merger	1,181	64	1,817	95
Consolidation	267	14	n/a	n/a
Failure	337	18	94	5
Other	64	3	1	<1
Total	1,849	100	1,912	100

Legend: n/a = not applicable.
Source: GAO analysis of data from the Federal Deposit Insurance Corporation (FDIC), National Credit Union Administration (NCUA), and Board of Governors of the Federal Reserve System. | GAO-18-312.
Notes: We defined community banks using FDIC's definition, which takes into account institutions' assets, foreign interests, specializations, and geographic characteristics. Community banks include banks with up to $39.5 billion in assets in 2017. We excluded large credit unions (those with total assets above an annual threshold equal to $201 million in 2001 and $994 million in 2017) from this analysis. Mergers are generally a means by which banks or credit unions can expand their size and geographic reach by combining with or acquiring other institutions that previously had different owners. Consolidations occur when an existing bank holding company combines related institutions holding separate charters. According to NCUA officials, no legal provision allows credit unions to consolidate. Institutions generally fail when their financial conditions have deteriorated to the point that they are unable to meet their obligations to depositors and others and they are closed by a federal or state regulator. Other exits include voluntary liquidations and unexplained closings. Percentages may not add up to 100 percent due to rounding.

merger to match those that were acquired based on their total asset size and used the matched pairs as our data in our model. Because it is difficult to measure the cumulative effect of changes in the regulatory environment, this model used data on these characteristics from 2003 through 2009 to forecast mergers from 2010 through 2016 based on these macroeconomic, local market, and bank characteristics. We then compared the mergers forecasted by the model to those that actually occurred over the period to capture the difference or residual. We drew conclusions about the influence of this residual (which we call "other factors"). Because the individual influence of each of these factors is unknown, our ability to determine the cumulative effect of changes in the regulatory environment on community bank mergers is limited. For more information on our econometric modeling methodology and results, see appendix II.

The actual numbers of mergers for this period were, on average, 20 percent higher than our model forecasted, based on macroeconomic, local market, and bank characteristics at the time (see Figure 10).[67] This difference between actual and forecasted mergers indicates that other factors likely had some effect, although the effect was relatively small. This effect was most pronounced from 2013 through 2016 where the difference ranged from 23 to 31 percent. Banks may choose to merge in order to achieve economies of scale —that is, to increase their size to generate additional revenues at lower costs.[68] Although the existence of economies of scale in banking has been the subject of debate, some research suggests that banks can lower their costs by expanding.[69] Some community bank representatives we spoke with said banks consider merging to increase profitability and operational efficiency by becoming larger institutions. In response to changes in the regulatory environment since 2010, representatives of one community bank told us that their bank merged as a way to increase resources and staff, while maintaining profitability.

---

[67] With the exception of 1 year, the actual number of community bank mergers were within the 95 percent confidence intervals for the forecasted number of mergers from 2010 through 2016. This suggests that the net effect on mergers from factors we included in our model (macroeconomic, local market, and bank characteristics) may not have fundamentally changed between the two periods we analyzed (2003 through 2009 and 2010 through 2016) and that the effect of other factors we did not include in our model were likely small from 2010 through 2016.

[68] Increasing returns to scale are created when an increase in bank size leads to increase revenues but with a less than proportionate increase in cost and, therefore, a decline in average costs. See GAO, *Community Banks and Credit Unions: Impact of the Dodd-Frank Act Depends Largely on Future Rule Makings*, GAO-12-881 (Washington, D.C.: Sept. 13, 2012).

[69] Research by the Federal Reserve found that banks of all sizes, but in particular smaller banks, appeared to benefit from economies of scale, see: David C. Wheelock and Paul W. Wilson, "Do Large Banks Have Lower Costs? New Estimates of Returns to Scale for U.S. Banks," Working Paper 2009-054E, Federal Reserve Bank of St. Louis, Revised (May 2011) and Gregory Elliehausen, "The Cost of Banking Regulation: A Review of the Evidence," Staff Study 171, Federal Reserve (Washington, D.C.: April 1998). In contrast, FDIC's 2012 research on the cost economies of scale for community banks found that economies of scale did not confer significant benefits on community banks with more than $500 million in total asset size for most lending specializations. See: Stefan Jacewitz and Paul Kupiec, *Community Bank Efficiency and Economies of Scale*, *FDIC*, December 2012.

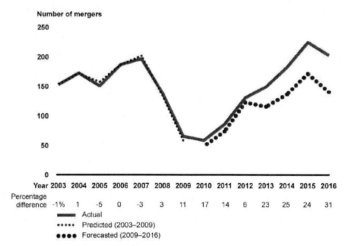

Source: GAO analysis of data from the Federal Deposit Insurance Corporation (FDIC), Board of Governors of the Federal Reserve System, Bureau of Economic Analysis, Bureau of Labor Statistics, Census Bureau, Federal Housing Finance Agency, and National Credit Union Administration. | GAO-18-312.

Notes: We defined community banks using FDIC's definition, which takes into account institutions' assets, foreign interests, specializations, and geographic characteristics. Community banks include banks with up to $39.5 billion in assets in 2017. To help control for potential differences in institutions' size between the banks that merged and those that did not, we randomly selected community banks that were not acquired through a merger to match those that were acquired based on their total asset size and used the matched pairs as our data in our model. From 2003 through 2009, the difference between the actual and predicted lines (given in percentage terms below the figure) represents the extent to which our model was a reasonable fit for the data; a smaller difference indicates a better fit. From 2010 through 2016, the difference between the actual and forecasted lines represents the combined influence of "other factors" we were unable to measure directly in our econometric model, which may include changes in the regulatory environment, the availability of banks for merger, and incentives to achieve economies of scale, among other things. Because the individual influence of each of these factors is unknown, our ability to determine the cumulative effect of changes in the regulatory environment on community bank mergers is limited. With the exception of 1 year, the actual number of community bank mergers was within the 95 percent confidence intervals for the forecasted number of mergers.

Figure 10. Actual Number of Community Bank Mergers Compared to Number Expected Based on Macroeconomic, Local Market, and Bank Characteristics, 2003–2016.

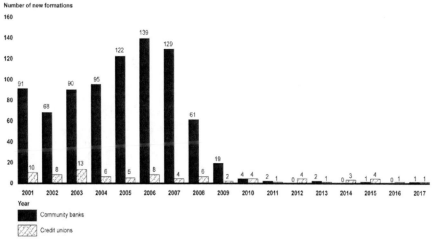

Source: GAO analysis of data from the Federal Deposit Insurance Corporation (FDIC), National Credit Union Administration, and Board of Governors of the Federal Reserve System. | GAO-18-312.

Notes: We define a new entrant as a new institution that is not a charter conversion or a new bank formed by an existing bank holding company. We defined community banks using FDIC's definition, which takes into account institutions' assets, foreign interests, specializations, and geographic characteristics. Community banks include banks with up to $39.5 billion in assets in 2017. We excluded large credit unions (those with total assets above an annual threshold equal to $201 million in 2001 and $994 million in 2017) from this analysis. Data we report for 2017 are as of June 2017.

Figure 11. Number of New Community Banks and Credit Unions, 2001–2017, by Type of Institution.

In addition, FDIC analysis found that the number of banks, including community banks, has been declining since the 1980s, when federal and state legislative changes began relaxing geographic restrictions on banking activities and allowed banks to operate across multiple states under a single charter, resulting in mergers that reduced the number of banks.[70] For example, FDIC researchers found that bank numbers were steady for several decades prior to the 1980s, but declined by around 66 percent from 1980 through 2013.

---

[70] Benjamin R. Backup and Richard A. Brown, "Community Banks Remain Resilient Amid Industry Consolidation," *FDIC Quarterly*, vol. 8, no. 2 (2014).

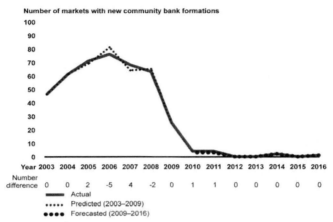

Source: GAO analysis of data from the Federal Deposit Insurance Corporation (FDIC), Board of Governors of the Federal Reserve System, Bureau of Economic Analysis, Bureau of Labor Statistics, Census Bureau, Federal Housing Finance Agency, and National Credit Union Administration. | GAO-18-312.

Notes: We defined community banks using FDIC's definition, which takes into account institutions' assets, foreign interests, specializations, and geographic characteristics. Community banks include banks with up to $39.5 billion in assets in 2017. To help control for the effect of differences in market sizes on new bank formation in markets, we randomly selected markets with no new community bank formations to match with markets with new community bank formations and used the matched pairs as the data in our model. There were no new community bank formations (measured as the period when the banks began collecting deposits) in 2012, 2013, and 2015. From 2003 through 2009, the difference between the actual and predicted lines represents the extent to which our model was a reasonable fit for the data; a smaller difference indicates a better fit. From 2010 through 2016, the difference between the actual and forecasted lines represents the combined influence of "other factors" we were unable to measure directly in our econometric model, which may include changes in the regulatory environment and incentives for new banks to enter, among other things. Because the individual influence of each of these factors is unknown, our ability to determine the cumulative effect of changes in the regulatory environment on new community bank formations is limited. The actual number of new community bank formations was within the 95 percent confidence intervals for the forecasted number of formations.

Figure 12. Actual Number of Markets with New Community Bank Formations Compared to Number Expected Based on Macroeconomic and Local Market Characteristics, 2003–2016.

The overall decline in the number of community banks and credit unions is also related to the rate at which new institutions form, which was lower from 2010 through 2017 than in prior periods.[71] According to bank regulator data, only 10 new community banks formed during this period—a rate of approximately one new community bank per year (see Figure 11). In contrast, 814 new community banks formed from 2001 through 2009—a rate of 90 per year. Similarly, according to our analysis of NCUA data, 19 new credit unions formed from 2010 through 2017 (a rate of about 2 per year), while 62 new credit unions formed from 2001 through 2009 (about 7 per year).

Our econometric analysis found that macroeconomic and local market characteristics were the primary factors affecting the rate of new community bank formations from 2010 through 2016. Specifically, our model forecast that the prevailing macroeconomic and local market characteristics would result in relatively few new community bank formations (no more than three markets with new bank formations in any one year) from 2010 through 2016; the actual number of new community bank formations that did occur exceeded this model's forecast, but only slightly (see Figure 12).[72] The similarity between the actual and forecasted

---

[71] For the purposes of this report, we consider a new bank formation to be a new community bank that was not a charter conversion and not a new bank formed by an existing bank holding company. For analyzing trends, we measured the number of new bank formations using the period when the bank was chartered.

[72] To determine the extent to which various factors explained new community bank formations, we constructed a model using macroeconomic and local market characteristics. To help control for the effect of differences in market sizes on new bank formation in markets, we randomly selected markets with no new community bank formations to match with markets with new community bank formations and used the matched pairs as the data in our model. Because it is difficult to measure the cumulative effect of changes in the regulatory environment, this model used data on these characteristics from 2003 through 2009 to forecast new community bank formations from 2010 through 2016 based on these macroeconomic and local market characteristics. We then compared the new community bank formations forecasted by the model to those that actually occurred over the period to capture the difference or residual. We drew conclusions about the influence of this residual (which we call the "other factors"). Because the individual influence of each of these factors is unknown, our ability to determine the cumulative effect of changes in the regulatory environment on new community bank formations is limited. For our modeling, we measured the number of new community bank formations annually based on the period when the bank began collecting deposits (as compared to the period when the bank was chartered). Since there were no new community bank formations in 2012, 2013, and 2015, the model was unable to generate results for these years. The actual number of community

numbers of new bank formations suggests that the effect of changes in the regulatory environment on new community bank formation was relatively small. This result was similar to a 2014 Federal Reserve study that found that economic conditions explained the majority of the decline in new banks.[73]

Number and Geographic Location of Community Bank Branches

From 2010 through 2017, the number of community bank branches — which are defined as all locations that accept deposits—declined, and our survey results and interviews suggest that these changes were due to various factors. According to our analysis of FDIC data, the number of community bank branches decreased by 15 percent from 2010 through 2017, from about 35,000 to about 30,000. This decrease reversed the previous trend of increasing numbers of branches leading up to the 2007–2009 financial crisis: according to FDIC data, from 2001 through 2009, the number of branches increased 6 percent, from about 33,000 to about 35,000.

Based on our survey results, we estimated that 20 percent of community banks closed one or more branches from January 2010 through August 2017.[74] Our survey results suggest that multiple factors, including changes in the regulatory environment, economic conditions, and

---

bank formations were within the 95 percent confidence intervals for the forecasted number of formations from 2010 through 2016. This suggests that the net effect on new community banks from factors we included in our model (macroeconomic and local market characteristics) may not have fundamentally changed between the two periods we analyzed (2003 through 2009 and 2010 through 2016) and that the effect of other factors we did not include in our model were likely small from 2010 through 2016. For more details on our economic modeling methodology and results, see appendix II.

[73] Robert M. Adams and Jacob P. Gramlich, "Where Are All the New Banks? The Role of Regulatory Burden in New Charter Creation," *Finance and Economics Discussion Series*, 2014-113 (Washington, D.C.: Dec. 16, 2014). This research analyzed new entrants from 1976 through 2013 and found that factors other than regulation, such as the low interest rate environment and weak economic conditions, explained at least 75 percent of the declines in new charters.

[74] We surveyed generalizable samples of community bank and credit union representatives about management decisions from January 2010 through August 2017. This estimate includes community banks that were in the process of closing an office at the time of the survey. The 95 percent confidence interval for this estimate is (16, 25). For additional information on our methodology and our results see appendixes I, III, and IV.

technological advances, influenced these closures.[75] Representatives from some community banks we interviewed said branch opening and closing decisions are often based on branch profitability and growth opportunities, which stem from economic conditions, and that closures did not have major effects on customers. In contrast, our prior work found that compliance with Bank Secrecy Act/anti-money laundering regulations along with other factors, including demographic factors, contributed to bank branch closures.[76]

The number of community bank branches in about half of U.S. counties increased or remained the same in 2010 and 2017, while the number decreased in the other half of counties (see Figure 13). Additionally, although small, the percentage of counties with no community bank branches increased slightly in 2017 as compared with 2010.[77]

The distribution of community bank branches between urban and rural areas appears to have remained largely unchanged from 2010 through 2017. The majority of community bank branches are located in urban areas—about 70 percent in 2017—and declines in the number of branches were largest in urban areas (see Table 5).[78]

---

[75] According to our community bank survey, of those institutions that closed one or more branches, an estimated 50 percent (38, 63) cited the regulatory environment, 49 percent (37, 61) cited changes in economic conditions, and 42 percent (30, 55) cited advances in technology as factors affecting their decision to a moderate or great extent.

[76] This analysis considered banks of all sizes (not just community banks). This analysis is subject to a number of important caveats. For more information about our methodology and results, see: GAO, *Bank Secrecy Act: Derisking Along the Southwest Border Highlights Need for Regulators to Enhance Retrospective Reviews*, GAO-18-263 (Washington, D.C.: Feb. 26, 2018). The Bank Secrecy Act established reporting, record keeping, and other anti-money laundering requirements for financial institutions to assist government agencies to detect and prevent money laundering and terrorist financing by, among other things, maintaining compliance policies, conducting ongoing monitoring of customers and transactions, and reporting suspicious financial activity.

[77] The percentage of counties with no community bank branches increased by about 2 percentage points, from 4 percent in 2010 (130 counties out of 3,141) to 6 percent in 2017 (173 counties out of 3,141).

[78] For the purposes of this report, we defined "urban" and "rural" areas using the Department of Agriculture's Rural-Urban Commuting Area codes. These codes classify all census tracts in the United States on a 10-tier continuum from rural to urban based on daily commuting patterns, urbanization, and population density. For our analysis, we collapsed the 10 tiers into 4, where 2 tiers are considered rural and the other 2 are considered urban.

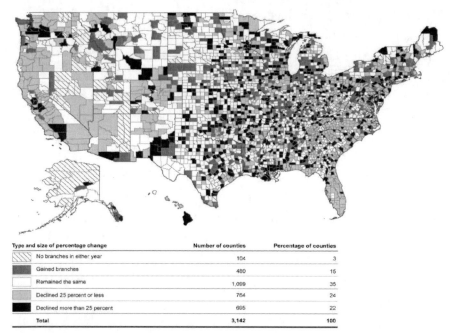

Type and size of percentage change	Number of counties	Percentage of counties
No branches in either year	104	3
Gained branches	480	15
Remained the same	1,099	35
Declined 25 percent or less	764	24
Declined more than 25 percent	695	22
Total	3,142	100

Source: GAO analysis of data from the Federal Deposit Insurance Corporation (FDIC); MapInfo (map). | GAO-18-312.

Notes: We defined community banks using FDIC's definition, which takes into account institutions' assets, foreign interests, specializations, and geographic characteristics. Community banks include banks with up to $39.5 billion in assets in 2017.

Figure 13. Changes in the Number of Community Bank Branches at the County Level, in 2010 and 2017.

Our analysis of NCUA data shows that from 2012 (the first year for which reliable data are available) through 2017, the number of credit union branches decreased by 5 percent, from about 16,000 to about 15,000. Based on our survey results, we estimated that 22 percent of credit unions closed one or more branches from January 2010 through August 2017 or were in the process of closing a branch.[79] Some credit union representatives we interviewed said credit unions make decisions about branch openings and closings based on the profitability of individual branches or member needs.

---

[79] The 95 percent confidence interval for this estimate is (16, 27).

Table 5. Number and Percentage of Urban and Rural Community Bank Branches, 2010 and 2017

Type	2010		2017	
	Number	Percent	Number	Percent
Urban branches	25,302	72	20,793	70
Rural branches	9,715	28	8,942	30
Total	35,017	100	29,735	100

Source: GAO analysis of Federal Deposit Insurance Corporation (FDIC) and Department of Agriculture data. | GAO-18-312.

Notes: We defined community banks using FDIC's definition, which takes into account institutions' assets, foreign interests, specializations, and geographic characteristics. Community banks include banks with up to $39.5 billion in assets in 2017. We define "urban" and "rural" areas using the Department of Agriculture's Rural-Urban Commuting Area codes. These codes classify all census tracts in the United Sates on a 10-tier continuum from rural to urban based on daily commuting patterns, urbanization, and population density. For our analysis, we collapsed the 10 tiers into 4, where 2 tiers are considered rural and the other 2 are considered urban. The totals in this table exclude 15 community bank branches in 2010 and 9 in 2017, because we were unable to classify the branch locations as urban or rural.

Market Share of Bank Activities

Along with decreases in the number of community banks, their market shares of banking activities—total banking assets, deposits, and loans and leases—decreased from 2010 through 2017.[80] For example, their share of total assets declined from 15 percent in 2010 to 13 percent in 2017, and their share of total deposits declined from 20 percent in 2010 to 15 percent in 2017.

These declines appear to be part of longer-term trends to some degree. As Figure 14 shows, although community banks' market shares rose during the 2007–2009 financial crisis, their slight declines since then continued an overall downward trend in community bank market shares from at least 2001. According to FDIC officials, the loss of market shares by community banks may, in part, be the result of the Federal Reserve expanding its balance sheet and providing hundreds of billions in additional balances into the banking system in response to the financial crisis.

---

[80] Data we report for 2017 are as of June 2017.

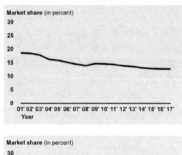
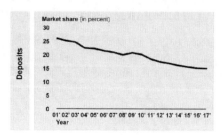
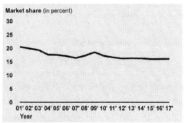

Source: GAO analysis of data from the Federal Deposit Insurance Corporation (FDIC). | GAO-18-312.

Notes: We defined community banks using FDIC's definition, which takes into account institutions' assets, foreign interests, specializations, and geographic characteristics. Community banks include banks with up to $39.5 billion in assets in 2017. Data we report for 2017 are as of June 2017.

Figure 14. Community Banks' Market Share of Total Assets, Deposits, and Loans and Leases, 2001–2017.

Credit unions' market shares of total assets, deposits, and loans and leases were largely unchanged.[81] From 2010 through 2017, their market shares of total assets, deposits, and loans and leases each changed by less than 1 percentage point.

The Effect of Regulatory Changes on Community Bank Financial Performance Is Likely Modest

In response to changes in the regulatory environment, community banks and credit unions may hire additional staff or outside consultants,

---

[81] As noted previously, for the purposes of this report, we define small and medium credit unions as those with assets of less than $994 million in 2017. See appendix I for our full definition of small and medium-sized credit unions.

invest in new software, or take other actions to help comply with new requirements. As a result, the number of employees and the administrative and personnel costs are likely to increase, and profits and performance are likely to decrease, all else being equal. However, while our survey results suggest many community banks and credit unions made such changes in response to regulations, these changes appear to have had minimal effects on community banks' and credit unions' total employment levels, expenses, and financial performance. Additionally, our econometric analysis suggests that the effects of changes in the regulatory environment on community bank profitability were likely small.

Changes in Employment

Our survey results indicated that most community banks and credit unions increased or reallocated staff from January 2010 through August 2017 to assist with changes in the regulatory environment, but FDIC and NCUA data for banks and credit unions showed no increases in total employment for these institutions.[82] Based on our survey, an estimated 73 percent of community banks hired additional staff and 86 percent reallocated existing staff to assist with changes in the regulatory environment.[83] However, our analysis of FDIC data found that total employment levels at these institutions decreased slightly from 2010 through 2017 (see Figure 15).[84] Based on our survey of credit unions, we estimated that most credit unions (61 percent) did not hire additional staff from January 2010 through August 2017, but that 61 percent of credit unions reallocated existing staff to assist with changes in the regulatory environment.[85] Similarly, our analysis of NCUA data shows that the median numbers of full-time and part-time credit union employees decreased during this period. Our survey results suggest that institutions' decisions to reallocate existing staff to assist with changes in the regulatory

---

[82] We surveyed generalizable samples of community bank and credit union representatives about management decisions and small business lending activities from January 2010 through August 2017. For additional information on our methodology and our results see appendixes I, III, and IV.

[83] The 95 percent confidence interval for these estimate are (68, 77) and (82, 90), respectively.

[84] Data we report for 2017 are as of June 2017.

[85] The 95 percent confidence intervals for these estimates are (55, 68) and (54, 68), respectively.

environment were driven or offset by other changes. For example, to help mitigate the negative effects of changes in staffing, institutions may have made greater use of technology. Of the community banks that decreased the time staff spend engaging directly with individual customers (an estimated 18 percent of community banks overall), an estimated 87 percent attribute that decision to technological advances.[86]

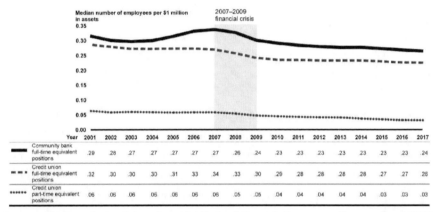

Source: GAO analysis of data from the Federal Deposit Insurance Corporation (FDIC) and National Credit Union Administration. | GAO-18-312.

Notes: We defined community banks using FDIC's definition, which takes into account institutions' assets, foreign interests, specializations, and geographic characteristics. Community banks include banks with up to $39.5 billion in assets in 2017. We excluded large credit unions (those with total assets above an annual threshold equal to $201 million in 2001 and $994 million in 2017) from this analysis. Dollar amounts are in constant 2016 dollars and data for 2017 are as of June 2017.

Figure 15. Median Number of Employees per $1 Million in Assets, 2001–2017 for Community Banks and Credit Unions, by Type of Institution.

Furthermore, an estimated 89 percent of community banks and 92 percent of credit unions increased their investments in customer-facing technologies, such as online or mobile banking.[87] Shifts in staffing allocations may also have resulted in decreased availability of products and

---

[86] The 95 percent confidence intervals for these estimates are (13, 22) and (76, 95), respectively.
[87] The 95 percent confidence intervals for these estimates are (85, 92) and (88, 95), respectively.

services; however, our survey results found that most community banks and credit unions did not decrease the time staff spend engaging with customers or identifying new and innovative products. Based on our survey, we estimated that 83 percent of community banks and 82 percent of credit unions increased or did not change the time staff spend engaging directly with individual customers during this period.[88] Similarly, an estimated 91 percent of community banks and 97 percent of credit unions increased or did not change the time staff spend identifying new or innovative products.[89]

Changes in Operating Expenses

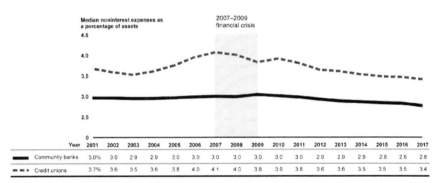

Source: GAO analysis of data from the Federal Deposit Insurance Corporation (FDIC) and National Credit Union Administration. | GAO-18-312.

Notes: Noninterest expenses include salaries, employee benefits, and consulting and advisory expenses. We defined community banks using FDIC's definition, which takes into account institutions' assets, foreign interests, specializations, and geographic characteristics. Community banks include banks with up to $39.5 billion in assets in 2017. We excluded large credit unions (those with total assets above an annual threshold equal to $201 million in 2001 and $994 million in 2017) from this analysis. Data we report for 2017 are as of June 2017.

Figure 16. Median Noninterest Expenses, 2001–2017 for Community Banks and Credit Unions, by Type of Institution.

---

[88] The 95 percent confidence intervals for these estimates are (78, 87) and (75, 87), respectively.
[89] The 95 percent confidence intervals for these estimates are (87, 94) and (93, 99), respectively.

Many survey respondents reported spending on outside services to help assist with changes in the regulatory environment, but our analysis found that noninterest expenses—a measure that includes these and other regulatory compliance costs, as well as salaries, employee benefits, and consulting and advisory expenses—decreased overall. According to our survey results, an estimated 96 percent of community banks and 78 percent of credit unions hired a third party or purchased additional software or automated systems to assist with changes in the regulatory environment from January 2010 through August 2017.[90]

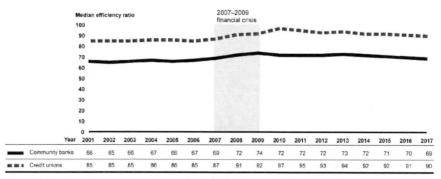

Source: GAO analysis of data from the Federal Deposit Insurance Corporation (FDIC) and National Credit Union Administration. | GAO-18-312.

Notes: The efficiency ratio is defined as noninterest expenses, less amortization of intangible assets, as a percentage of net interest income plus noninterest income. This ratio measures the proportion of net operating revenues that are absorbed by operating expenses, so that a lower value indicates greater efficiency. We defined community banks using FDIC's definition, which takes into account institutions' assets, foreign interests, specializations, and geographic characteristics. Community banks include banks with up to $39.5 billion in assets in 2017. We excluded large credit unions (those with total assets above an annual threshold equal to $201 million in 2001 and $994 million in 2017) from this analysis. Data we report for 2017 are as of June 2017.

Figure 17. Median Efficiency Ratio, 2001–2017 for Community Banks and Credit Unions, by Type of Institution.

---

[90] The 95 percent confidence intervals for these estimates are (93, 98) and (72, 84), respectively.

Community Banks

As Figure 16 shows, median noninterest expenses as a percentage of assets for community banks increased prior to and during the 2007–2009 financial crisis but then declined through 2017.[91] Similarly, credit unions' median noninterest expenses as a percentage of assets increased leading up to the financial crisis but have since declined to below precrisis levels. Community bank and credit union financial performance also improved from 2010 through 2017. In the prior period from 2001 through 2009, community banks' median efficiency ratio—a measure of operating expenses as a proportion of income—increased from 66 percent to 74 percent (see Figure 17), suggesting a decline in efficiency.[92] However, the ratio for these institutions has since decreased to 69 percent in 2017, indicating slightly greater efficiency. Similarly, from 2001 through 2009, credit unions' median efficiency ratio increased from about 85 percent to about 92 percent; however, it then improved to about 90 percent in 2017.

Changes in Profitability

Our analysis of FDIC data suggests that community bank profitability is increasing and that regulatory environment has likely not negatively affected profitability significantly. Specifically, the median pretax return on assets—a measure of profitability—for the population of all community banks decreased leading up to and during the 2007–2009 financial crisis (see Figure 18).[93] From 2010 through 2017, however, the median return on assets for the population increased, although it remains below precrisis levels.[94] Similarly, credit unions' median return on assets decreased during the financial crisis but increased from 2010 through 2017.

---

[91] Data we report for 2017 are as of June 2017.

[92] The efficiency ratio is defined as noninterest expenses, less amortization of intangible assets, as a percentage of net interest income plus noninterest income. This ratio measures the proportion of net operating revenues that are absorbed by operating expenses, so that a lower value indicates greater efficiency of operations.

[93] Return on assets is defined for banks as net income before income taxes, extraordinary income, and other adjustments as a percentage of average total assets. We define it for credit unions as net income as a percentage of total assets.

[94] Data we report for 2017 are as of June 2017. In a study published in 2016, FDIC analyzed the core profitability of community banks (which FDIC defined as the portion of return on assets attributable to structural factors that reflect the operating environment and business practices of banks and excludes macroeconomic factors) from 1985 to 2015. The study found that, while average community bank return on assets had generally remained lower

Our econometric analysis found that community bank profitability was higher from 2010 through 2016 than would have been expected based on macroeconomic, local market, and bank characteristics at the time.[95] Specifically, our model found that, on average, community banks' actual return on assets was 40 basis points higher than our model forecasted given the macroeconomic, local market, and bank characteristics in place during the post-crisis period from 2010 through 2016 and despite any change in the regulatory environment.[96] This effect was most pronounced in 2010 (immediately after the crisis), when the actual return on assets did not dip as low as our model forecasted, and in 2012 and 2013— community banks' return on assets was 70 basis points higher than would have been expected. From 2014 through 2016, actual return on assets continued to be higher than our model forecasted, but the difference was smaller.

The difference between actual community bank return on assets and what the model forecasted is attributable to the influence of the "other factors" category, which could include the influence of weaker banks exiting from the population. For example, FDIC reported that from 2009 through 2012 (during and following the crisis), many weaker banks exited, which may have contributed to an upturn in overall community bank

---

than its levels before the 2007–2009 financial crisis, core profitability has returned to levels comparable to those experienced prior to the financial crisis. See Jared Fronk, "Core Profitability of Community Banks: 1985–2015," *FDIC Quarterly*, vol. 10, no. 4 (2016).

[95] To determine the extent to which various factors explained community banks' pretax return on assets, we constructed a model using macroeconomic, local market, and bank characteristics. Because it is difficult to measure the cumulative effect of changes in the regulatory environment, this model used data on these characteristics from 2003 through 2009 to forecast community banks' return on assets from 2010 through 2016 based on these macroeconomic, local market, and bank characteristics. We then compared community banks' return on assets forecasted by the model to those that actually cover the period to capture the difference or residual. We drew conclusions about the influence of this residual (which we call the "other factors"). For more information on our econometric modeling methodology and results, see appendix II.

[96] With the exception of 2 years, the actual community bank return on assets was within the 95 percent confidence intervals for the forecasted return on assets from 2010 through 2016. This suggests that the net effect on community banks' return on assets from factors we included in our model (macroeconomic, local market, and bank characteristics) may not have fundamentally changed between the two periods we analyzed (2003 through 2009 and 2010 through 2016) and that the effect of other factors we did not include in our model were likely small from 2010 through 2016.

profitability.[97] In addition, FDIC found that banks acquired during a merger from 2010 through 2016 had lower profitability than their peers—removing these weaker institutions from the population of community banks could also explain the higher-than-forecasted return on assets.[98] However, the individual influence of the other factors is unknown, which limits our ability to determine the cumulative effect of these other factors on community bank return on assets.

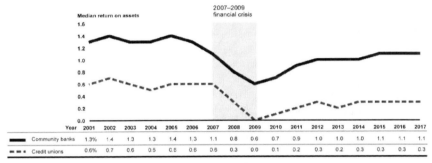

Source: GAO analysis of data from the Federal Deposit Insurance Corporation (FDIC) and National Credit Union Administration. | GAO-18-312.

Notes: Return on assets is defined for banks as net income before income taxes, extraordinary income, and other adjustments as a percentage of average total assets. We define it for credit unions as net income as a percentage of total assets. We defined community banks using FDIC's definition, which takes into account institutions' assets, foreign interests, specializations, and geographic characteristics. Community banks include banks with up to $39.5 billion in assets in 2017. We excluded large credit unions (those with total assets above an annual threshold equal to $201 million in 2001 and $994 million in 2017) from this analysis. Data we report for 2017 are as of June 2017.

Figure 18. Median Return on Assets, 2001–2017 for Community Banks and Credit Unions, by Type of Institution.

---

[97] Jared Fronk, "Core Profitability of Community Banks: 1985–2015," *FDIC Quarterly*, vol. 10, no. 4 (2016).

[98] Eric C. Breitenstein and Nathan L. Hinton, "Community Bank Mergers Since the Financial Crisis: How Acquired Community Banks Compared with their Peers," *FDIC Quarterly*, vol. 11, no. 4 (2017).

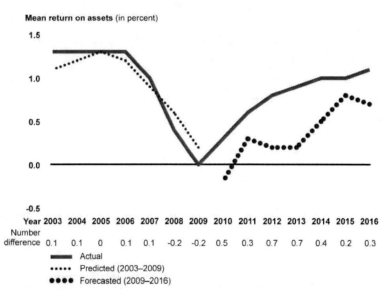

Source: GAO analysis of data from the Federal Deposit Insurance Corporation (FDIC), Board of Governors of the Federal Reserve System, Bureau of Economic Analysis, Bureau of Labor Statistics, Census Bureau, Federal Housing Finance Agency, and National Credit Union Administration. | GAO-18-312.

Notes: We defined community banks using FDIC's definition, which takes into account institutions' asset, foreign interests, specializations, and geographic characteristics. Community banks includes banks with up to $39.5 billion in assets in 2017. From 2003 through 2009, the difference between the actual and predicted lines represents the extent to which our model was a reasonable fit for the data; a smaller difference indicates a better fit. From 2010 through 2016, the difference between the actual and forecasted lines represents the combined influence of "other factors" we were unable to measure directly in our econometric model, which may include changes in the regulatory environment and the elimination of underperforming community banks through mergers or failures, among other things. Because the individual influence of each of these factors is unknown, our ability to determine the cumulative effect of changes in the regulatory environment on community bank return on assets is unknown. With the exception of 2 years, community banks' actual return on assets was within the 95 percent confidence intervals for the forecasted returns.

Figure 19. Actual Community Bank Pretax Return on Assets Compared to Returns Expected Based on Macroeconomic, Local Market, and Bank Characteristics, 2003–2016.

Finally, the influence of changes in the regulatory environment on the number and financial performance of community banks and credit unions is not necessarily an indication of undue burden; such changes could also result in benefits to individual institutions and the overall financial system. A change in a bank's or credit union's behavior may be the appropriate result of the regulators addressing weak business practices, and federal oversight serves, in part, to help ensure that these institutions do not take excessive risks that could undermine their safety and soundness.

REGULATORS HAVE TAKEN STEPS TO ANALYZE AND MITIGATE THE EFFECTS OF REGULATORY CHANGES ON SMALL BUSINESS LENDING

In response to the 2007–2009 financial crisis, the financial banking regulators—the Federal Reserve, FDIC, and OCC—have taken various actions to identify and mitigate effects of changes in the regulatory environment on community banks and small business lending. In a policy statement published in February 2010, regulators underscored the importance of ensuring that financial institutions, including community banks, continued to make credit available to small businesses.[99] In particular, the policy stated that supervisory policies or actions should not inadvertently curtail the availability of credit to sound small businesses.[100]

Federal Reserve and FDIC officials told us that to help assess the extent to which credit has continued to reach small businesses following

---

[99] The Board of Governors of the Federal Reserve System, the Federal Deposit Insurance Corporation, the National Credit Union Administration, the Office of the Comptroller of the Currency, and the Office of Thrift Supervision, Interagency Statement on Meeting the Credit Needs of Creditworthy Small Business Borrowers (Washington, D.C.: Feb. 12, 2010).

[100] In their policy statement, regulators noted that institutions that engage in prudent small business lending after performing a comprehensive review of a borrower's financial condition will not be subject to criticism for loans made on that basis. They cautioned that institutions should avoid excessive tightening of underwriting standards and that sound small business borrowers should not automatically be refused credit because of borrowers' particular industry.

the crisis, they have regularly monitored small business lending trends, including external data sources that assess small business demand for credit. For example, Federal Reserve officials analyzed data published by the National Federation of Independent Business on small business owners' perceptions of credit market conditions.[101] Similarly, FDIC officials told us that to monitor the effect of changes in the regulatory environment on small business lending, FDIC compared community banks' total business loan growth (as a measure of small business lending) to growth in gross domestic product and found that community banks' lending outpaced overall economic output. In addition, in December 2017, the Federal Reserve took steps to help strengthen its ability to monitor small business lending activity through a new quarterly survey of banks.[102] This initiative is designed to collect information on the availability and cost of loans to small businesses, the role of community banks in providing loans to small businesses, and small businesses' access to credit in their local communities.

To complement their data analysis, Federal Reserve and FDIC officials told us they have also gathered information directly from community banks to help identify any potential effects of changes in the regulatory environment on small business lending activities. For example, the Federal Reserve has met twice yearly since 2013 with an advisory council of community bank and other representatives, where they ask for information on changes in the availability of small business loans and the effects of examination practices on access to credit, among other issues.[103] Additionally, in 2017 FDIC issued preliminary results of a survey of banks'

---

[101] The National Federation of Independent Business Research Foundation has collected data on small business economic trends with quarterly surveys since 1974 and monthly surveys since 1986. The survey asks members about economic outlook and credit conditions, among other things. According to Federal Reserve officials, they also monitored small business lending demand using the Wells Fargo/Gallup Small Business Index, which measures small business owners' optimism.

[102] The Federal Reserve's Small Business Lending Survey (FR 2028D) replaces the Survey of Terms of Business Lending (FR 2028A), which the Federal Reserve determined was insufficient for addressing questions about small business lending during the financial crisis, ensuing recession, or economic recovery.

[103] The Federal Reserve established its Community Depository Institutions Advisory Council in 2010 and it held its first meeting in 2013. The council provides first-hand input on the economy, lending conditions, and other issues.

small business lending products and processes.[104] According to FDIC officials, this survey was designed to help improve their understanding of the types of small business loans provided by banks, including community banks.

Although OCC officials told us that they have not analyzed the effects of changes in the regulatory environment on community banks' small business lending, they are considering analyzing the cumulative effect of regulatory changes on the overall performance and activities of smaller banks in 2018 or 2019. OCC officials said that the scope and methodology of this study, including the extent to which it will include specific analysis of the effect of regulatory changes on small business lending activities, have not yet been determined.

The Federal Reserve and FDIC have also taken steps to assess the effects of changes in the regulatory environment on the number and performance of community banks. For example, Federal Reserve researchers assessed the effects of regulatory changes on the formation of new community banks and found that the effect was relatively small.[105] In addition, a 2016 FDIC study analyzed the effects of changes in macroeconomic factors relative to core profitability (a measure that includes the regulatory environment) on the overall profitability of community banks and found that macroeconomic shocks, such as unemployment levels and interest rates, explained the majority of the change.[106] A Federal Reserve study and a survey conducted by FDIC also analyzed how changes in the regulatory environment affected community banks' compliance costs, performance, and operations.[107] According to

---

[104] FDIC defined small banks as those with less than $10 billion in assets, a group that includes many community banks. For preliminary results of their research, see Federal Deposit Insurance Corporation, CBAC 2018 Preview: FDIC Small Business Lending Survey (Washington, D.C.: Nov. 1, 2017). According to FDIC officials, they anticipate issuing their final report in 2018.

[105] Robert M. Adams and Jacob P. Gramlich, "Where Are All the New Banks? The Role of Regulatory Burden in New Charter Creation," Finance and Economics Discussion Series 2014-113 (Washington, D.C.: Dec. 16, 2014).

[106] In this study, community bank profitability is measured using pretax return on assets. Jared Fronk, "Core Profitability of Community Banks: 1985-2015," FDIC Quarterly, vol. 10, no. 4 (2016).

[107] The Federal Reserve and the Conference of State Bank Supervisors conducted an annual survey of community banks from 2014 through 2017. According to Federal Reserve

Federal Reserve officials, the results of their study were largely inconclusive. Similarly, FDIC's survey of the factors affecting regulatory compliance costs at nine community banks found that data limitations prevented them from identifying any specific effects.[108]

Banking regulators have also taken steps to try to mitigate potential effects of changes in the regulatory environment on small business lending. For example, to reduce the time and resources community banks use for compliance activities, Federal Reserve, FDIC, and OCC officials said they made changes to the duration of examinations and provided technical assistance related to regulatory compliance and bank management.[109] Community bank representatives and policy and advocacy groups have also suggested that the cost of complying with new capital rules reduced the ability of community banks to lend to small businesses. In response, regulators proposed changes to certain capital rules, adopted in 2013, for institutions with total assets under $1 billion.[110]

---

officials, this research was intended to assess anecdotal reports from banks that regulatory changes required banks to add staff and expenses. The survey results are available at https://www.communitybanking.org/ (last accessed on Jan. 5, 2018). FDIC's Division of Insurance and Research conducted interviews with nine community bankers to understand the factors affecting the cost of regulatory compliance and to obtain financial data to better understand how regulation and supervision affect bank performance. The interviews were conducted in October and November 2012. Federal Deposit Insurance Corporation, FDIC Community Banking Study (Washington, D.C.: December 2012).

[108] FDIC found that the study participants in general did not separately track the cost of regulatory compliance, and the majority of the nine study participants indicated that it was costly to separate out the indirect costs of compliance from normal operating costs. As a result, FDIC was unable to obtain specific information about what drives the cost of regulatory compliance.

[109] In 2014 and 2015, the Federal Reserve revised its examination guidelines to more closely align the expected examination activities with the size, complexity, and risk profile of the institution (see: Board of Governors of the Federal Reserve System, Community Bank Risk-Focused Consumer Compliance Supervision Program, Consumer Affairs Letter CA 13-19 (Nov. 18, 2013) and Enhancements to the Federal Reserve System's Surveillance Program, Supervision and Regulation Letters SR 15-16 (Dec. 10, 2015)). According to Federal Reserve officials, they also began conducting more examinations from off-site locations. In 2016, in response to a legislative change allowing regulators to decrease the frequency of examinations for certain institutions, FDIC, the Federal Reserve, and OCC decreased the frequency of on-site examinations for institutions with total assets under $1 billion (a population that is primarily composed of community banks).

[110] See Simplifications to the Capital Rule Pursuant to the Economic Growth and Regulatory Paperwork Reduction Act of 1996, 82 Fed. Reg. 49984 (Oct. 27, 2017). The 2013 rules were designed to strengthen the capital requirements of banks and certain banking organizations by improving the quality and quantity of regulatory capital and increasing the

Community Banks 69

Similar to community bank regulators, NCUA has also taken steps to monitor and assess the effects of changes in the regulatory environment on credit unions' activities, including small business lending.[111] According to NCUA officials, they monitor trend data, conduct 3-year rolling reviews of their regulations, and convene special working groups to monitor implementation of new rules.

- Data monitoring. NCUA officials told us that to identify any potential effects of changes in the regulatory environment on credit unions' small business lending, they monitor institutions' small business lending activities.[112] NCUA officials found that credit unions' small business lending has steadily increased since 2001 and was the fastest growing segment of credit unions' loan portfolio.
- Review of regulations. In addition, NCUA conducts an annual retrospective review of its regulations, whereby credit union representatives, other stakeholders, and the public are invited to identify opportunities to reduce the burden of NCUA's regulations.[113] According to NCUA officials, credit union and industry group representatives use this process to help identify unintended consequences of regulatory changes. For example, NCUA's updated small business lending rule went into effect in January 2017, and NCUA officials said they plan to use the annual

---

risk-sensitivity of the capital rule. The proposal addresses aspects of the generally applicable capital rules related to the treatment of acquisition, development, or construction loans; items subject to threshold deduction; and minority interests included in regulatory capital, among other things.

[111] For the purpose of our review, all loans made by credit unions for business activities are considered small business loans.

[112] NCUA collects quarterly data from credit unions on their financial condition, income and expenses, and lending activities (among other things).

[113] Annually, NCUA solicits public comments on opportunities to modernize, improve the applicability, or reduce the burden of approximately one-third of their regulations. According to NCUA officials, the process is structured so that each NCUA regulation is considered for public comment every 3 years.

retrospective review process to identify any unexpected effects on credit unions' small business lending from this change.[114]
- Monitor implementation. Finally, NCUA officials told us that in 2017, following the issuance of NCUA's updated small business lending rule, they created a working group of credit union representatives, state regulators, and NCUA staff to discuss the implementation of the new rule, including how credit unions are adapting to the new requirements. Among other things, the group is intended to increase understanding of supervisory expectations, identify concerns with interpretation and enforcement of the regulation, and identify opportunities to improve NCUA's guidance related to the regulation.

CONCLUSION

Financial regulation helps ensure the safety and soundness of the financial system but can also have unintended effects. Although recent regulatory changes have generally targeted larger institutions, these changes have the potential to affect community banks' small business lending as well. It is therefore important for regulators to understand how regulation may be affecting community banks and their small business customers. However, the data banks are required to report to regulators do not accurately capture community banks' lending to small businesses because they exclude a portion of these loans and may include loans to large businesses. Federal internal control standards require regulators to obtain relevant and reliable data from external sources. Bank regulators have not reassessed the reporting requirement since 1992 (when it was established as mandated by Congress), but technological changes since then may allow regulators to change the requirement to better reflect lending to small businesses without unduly increasing reporting burdens on

---

[114] See Member Business Loans; Commercial Lending, 81 Fed. Reg. 13530 (Mar. 14, 2016). According to NCUA officials, they anticipate that the annual review process will include the updated small business lending rule in 2019 or 2020.

banks. Without data that better reflect community banks' lending to small businesses, regulators and policymakers are limited in their ability to assess the availability of credit to small businesses as Congress envisioned and to understand how regulation may be affecting these institutions.

AGENCY COMMENTS AND OUR EVALUATION

We provided a draft of this chapter to the Federal Reserve, BCFP, FDIC, NCUA, OCC, and SBA for review and comment. We received written comments from the Federal Reserve, FDIC, and OCC, which we have reprinted in appendixes V through VII. The Federal Reserve, BCFP, and FDIC also provided technical comments, which we incorporated as appropriate.

In their written comments, the Federal Reserve, FDIC, and OCC agreed with the recommendation made to each regulator to collaborate to reevaluate and modify (as needed) the requirements for the data banks report in the Call Reports to better reflect lending to small businesses. Each agency stated its intent to coordinate through the Federal Financial Institution Examination Council to reassess and potentially modify the reporting requirements. The regulators also noted that in considering revisions to the reporting requirements they would attempt to balance the importance of maximizing information collection with the potential burden changes would place on banks. In addition, OCC noted that any changes to the reporting requirements would be issued for public comment prior to taking effect. As agreed with your office, unless you publicly announce the contents of this chapter earlier, we plan no further distribution until 30 days from the report date. At that time, we will send copies to the Federal Reserve, BCFP, FDIC, NCUA, OCC, and SBA, and other interested parties. Sincerely yours,

Lawrance L. Evans, Jr.
Managing Director
Financial Markets and Community Investment

Oliver Richard
Director, Center for Economics
Applied Research and Methodology

CONGRESSIONAL ADDRESSEES

Addressees

The Honorable Steve Chabot Chairman
Committee on Small Business House of Representatives

APPENDIX I: OBJECTIVES, SCOPE, AND METHODOLOGY

This chapter examines the effect of changes in the regulatory environment on community banks and credit unions and their ability to meet the credit needs of small businesses. It examines, for the period from 2010 through 2017, the effect of changes in the regulatory environment, including (1) the data regulators use to measure the volume of small business lending and how and why small business lending volumes changed, (2) how and why small business lending processes changed among these institutions, and (3) how and why the number of institutions and their financial performance changed, as well as (4) actions regulators took to identify and mitigate the effects of changes in the regulatory environment on these institutions and their small business customers.[115]

Data Used for Our Analysis

To address these four objectives, we compiled regulator data on community banks and credit unions from January 2001 through June 2017.

---

[115] Data we report on banks and credit unions are as of June 2017.

Data on Banks

For this chapter, we defined community banks using the Federal Deposit Insurance Corporation's (FDIC) definition, which takes into account a bank's business activities, asset size, office structure, and geographic scope of operations to determine the extent to which it focuses on traditional lending and deposit gathering.[116] Specifically, to identify community banks, FDIC:

1) Aggregates all charter-level data reported under each holding company into a single banking organization.
2) Excludes any banking organization with (a) no loans or no core deposits; (b) foreign assets greater then or equal to 10 percent of total assets; or (c) more than 50 percent of assets in certain specialty banks, including credit card specialists and industrial loan companies, among others.
3) Includes all remaining banking organizations that engage in basic banking activities as measured by a total loans-to-asset ratio greater than 33 percent and a ratio of core deposits to assets greater than 50 percent.
4) Includes all remaining banking organizations that operate within a limited geographic scope. This is measured as having: (a) at least one branch and not more than an indexed maximum number of branches (the indexed maximum was 75 branches in 2010), (b) no more than the indexed maximum level of deposits for any one branch (the indexed maximum was $5 billion in 2010), (c) branches in no more than two large metropolitan statistical areas, and (d) branches in no more than three states.
5) Includes all banking organizations (even those previously excluded due to limited banking activities or geographic scope) under an indexed maximum asset size threshold (the indexed maximum was $1 billion in 2010).

---

[116] Community banks include banks with up to $39.5 billion in assets in 2017. For additional information on FDIC's definition of community banks, see: Federal Deposit Insurance Corporation, FDIC Community Banking Study (December 2012).

To identify community banks from 2001 through 2017, we used the community bank indicator in FDIC's Statistics on Depository Institutions and their Historical Community Banking Reference Data.[117] In total, we identified 9,914 unique community banks from the first quarter of 2001 through the second quarter of 2017 for analysis. We assessed the reliability of these data for the purposes of identifying community banks by reviewing relevant documentation; interviewing knowledgeable officials; and electronically testing the data for missing values, outliers, and invalid values, and we found the data to be sufficiently reliable for that purpose.

We subsequently compiled quarterly bank-level data on both community banks and large banks (that is, all banks that were not community banks), including information on their loans and leases, assets, deposits, employment, return on assets, and other characteristics from FDIC's Statistics on Depository Institutions. These data are submitted quarterly by all FDIC-insured banks through the Federal Financial Institution Examination Council's Consolidated Reports of Condition and Income (Call Reports) and, prior to March 2012, from Thrift Financial Reports.[118] We compiled these data for every quarter from the first quarter of 2001 through the second quarter of 2017. We assessed the reliability of these data by reviewing relevant documentation; interviewing knowledgeable officials; and electronically testing the data for missing values, outliers, and invalid values, and we found the data to be sufficiently reliable for the purpose of identifying community banks and constructing indicators associated with compliance costs and business lines for banks.

In addition, we used FDIC's Community Banking Study Structure data to determine, from the first quarter of 2001 through the second quarter of 2017, the number of exits from the pool of community banks each year, the

---

[117] These publicly available data contain quarterly records for all FDIC-insured banks.

[118] Call Reports are a primary source of financial data used for the supervision and regulation of banks. They consist of a balance sheet, an income statement, and supporting schedules. Every national bank, state member bank, and insured state nonmember bank, is required to file a consolidated Call Report. The specific reporting requirements depend on the size of the institutions and whether they have any foreign offices. All institutions file a Call Report normally as of the close of business on the last calendar day of each calendar year. As of March 2012, savings associations no longer filed Thrift Financial Reports and instead were required to file Call Reports.

reason for the exit, and, for mergers, whether the acquiring bank was a community bank.[119] We assessed the reliability of these data by reviewing relevant documentation; interviewing knowledgeable officials; and electronically testing the data for missing values, outliers, and invalid values, and we found the data to be sufficiently reliable for the purpose of identifying bank mergers, failures, and other exits.

To identify the number of new community banks formed each year, we used the Board of Governors of the Federal Reserve System's (Federal Reserve) National Information Center Bulk Structure data, which contain a variable indicating the date on which each community bank became active. Specifically, we matched these data with our data set of community banks using the Federal Reserve's identification number for each bank to count the number of new community bank formations in each year.[120] We assessed the reliability of these data by reviewing relevant documentation and electronically testing the data for missing values, outliers, and invalid values, and we found the data to be sufficiently reliable for the purpose of identifying new banks.

To identify the number of bank branches and their locations, we used FDIC's Summary of Deposits data from 2001 through 2017. Banks submit information on each of their branches annually to FDIC. These data are available as of June of each year. For our purposes, we defined a branch as any bank branch or location that accepts deposits. We assessed the reliability of these data by reviewing relevant documentation and electronically testing the data for missing values, outliers, and invalid values, and we found the data to be sufficiently reliable for the purpose of determining the number and location of bank branches.

Finally, we placed community banks into four size categories based on total assets (measured in 2016 dollars) in a given year. We defined micro community banks as having less than $100 million in assets, small

---

[119] These data contain records identifying each instance an FDIC-insured bank enters or exits the universe of banks filling Call Reports beginning in the second quarter of 1984.

[120] Institutional identification numbers are assigned by the Federal Reserve when an institution becomes active and are unique to that institution. The identification numbers stay with an institution during a charter conversion (such as, a credit union converting to a bank) and are not reused.

community banks as having at least $100 million but less than $300 million in assets, medium community banks as having at least $300 million but less than $1 billion in assets, and large community banks as all community banks having $1 billion or more in assets.

Data on Credit Unions

We also assembled data on credit unions that we obtained from regulators' public websites and directly from the National Credit Union Administration (NCUA). We analyzed small and medium (based on total assets) natural person credit unions and excluded large credit unions from our analysis.[121] To identify large credit unions, we used a methodology similar to that used by FDIC to define community banks.[122] Mirroring FDIC's approach, we used NCUA Call Report data to determine that the largest 5 percent of credit unions had total assets greater than about $100 million in 1994 and $900 million in 2016. We used these thresholds—$100 million and $900 million— to exclude the largest credit unions in 1994 and 2016, respectively. Moreover, we calculated that growth from $100 million in 1994 to $900 million in 2016 represented an approximately 10.5 percent annual growth rate. To determine which credit unions to exclude in the years from 1994 through 2016, we applied this annual growth rate to our 1994 base of $100 million, which allowed us to calculate asset-size thresholds for 1994 through 2017. To identify the credit unions for our analysis, we applied these asset-size thresholds to all federally, state-, and privately insured credit unions that filed an NCUA Call Report in each quarter from the first quarter of 2001 through the second quarter of 2017. The remaining credit unions included in our population represented approximately 95 percent of all credit unions as of June 2017. To better ensure the validity of this methodology, we shared our approach with

---

[121] Natural person credit unions are credit unions whose members (and owners) are individuals.
[122] To account for changes in bank size over time due to economic conditions, inflation, and the size of the banking industry, FDIC used a compound annual growth rate of 5.7 percent to adjust the asset size threshold each year for its community bank definition. It made the size threshold $250 million in 1985 and $1 billion in 2010. Approximately 90 percent of all banking organizations fell within these asset-size thresholds in both 1985 and 2010, the base years for their compound annual growth calculation.

officials from NCUA and incorporated their comments into our methodology.

We then compiled quarterly Call Report data on these credit unions' loans and leases, assets, deposits, employment, return on assets, and other characteristics from the first quarter of 2001 through the second quarter of 2017. We assessed the reliability of these data by reviewing relevant documentation; interviewing knowledgeable officials; and electronically testing the data for missing values, outliers, and invalid values. We found the data to be sufficiently reliable for the purpose of identifying small and medium credit unions and constructing indicators of the number of institutions, their lending activities, and financial performance.

To identify the number of new credit unions and credit union mergers, for each year in the period, we obtained data from NCUA. These data identify the name of the new, acquiring, and acquired credit unions and the date the event occurred. We assessed the data for reliability by electronically testing these data for missing values, outliers, and invalid values, and found the data to be sufficiently reliable for the purpose of constructing indicators on credit union mergers and new entrants. Finally, we used the Federal Reserve's National Information Center Bulk Structure data to count the number of credit unions that failed each year.[123] As noted previously, we determined that these data were sufficiently reliable for identifying credit union failures.

Finally, to facilitate our comparison of bank and credit union data across multiple years, we adjusted dollar figures for inflation using the Bureau of Economic Analysis's Gross Domestic Product Implicit Price Deflator. All dollar figures in the report are in 2016 dollars.

Data on Small Business Lending

While conducting our analyses, we found that the reported regulatory measure of community banks' small business lending using bank

---

[123] These data contain structural information on banks, credit unions, and other institutions for which the Federal Reserve has supervisory, regulatory, or research interest. Information is available for all active banks and credit unions and the last instance of closed institutions. Among other things, these data contain information identifying the reason for a credit union failure and the date on which the exit occurred.

regulators' data on "loans to small businesses" had limitations for accurately measuring small business lending. For example, the $1 million threshold that defines small business loans and the $500,000 threshold that defines small business farm loans are not indexed to inflation. As a result, the number of loans that fall under these thresholds decreases over time due to inflation alone, regardless of any actual changes in lending levels, which may cause the data to underestimate the volume of small business lending. In addition, these data include small loans to large businesses and exclude larger loans to small businesses, which may result in an over- or underestimation of the volume of small business lending. To further explore the limitations of these data, we reviewed regulator analyses that used these data, including Federal Reserve reports to Congress.[124] We also used the Bureau of Economic Analysis's Implicit Price Deflator to show how the value of the small business loan threshold would have changed over time if it had been indexed to inflation when it was established. Although the data were limited in their ability to measure small business lending, we determined that the data were generally a reliable measure of business loans with original principal balances of $1 million or less.

As we were unable to measure banks' small business lending directly, we identified two additional proxy measures of small business lending (business loans with original principal balances of $1 million or less made by survivor community banks and total business lending) and used these measures together to analyze community banks' small business lending. We identified these alternative measures based on our internal analyses and conversations with bank regulators and believe these are suitable alternative measures of small business lending. Specific information on our methodology follows:

Survivor Community Banks' Business Loans of $1 Million or Less

Our first measure used as its basis the data regulators collected from institutions on small business lending defined as commercial real estate loans and commercial and industrial loans with original principal balances

---

[124] For example, Board of Governors of the Federal Reserve System, Report to the Congress on the Availability of Credit to Small Businesses (Washington, D.C.: September 2017).

of $1 million or less and farm loans with original principal balances of $500,000 or less, regardless of the size of the borrowing business or farm. These data were available through FDIC's Statistics on Depository Institutions annually (as of the second quarter of each year) from 2001 through 2009, quarterly from 2010 through 2016, semi-annually for banks with less than $1 billion in assets in 2017, and quarterly for banks with $1 billion or more in assets in 2017.[125]

To help ensure that our analysis of trends in Call Report data on business loans of $1 million or less captured lending levels rather than changes in the population of community banks, we adjusted the data regulators collected on small loans to business to account for the effect of exits from the population of community banks.[126] Exits occur due to a community bank becoming a large bank or merging with a large bank, voluntarily exiting the market, or failing during the period we examined. To account for these exits, we identified those banks that were in operation through the entire period from 2001 through June 2017 and were community banks in June 2017, were new entrants during this period and were community banks in June 2017, or merged with another community bank where the merged entity continued to exist until June 2017 and was a community bank at that time. This population is known as "survivor" community banks. To identify these survivor community banks, we first started with the quarterly Statistics on Depository Institutions data for all community and large banks from the first quarter of 2001 through the second quarter of 2017. We then matched these data with FDIC's Community Banking Structure data and (1) eliminated all institutions that exited for some reason other than a merger (such as from a failure, a voluntary exit, or an unexplained exit) and (2) replaced the FDIC identification numbers of institutions that exited due to a merger or

---

[125] Effective March 2017, regulators changed the frequency for reporting on loans to small businesses of eligible institutions (generally, those with only domestic offices and total assets less than $1 billion) from quarterly to semi-annually. All other institutions continue to file quarterly reports.

[126] According to FDIC and OCC officials, when comparing a subpopulation of institutions, they sometimes adjust the population being analyzed to take into account entries and exits from the population—this is known as merger-adjusting. Merger-adjusting has advantages and disadvantages, including introducing survivor bias into the analysis.

consolidation with the identification numbers of their ultimate owner at the end of the study period (the second quarter of 2017). We considered an institution to be a community bank for our entire study period if it or its ultimate owner met FDIC's definition of a community bank in the second quarter of 2017. We then calculated the annual amount of outstanding business loans of $1 million or less for the survivor population of community banks as of the second quarter of each year from 2001 through 2009, the fourth quarter of each year from 2010 through 2016, and the second quarter of 2017 and analyzed changes for these institutions for the periods from 2001 through 2017.[127] To address the potential for survivor bias with this measure, we also analyzed total business lending without adjusting for exits from the population of institutions.

Total Business Lending

Our second proxy measure of small business lending used data collected from community banks on all commercial real estate, commercial and industrial, and farm loans. These data are collected in the quarterly Call Reports and are available through FDIC's Statistics on Depository Institutions. This alternative measure of small business lending also has limitations. In particular, it overestimates small business lending by community banks by including loans to large businesses. As large businesses are more likely than small businesses to obtain large business loans, the small number of large business loans could be disproportionally represented in data on total business lending by community banks.

Although both of these proxies for measuring community banks' small business lending have limitations, we determined that these data, used in combination, are appropriate measures for providing perspective on community banks' small business lending.

For credit unions, the Call Report definition of a member business loan includes any loan, line of credit, or letter of credit where the proceeds will be used for a commercial, corporate, or agricultural purpose and the net balance is $50,000 or greater. For the purpose of our review, all member

---

[127] The quarters analyzed varied because of changes to the frequency and timing of regulators' collection of small business lending data from 2001 through the second quarter of 2017.

business loans made by credit unions are considered small business loans. Because loans for less than $50,000 are not included in this definition of business loans, this approach likely underestimates small business lending by credit unions. Additionally, we analyzed data on Small Business Administration (SBA) section 7(a) loans from 1992 through 2017, which were provided to us by SBA. We assessed the community bank, credit union, and SBA data for reliability by electronically testing these data for missing values, outliers, and invalid values, and we found the data to be sufficiently reliable for the purpose of analyzing community banks' and credit unions' small business lending.

Changes in Community Banks' and Credit Unions' Small Business Lending, Number of Institutions, and Financial Performance

To identify how and why community banks' and credit unions' small business lending, the number of institutions, and financial performance changed from 2001 through 2017, we conducted a literature review; interviewed key stakeholders; analyzed data we compiled on banks and credit unions, including developing and estimating econometric models; and conducted generalizable surveys of community bank and credit union representatives.[128]

Literature Review

We conducted a literature review to identify (1) potential indicators and data sources to analyze and describe the number of community banks and credit unions and these institutions' small business lending and financial performance and (2) analysis, research, and other statements made by researchers, market participants, stakeholders, and agency officials about factors, including the effects of changes in the regulatory environment, which could influence changes in community bank and credit

---

[128] Data we report on community banks and credit unions are as of June 2017.

union activities since 2010. To identify existing research, analysis, and statements, we conducted searches of various databases, such as ProQuest, Scopus, Public Affairs Information Service, Policy File, Econlit, and the Harvard Kennedy School's Think Tank and federal agency websites. Our literature review primarily covered sources from 2010 onward. From these sources, we identified studies and articles that appeared in journals or were published by federal agencies, stakeholders, universities, or public policy organizations that were relevant to our research. We performed these searches and identified articles from November 2016 to April 2017. We reviewed the methodologies of these studies and determined that they were sufficiently reliable for identifying indicators and data sources for our analysis and potential explanations for trends in community bank and credit union activities since 2010. We used the results of this literature review to help inform our analysis of trends in community banks' and credit unions' activities, including by identifying data sources and indicators of bank and credit union performance used in these analyses. To supplement our identification of potential indicators and data sources, we also asked regulators (Bureau of Consumer Financial Protection (BCFP), the Federal Reserve, FDIC, NCUA, and the Office of the Comptroller of the Currency (OCC)) and SBA officials about the indicators and data sources they use to monitor the number of institutions and activities of banks and credit unions.

We also used the results of this literature review to develop a list of potential effects of changes in the regulatory environment on community banks and credit unions, including effects on lending products and services (e.g., changes in the time to make loans, the products offered, the cost of these products, the availability of these products to certain types of borrowers); the number of institutions (e.g., decisions to merge, close branch offices, open branch offices); and services provided to customers (e.g., time to serve customers, develop new products and services, innovate). We also used the literature review to identify alternative explanations for changes in the number and activities of community banks and credit unions, such as changes in the economic environment, competition, and technological changes in the industry. To further inform the initial list of potential effects, we also included a question about the effects of changes in the regulatory environment on community banks and credit unions during five focus groups held with community bank and credit union representatives as part of GAO's work on a related engagement assessing which regulations created the most burden for community banks and credit unions.[129]

Interviews

We also conducted semi-structured interviews with a range of market participants and regulators to obtain additional information about the effects of changes in the regulatory environment, as well as other factors that may influence small business lending, the number of community banks and credit unions, and the financial performance of these institutions and to help inform our survey questions. Specifically, we interviewed representatives of 10 community banks and 8 credit unions, selected to include in our sample institutions with a range of asset sizes, geographic locations, and urban and rural locations. We also interviewed representatives of one of the largest U.S. banks (based on total asset size) with significant small business lending. To supplement our interviews with financial institutions, we interviewed representatives of 4 consumer groups and 3 financial services advocacy groups, selected because of their familiarity with community banks and credit unions and changes in the regulatory environment. In addition, we interviewed officials from the Federal Reserve, BCFP, FDIC, NCUA, and OCC. To obtain the perspective of small businesses on changes in the availability and cost of small business credit, we interviewed a judgmentally selected sample of small business advisers from six states' Small Business Development

---

[129] Specifically, we asked two focus groups of community bank officials and three focus groups of credit union officials about the impact of compliance with changes to the Bank Secrecy Act/anti-money laundering requirements, the TILA-RESPA Integrated Disclosure requirements (a mortgage-related regulation), and Home Mortgage Disclosure Act of 1975 reporting requirements on community banks' and credit unions' activities. Focus group participants were selected to represent a range of total asset sizes. For additional information on the focus group methodology, see: GAO, Community Banks and Credit Unions: Regulators Could Take Additional Steps to Address Compliance Burdens, GAO-18-213 (Washington, D.C.: Feb. 13, 2018).

Centers, including at least one state from each of the four Census regions and representatives of six small business advocacy groups.[130] To select small business advocacy groups to interview, we judgmentally chose organizations representing a range of membership types (e.g., start-ups, established businesses, organizations serving minority- or women-owned businesses). Finally, we interviewed SBA officials about changes in the availability of small business lending and the factors that may have affected any changes.

Analysis of Bank and Credit Union Data

In addition, we analyzed trend data on banks' and credit unions' small business lending, the number of these institutions, and their financial performance from 2001 through 2017, and we developed econometric models to describe the extent to which changes in the regulatory environment may have contributed to these trends for community banks.[131] To analyze changes in community banks' small business lending, we analyzed data on their business loans of $1 million or less and total business lending both before and after adjusting for exits. Specifically, for Call Report data on business loans of $1 million or less, we calculated the total number and dollar amount (adjusted for inflation) of community banks' loans as of the second quarter of each year from 2001 through 2009, the fourth quarter of each year from 2010 through 2016, and the second quarter of 2017. We also calculated the amount of business loans of $1 million or less for survivor community banks and by community bank size category. For total business lending, we calculated the dollar amount (adjusted for inflation) of community banks' total business lending both for all community banks and survivor community banks. Finally, for credit unions, we calculated the total number and dollar amount (adjusted for inflation) of small business loans. We then analyzed how these trends changed over the period from 2001 through 2017 (including the changes

---

[130] Small business advisers are staff from Small Business Development Centers who provide coaching and other assistance to aspiring and existing small business owners throughout the country. We interviewed advisers in Connecticut, Ohio, Arkansas, Texas, Nevada, and Oregon.

[131] Data we report on community banks and credit unions are as of June 2017.

during the period from 2010 through 2016, which we identified because they represent periods of key changes in the operating and regulatory environment for financial institutions). We also compared community banks' trends in the amount and number of loans to small businesses and amount of all business loans to those of large banks, and compared community banks' amount of loans to small businesses to that of credit unions.[132]

To further analyze the trends in small business lending, we also analyzed the lending of small business loans guaranteed by SBA. Specifically, we calculated the total dollar amount (adjusted for inflation) of SBA-guaranteed loans that community banks disbursed each year from January 1992 through December 2017 using loan-level data provided by SBA. These data contained the FDIC certification number of the lending bank for each bank loan. Using this number, we were able to identify banks and calculate their amount of SBA-guaranteed lending from 1992 through 2017.

To analyze changes in the number of banks and credit unions and the financial performance of banks and credit unions from 2001 through 2017, we compared trends occurring during this period. Specifically, for community banks, large banks, and credit unions, we calculated the percentage change in the number of institutions from 2001 through 2009, and from 2010 through 2017, and compared trends for these two periods and also compared trends between community banks and large banks. To better understand the extent to which institutional growth, mergers, failures, and new entrants contributed to changes in the number of institutions, we counted the number of community bank and credit union exits annually by reason (consolidations, mergers with an existing community bank, mergers with a large bank, failures, and other unexplained exits) and the number of new entrants for the period from 2001 through 2017.[133] We then calculated the percentage change in the

---

[132] Our large bank analysis of Call Report data on business loans of $1 million or less is not adjusted for exits because we judged that relatively few large banks became community banks during this period.

[133] Consolidations occur when an existing bank holding company combines related institutions. According to NCUA officials, there is no legal provision for the consolidation of credit

number of institutional exits (by exit reason) and entrances for the two periods and compared the results.

To complement our analysis of changes in the number of institutions, we also analyzed changes in the number of bank and credit union branches and their locations. To identify the number of bank branches and their locations, we used FDIC's Summary of Deposits data from 2001 through 2017 to count the number of community and large bank branches in each year. We then compared trends in the number of community bank branches for the periods from 2001 through 2009, and 2010 through 2017. To determine how many counties had no community bank branches in 2010 and 2017, we combined FDIC's data with county-level unemployment data from the Bureau of Labor Statistics for these years, which allowed us to identify all U.S. counties, including those without community bank branches. This allowed us to determine whether the number of counties with no community banks had increased or decreased during this period. We assessed the reliability of these data by reviewing relevant documentation and electronically testing the data for missing values, outliers, and invalid values, and determined they were sufficiently reliable for purposes of counting and identifying the geographic location of community bank offices.

Using FDIC data and MapInfo, we also calculated the percentage changes in the number of community banks in each county between 2010 and 2017 and determined the number and portion of counties that gained community banks, had no change in the number of community banks, declined by no more than 10 percent, declined by more than 10 percent but not more than 25 percent, and declined by more than 25 percent.

For our analysis of community bank branch data, we categorized branches as rural or urban based on their physical addresses in 2010 and 2017 using the Department of Agriculture's Rural-Urban Commuting Area

---

unions; therefore, we did not count consolidations for credit unions. Banks or credit unions fail when their financial conditions have deteriorated to the point that they are unable to meet their obligations to depositors and others and they are closed by federal or state regulators. Mergers are generally a means by which banks and credit unions can expand their size and geographic reach by combining with or acquiring other banks or credit unions that previously had different owners.

codes. The codes classify all Census tracts in the United States into 10 tiers from rural to urban based on daily commuting patterns, urbanization, and population density. For ease of presentation, we consolidated these 10 tiers into two categories where "rural" consists of loans in large rural towns and small towns and isolated rural areas and "urban" consist of loans in urban and suburban areas. We assessed the reliability of these data by reviewing relevant documentation and electronically testing the data for missing values, outliers, and invalid values, and we found the data to be sufficiently reliable for the purpose of categorizing institutions as urban or rural. We then analyzed how the number and percentage of community bank offices in urban and rural areas changed during this period. To identify the number of credit union offices, we used NCUA's Call Report data to count the number of credit unions in each year from 2012 through 2016, the only years for which reliable data were available.[134] We then analyzed the percentage change in the number of credit union offices during this period. We did not analyze the location of credit union offices because of the limited number of years for which the data were available.

We also analyzed the financial performance of community banks and credit unions by identifying key indicators of financial institution performance and comparing trends in these indicators for the period from 2001 through 2017 (we calculated these indicators as of the fourth quarter of each year from 2001 through 2016 and as of the second quarter of 2017).[135] To identify indicators of financial performance, we used the results of our literature review (described previously) to identify indicators used by researchers, market participants, and other stakeholders to describe the financial performance of community banks and credit unions. We also considered indicators used in our prior work analyzing the financial

---

[134] NCUA collects information on credit union branches. However, NCUA officials said they believed this information is only reliable for the purposes of calculating trends in credit union branches starting in 2012.

[135] We did not merger-adjust the bank or credit union data for these analyses. As noted previously, according to FDIC and OCC officials, when comparing a subpopulation of institutions, they sometimes adjust the population being analyzed to take into account entries and exits from the population—this is known as merger-adjusting. Merger-adjusting has advantages and disadvantages, including introducing survivor bias into the analysis.

performance of community banks and credit unions.[136] We selected indicators for analysis that provided information on key community bank and credit union performance measures that our literature review and interviews with stakeholders identified as potentially affected by changes in the regulatory environment or other changes following the crisis. For example, in response to changes in the regulatory environment, community banks and credit unions may have hired additional staff or outside counsel or consultants, invested in new software, or taken other actions that may have increased the number of employees and the cost of resources and also, potentially, decreased institutions' profits and performance. To measure these changes, we selected indicators of the market shares of financial institution activities (including total assets, deposits, and loans and leases); cost of resources (using the median ratio of noninterest expenses to assets); employment (using the median number of employees per $1 million assets); profitability (measured by the median pretax return on assets); and institutional efficiency (measured as the median proportion of net operating expenses that are absorbed by overhead expenses).[137] We then analyzed how these indicators changed over the period from 2001 through 2017.

Finally, to help determine the extent to which changes in the regulatory environment may have affected changes in community banks' small business lending, the number of institutions, and their financial performance, we constructed econometric models. These models considered the extent to which macroeconomic, local market, and bank characteristics or other factors (including changes in the regulatory environment, demand for small business loans, and technological changes) affected changes in community bank small business lending; merger activities; new bank formation; and return on assets. For more information

---

[136] GAO, *Dodd-Frank Regulations: Impacts on Community Banks, Credit Unions and Systemically Important Institutions*, GAO-16-169 (Washington, D.C.: Dec. 30, 2015) and *Troubled Asset Relief Program: Most Community Development Capital Initiative Investments Remain Outstanding*, GAO-16-626 (Washington, D.C.: July 5, 2016).

[137] For our analysis of market share of deposits, we only considered domestic deposits. The efficiency ratio is defined as noninterest expenses, less amortization of intangible assets, as a percentage of net interest income plus noninterest income. A lower value indicates greater efficiency.

about our econometric modeling, including model specifications, data sources, and results, see appendix II.

National Survey of Community Banks and Credit Unions

To obtain information on the changes community banks and credit unions made to their small business and residential mortgage lending products and management activities since the 2007–2009 financial crisis and the factors that influenced those changes, we administered web-based surveys to nationally representative samples of community bank and credit union chief executive officers.

Community Bank Survey

We administered our community bank survey to a generalizable sample of 466 community bank chief executive officers from July 10, 2017, to August 25, 2017. We used publicly available FDIC Call Report data to build our population frame. We then stratified by three different asset size categories and a two-level urban/rural categorization. This resulted in 6 sampling strata. We then sorted the banks geographically by Census division within each stratum and selected a systematic random sample within each stratum to ensure that our selection of banks was geographically representative. The asset size categories we used were small (less than $100 million in total assets), medium (between $100 million and $300 million in total assets), and large (more than $300 million in total assets). To designate community banks as urban or rural, we used Rural-Urban Commuting Area codes. We excluded community banks without Rural-Urban Commuting Area codes and community banks that conducted no business lending in 2016 from our sample. FDIC provided contact information for selected community banks so that we could request their participation in our survey.

We allocated sufficient sample size to the 6 strata to support estimation for an attribute measure with a margin of error no greater than plus or minus 10 percentage points at the 95 percent level of confidence for small, medium, large, urban, and rural banks. We then adjusted the initial stratum sample size allocations upward further for an assumed response rate of 60 percent. Our original sample size was 474; however, 6 banks had gone out of business or been acquired between the time the 2016 FDIC Call Reports were filed and when we contacted FDIC for the bank representative information and, in their survey responses, an additional 2 banks indicated that they had not originated any small business or residential mortgage loans since 2010. We treated these 8 banks as out-of-scope. In addition, 19 of the banks selected in our sample had already been selected to receive a survey for another GAO engagement running concurrently with ours. These 19 banks were not contacted as part of our survey to minimize respondent burden and subsequently were treated as nonrespondents for this survey. Our community bank survey had a weighted response rate of 68 percent. Because our survey instrument subdivided respondents into banks that answered "increased," "decreased," or "no change" to top-level check questions, we were not able to report survey results by all subpopulations. For information on the specific questions asked in the survey, see appendix III.

Credit Union Survey

We administered our credit union survey to a generalizable sample of 470 credit union chief executive officers from July 17, 2017, to August 25, 2017. We built our population frame from publicly available NCUA Call Report data. We stratified the credit unions that engaged in both business and residential mortgage lending in the first quarter of 2016 by two asset size categories and a two-level urban/rural categorization. This resulted in four strata. We then placed all credit unions that engaged in residential mortgage lending only in the first quarter of 2016 into a fifth stratum. We then sorted the credit unions geographically by Census division within each stratum and selected a systematic random sample within each stratum to ensure that our selection of credit unions was geographically representative. We used this stratified design to ensure that we would be able to collect information on residential mortgage lending as well as small business lending by credit unions. Given that credit unions are generally smaller institutions than community banks, the asset size categories we used to stratify the credit union sample were smaller than the categories we used to stratify the community bank sample. Specifically, the two asset size categories we used were small (less than $50 million in total assets) and large (more than $50 million in total assets). We also used Rural-Urban Commuting Area codes to designate credit unions as urban or rural. We excluded credit unions without Rural-Urban Commuting Area codes and credit unions that conducted no business or residential mortgage lending in the first quarter of 2016 from our sample. NCUA provided contact information for the selected credit unions so that we could request their participation in our survey.

We allocated sufficient sample size to the five strata to support estimation for an attribute measure with a margin of error no greater than plus or minus 10 percentage points at the 95 percent level of confidence for small, large, urban, and rural credit unions and credit unions that conducted only residential mortgage lending. We then adjusted the initial stratum sample size allocations upward further for an assumed response rate of 60 percent. Our original sample size was 513; however, 8 credit unions had gone out of business or been acquired between the time the 2016 NCUA Call Reports were filed and when the sample was fielded. We treated these 8 credit unions as out-of-scope. Finally, 35 credit unions indicated on the survey that they had not originated a small business loan or a residential loan since 2010. We treated these 35 credit unions as out-of-scope. Our credit union survey had a weighted response rate of 61 percent. Because our survey instrument subdivided respondents into credit unions that answered "increased," "decreased," or "no change" to top-level check questions, we were not able to report survey results by all subpopulations. For information on the specific questions asked in the survey, see appendix IV.

Both surveys included questions on small business lending activities, management decisions, and residential mortgage lending. Aside from some terminology, the survey questions were identical and included both multiple choice and open-ended questions.[138] To develop the survey questions, we considered information obtained from interviews and focus

---

[138] For example, in the credit union survey, the small business lending section was labeled "member business lending" to reflect the terminology used in credit union lending.

groups with community banks, credit unions, industry groups, and regulators; a literature review; a review of topical congressional hearings; and a review of regulators' strategic plans since 2010. To ensure that our questions were relevant and reasonable and that survey respondents could provide reliable and valid responses, we conducted pretests of both surveys with four banks and three credit unions. Our survey expert also reviewed both instruments and provided feedback. To encourage participation, we conducted follow-up efforts, including multiple email and phone call reminders, throughout the survey period. These reminders allowed us to encourage respondents to complete the survey and provide support in accessing the survey questionnaire.

To analyze the results of each survey, we examined responses to multiple choice and open-ended questions separately. For multiple choice questions, we constructed 95 percent confidence intervals around each estimate and examined the extent to which institutions cited a variety of factors, including the regulatory environment, as having contributed to changes in their small business lending, residential mortgage lending, and overall management. For open-ended questions, we categorized written comments by the topic(s) they addressed and examined which topics institutions addressed most frequently in their comments. For the community bank survey results, see appendix III. For the credit union survey results, see appendix IV.

Because we followed a probability procedure based on random selections, our sample is only one of a large number of samples that we might have drawn. Since each sample could have provided different estimates, we express our confidence in the precision of our particular sample's results as a 95 percent confidence interval (for example, plus or minus 7 percentage points). This is the interval that would contain the actual population value for 95 percent of the samples we could have drawn. Confidence intervals are provided along with each sample estimate in the report. All survey results presented in the report are generalizeable to the respective population of in-scope community financial institutions, except where otherwise noted.

In addition to the reported sampling errors, the practical difficulties of conducting any survey may introduce other types of errors, commonly referred to as nonsampling errors. For example, differences in how a particular question is interpreted, the sources of information available to respondents, or the types of people who do not respond can introduce unwanted variability into the survey results. We included steps in both the data collection and data analysis stages for the purpose of minimizing such nonsampling errors.

Regulators' Identification of the Effects of Changes in the Regulatory Environment and Mitigating Steps

To evaluate the extent to which regulators took steps to identify and address any effects of changes in the regulatory environment on community banks and credit unions, we reviewed regulators' collection and analysis of information on any effects and the steps they took to mitigate any effects. We then compared these actions with standards for using quality information to inform decision making.[139] To identify actions regulators took to assess the effects of changes in the regulatory environment on community banks and credit unions, we collected and reviewed regulators' research on effects; reviewed documentation of regulators' outreach activities with institutional representatives and other stakeholders; and interviewed regulators, community bank and credit union representatives, and other stakeholders. To identify regulators' research, we conducted a literature review to identify works published by regulators from 2010 through 2017 that assessed trends in the number of institutions, their financial performance, and their small business lending products and processes. To identify existing research, we conducted searches of the ProQuest database. We supplemented our search with a review of regulators' websites and confirmed our list of research papers with regulators. We then reviewed each research paper to assess the extent to

---

[139] GAO, *Standards for Internal Control in the Federal Government*, GAO-14-704G (Washington, D.C.: September 2014).

which they evaluated trends in the number of institutions (e.g., decisions about acquiring or being acquired, branch closure or opening, changes in staff time and activities, profits); their financial performance; or institutions' lending activities (e.g., changes in the time period to make loans, number of lending products and services offered, minimum credit quality criteria, borrower documentation requirements, access to credit for certain types of borrowers) and the extent to which regulators considered the effects of changes in the regulatory environment as a factor affecting those trends.

To identify actions regulators took to collect and analyze information from community bank and credit union representatives and other stakeholders, we reviewed regulators' websites and interviewed regulators about efforts to collect information, including the extent to which they collected information on effects as part of the examination process. We analyzed (where available) the agendas, transcripts, and notes from outreach meetings with institutional representatives and other stakeholders to assess the extent to which regulators asked about the effects of changes in the regulatory environment on community banks' and credit unions' management decisions and lending activities and the extent to which participants highlighted challenges. Specifically, we analyzed documents associated with the Federal Reserve's Community Depository Institutions Advisory Council and FDIC's Advisory Committee on Community Banking; regulators' outreach meetings with industry representatives, including the Federal Reserve's, FDIC's, and OCC's Economic Growth and Regulatory Paperwork Reduction Act outreach meetings (the process used input from the public to identify ways to reduce regulatory burden on institutions); and the 2012–2016 comment letters NCUA received as part of its annual regulatory review process. For each of these documents, we used a data collection instrument to assess the extent to which regulators explicitly asked about the effects of changes in the regulatory environment on their activities and the extent to which participants or letter writers identified specific effects on institutions' management activities, financial performance, or lending activities.

To complement these reviews, we also interviewed institutional representatives and regulators. Specifically, we interviewed 10 community bank and 8 credit union representatives and asked about the extent to which regulators asked about any effects of changes in the regulatory environment on the number of institutions, their performance, and their small-business lending activities. As noted previously, these institutional representatives were selected to provide a mix of institutions of various size (based on total asset size) and geographic locations (both urban and rural and throughout the United States). We also interviewed Federal Reserve, FDIC, NCUA, and OCC officials about their efforts to identify any effects of changes in the regulatory environment on community banks and credit unions. Finally, we interviewed officials from BCFP and SBA about their efforts to identify and analyze any effects of changes in the regulatory environment, including BCFP's changes to rules governing residential mortgage lending, on the number and financial performance of community banks and credit unions and their small business lending.

To assess the extent to which regulators took steps to mitigate any effects from changes in the regulatory environment on community banks and credit unions, we interviewed regulators about the steps they took and reviewed related documentation. Specifically, we asked regulators to provide information and documentation of actions they took in response to concerns raised by institutions and their customers about the effects of changes in the regulatory environment, including the elimination of certain lending products or services and decreased staff time to engage with customers. We reviewed regulators' documents, such as notifications of policy change, to assess the extent to which regulators identified the effect of changes in the regulatory environment as motivating the adjustment to policies or processes.

We conducted this performance audit from November 2016 to August 2018 in accordance with generally acceptable government auditing standards. Those standards require that we plan and perform the audit to obtain sufficient, appropriate evidence to provide a reasonable basis for our findings and conclusions based on our audit objectives. We believe that the evidence obtained provides a reasonable basis for our findings and conclusions based on our audit objectives.

APPENDIX II: DESCRIPTION OF GAO'S ECONOMETRIC MODELS OF FACTORS AFFECTING COMMUNITY BANK OUTCOMES SINCE 2010

Introduction

The regulatory environment of banks has changed since the 2007–2009 financial crisis as Congress enacted new legislation and regulators have implemented additional regulatory requirements. In particular, the Dodd-Frank Wall Street Reform and Consumer Protection Act (Dodd-Frank Act) imposed new requirements on banks of all sizes, and although these requirements were directed primarily at large banks, questions exist over the extent to which this act and regulations implemented since then, such as new capital requirements, have affected community banks.[140] This appendix provides detail on our analysis of the effects of changes in the regulatory environment since 2010 on various community bank outcomes, specifically mergers, formation of new institutions or charters, small business lending, and pretax return on assets.[141]

It is generally difficult to determine the effects of changes in the regulatory environment on community banking outcomes for a number of reasons. First, the regulatory environment comprises changes in laws and their implementation, enforcement by supervisory agencies, and regulatory uncertainty on the part of community banks in the aftermath of the financial crisis. Second, apart from the financial crisis, concurrent events that could confound the effects of changes in the regulatory environment include changes in risk aversion on the part of community banks pertaining

---

[140] Pub. L. No. 111-203, 124 Stat. 1376 (2010).
[141] In this report, we define community banks' using FDIC's definition, which takes into account institutions' assets, foreign interests, and geographic characteristics. Community banks include banks with up to $39.5 billion in assets in 2017.

to credit, changes in technology such as innovations in online banking, and competition from alternative or nonbank lenders. Third, the ability to credibly identify the cumulative effect of regulation is limited by the data and available estimation methodologies.

Although it is difficult to determine a direct link between changes in the regulatory environment and subsequent community banking outcomes, regulations could impose compliance costs if they increase regulatory reporting and compliance requirements and likely reduce the profitability of community banks. We reported in 2012 that, although the Dodd-Frank Act reforms are directed primarily at large, complex U.S. financial institutions, regulators, industry officials, and others collectively identified provisions within the act that they expected to have both positive and negative effects on community banks.[142] At the same time, it is difficult to know for sure which provisions would affect community banks because the outcome would depend largely on how agencies have implemented certain provisions through their rules.[143] Furthermore, not all of the rules had been finalized at the time of our review, and others had probably not had sufficient time to materially influence bank activity.[144]

GAO's Econometric Models of Community Bank Outcomes

We used econometric models to examine, to the extent possible, potential effects of changes in the regulatory environment on community

---

[142] GAO, *Community Banks and Credit Unions: Impact of the Dodd-Frank Act Depends Largely on Future Rule Makings*, GAO-12-881 (Washington, D.C.: September 2012).

[143] The rules that were expected to affect community banks include depository insurance reforms and Bureau of Consumer Financial Protection supervision of nonbank providers of financial services and products, certain mortgage reforms mandated by the Dodd-Frank Act, and risk retention provision for securitizations.

[144] In a study in which FDIC conducted interviews with nine community banks to better understand what drives the cost of regulatory compliance at their banks, most interview participants stated that while no one regulation or practice had a significant effect on their institution, the cumulative effects of regulatory requirements led them to increase staff over the past 10 years. Moreover, the interviews indicated that it would be costly in itself to collect more detailed information about regulatory costs. As a result, measuring the effect of regulation remains an important question that presents substantial challenges. See Federal Deposit Insurance Corporation, FDIC Community Banking Study (December 2012).

bank outcomes from 2010 through 2016, the period when the Dodd-Frank Act was enacted and other regulatory and supervisory changes were made. Because it is difficult to directly estimate the cumulative effects of changes in the regulatory environment on community banking outcomes, we focused on the role of nonregulatory factors (such as macroeconomic, local market, and bank characteristics) and inferred from that the potential role of regulations.

Description of Estimation Methodology

Our approach was developed under the premise that it is difficult to measure directly the cumulative effect of the regulatory environment. We developed econometric models to better understand the extent to which community bank outcomes (such as mergers, new bank formations, small business lending, and return on assets) could potentially be attributable to changes in the regulatory environment since 2010. Because measuring the cumulative effect of changes in the regulatory environment is difficult, we used a two-step approach that did not require us to estimate regulatory effects directly.

- First, we estimated models that used data on macroeconomic, local market conditions (consisting of local market demographics and local market competition), and bank characteristics, which represent factors that we could measure, prior to 2010 (from 2003 through 2009) to help forecast community bank outcomes from 2010 to 2016; that is, we forecasted the counterfactuals since 2010 based on the regression models in the absence of all the factors not included in the model ("other factors") that include the effects of the regulatory environment.
- Second, by comparing the actual outcomes that occurred during the period to the outcomes forecasted by the models, we drew conclusions about the influence of other factors that represent the difference between the actual and forecasted outcomes.[145] These

---

[145] Adams and Gramlich (2014) used a similar approach in their study of new bank formations.

other factors represent the combined effect of all the variables that we did not include in our model and would include changes in the regulatory environment since 2010, and depending on the model, factors such as demand for small business loans, credit standards applied by banks, innovations in online banking and competition from nonbank lenders, technological changes, and scale economies.[146]

In addition to the limitations of the models mentioned earlier, it is implicit in our approach that the preferences of the marketplace participants did not generally change between the two periods. More important, we could not determine the contribution of the regulatory environment that would be part of the other factors. We acknowledge this study's inherent weaknesses with respect to these aspects.

General Structure of Models Used

Following the existing literature, we hypothesized that the factors that could affect community bank outcomes and that we could adequately measure are macroeconomic conditions (MACRO), local market demographics (LDEMOG), local market competition (LCOMP), and community bank characteristics (BANKCHAR). In general, all these factors are intended to capture the role of nonregulatory factors.[147] The general specification of the models we used is as follows:

$$Y_{imt} = B0 + \text{MACRO}_t\ B1 + \text{LDEMOG}_{mt}\ B2 + \text{LCOMP}_{mt}\ B3 + \text{BANKCHAR}_{it}\ B4 + e_{imt}.$$

Y is the dependent variable representing the community bank outcome. It represents outcomes or trends of community bank (i) in market (m) in

---

[146] The impact of the costs of regulatory compliance is expected to be included in the effects of regulatory changes.

[147] Because local market competition and bank characteristics could be affected by regulatory changes and some of the other factors, we also estimated the effects of only macroeconomic factors and local market demographics, which are not likely to be influenced by these other factors. We obtained similar results.

year (t). The parameters to be estimated are represented by the Bs (where B_0 is the constant term), and "e" is the regression error term.

The community banks are identified based on the Federal Deposit Insurance Corporation's (FDIC) methodology (see app. I).[148] We defined a local market to be a metropolitan statistical area (MSA) or a non-MSA county for an area that is not part of an MSA. All the variables were measured on an annual basis, and dollar values are in billions (unless indicated otherwise) and in 2016 dollars. We developed models for four community bank outcomes.

Mergers Model

We modeled whether a community bank (i) was acquired by another bank (community bank or large bank) in year (t).[149] The data are bank-year observations that equal 1 if a community bank was acquired and 0 if not acquired. The likelihood of a merger acquisition depends generally on the difference in perceived postmerger valuation of the target community bank between the acquirer community bank or large bank and the target community bank. Thus, factors affecting the current performance of the target community bank are important.[150] We identified two groups of community banks: those that were acquired (treatment banks) and those that were not acquired (control banks) during the sample period. We used matched pairs data where the control banks were randomly selected to match the number of treatment banks for each year. The explanatory variables are 1-year lags prior to the merger years because of potential endogeneity concerns and data limitation.[151] We estimated the model using a logistic regression technique.

---

[148] Federal Deposit Insurance Corporation, FDIC Community Banking Study, December 2012.
[149] The FDIC estimated that about 3 percent of the acquisitions were government assisted but they were not identified in the data.
[150] See, for example, studies by Akhigbe, Madura, and Whyte (2004), and Ballew, Iselin, and Nicoletti (2017).
[151] The data reported for the acquired bank generally stopped one quarter before the reported merger date, meaning that sufficient data on the bank were not generally available in the year of the merger.

New Bank Formations Model

We modeled whether new community banks were formed in market (m) in year (t).[152] The data are market-year observations that equal 1 if a market had new community banks formed and 0 if no new community banks were formed. The likelihood of new bank formation in a market generally depends on factors affecting the new bank's expected profits upon entry, which would depend on local market conditions, including competition.[153] We identified two groups of markets: those where a new community bank was formed (treatment markets) and those where no new community banks were formed (control markets) during the sample period. We used matched pairs data where the control markets were randomly selected to match the number of treatment markets for each year. The explanatory variables are the average of the 2 years prior to the new bank formation because of potential endogeneity concerns and data limitation.[154] We estimated the model using a logistic regression technique.

Small Business Lending Model

We modeled small business lending by a community bank (i) in year (t). Small business loans are proxied by loans of $1 million or less at origination for commercial and industrial loans and for commercial real estate loans, and $500,000 or less at origination for farm loans (i.e., agricultural farmland or production finance loans). Small business lending by community banks tended to fall over time due to exits from failures or when a community bank becomes a large bank through growth or a merger, it does not capture lending to small businesses of loans over $1 million, and the thresholds as reported in the Call Reports are not adjusted for inflation. We therefore modeled loans within the threshold made by "survivor" community banks— community banks that existed or formed

---

[152] For the purposes of this report, we consider a new bank formation to be a new community bank that was not a charter conversion and not a new bank formed by an existing bank holding company. We measured the number of new community bank formations based on the period when the bank began collecting deposits (as compared to when the bank was chartered) in order to match the data to the bank branches data.

[153] See, for example, studies by Seelig and Critchfield (2003) and Adams and Gramlich (2014).

[154] For instance, the treatment market for 2016, when there was a single new bank formation, did not have data available for 2015.

since 2001 and remained in existence through 2017, and we excluded banks that exited the population of community banks at any time from 2001 through 2017. We also modeled total business loans by community banks, which are not subject to the potential bias due to lack of inflation-adjustment of the threshold but have other limitations discussed in the body of this chapter. The volume of lending by community banks depends generally on factors affecting the supply of and demand for loans by businesses.[155] We estimated the models using an unbalanced panel consisting of data on bank-market-year observations. The explanatory variables are 1-year lags because of potential endogeneity concerns and data limitation.[156] We estimated the models using an ordinary least square regression technique.

Pretax Return on Assets Model

We modeled pretax return on assets of community bank (i) in year (t). It is the annualized pretax net income as a percentage of total assets. The profitability of community banks depends generally on macroeconomic conditions and structural factors such as business practices and competitive environment.[157] We estimated the models using an unbalanced panel consisting of data on bank-market-year observations. The explanatory variables are 1-year lags because of potential endogeneity concerns. We estimated the model using an ordinary least square regression technique.

List of Explanatory Variables Used

The list of the explanatory variables we used in the models is provided below.

The macroeconomic (MACRO) factors consist of the following variables:

---

[155] See, for example, studies by Kiser, Prager, and Scott (2012), and Berrospide and Edge (2010).
[156] Prior to 2010 the data for business lending were reported only in the second quarter, thus the reported loans were between July 1 of that year and June 30 of the subsequent year. Therefore it is appropriate to forward the outcome variable of our regression model by 1 year.
[157] See, for example, Fronk (2016) and Athanasoglu, Brissimis, and Delis (2008).

- Federal funds rate: the effective federal funds rate (percent).
- Rate spread: the difference between the 10-year and 1-year Treasury notes (percent).
- Gross state product growth rate: percentage change in gross state product (percent).

The local market (LDEMOG) factors consist of the following variables:[158]

- Market size: the market in which a community bank operates is assigned to one of four categories based on the total assets of all the community banks in that market—1st (1), 2nd (2), 3rd (3), and 4th (4) quartiles (indicators).
- MSA markets: equals one for counties in MSAs and equals zero for non-MSA counties (an indicator).
- Income per capita growth rate in the market: percentage change in per capita income (ratio of personal income to population).
- Unemployment rate in the market (percent).
- Population growth rate in the market: percentage change in population.
- Population density in the market: ratio of population to land area (population per square mile).
- House price percentage change in the market: percentage change in house price index.

The local market competition (LCOMP) factors consist of the following variables:

---

[158] We included market fixed-effects, which are market-level characteristics unique to each market that do not vary over time, in the lending and pretax return on assets models, which used panel data. We did not include state fixed-effects because they could include state regulations; however, we note that the market fixed-effects could capture state regulations that have not changed over the period of our study.

- Market concentration of bank deposits: Herfindahl-Hirschman Index of market concentration of bank deposits.
- Market concentration of bank branches: Herfindahl-Hirschman Index of market concentration of bank branches.
- Credit union assets: credit unions' total market assets (in logs).
- Number of credit unions in the market.

The bank characteristics (BANKCHAR) consist of the following variables:[159]

- Community bank size: each bank is assigned to one of four categories based on the bank's total assets size—micro (less than $100 million), small (equal to or greater than $100 million and less than $300 million), medium (equal to or greater than $300 million and less than $1 billion), and large (equal to or greater than $1 billion), (indicators).
- Total equity capital: equity capital (percent of total assets).
- Nonperforming assets: net charge-offs (percent of total loans and leases).
- Core deposits: core or retail deposits (percent of total assets).
- Brokered deposits: brokered deposits (percent of total assets).
- Current loans: loans that are less than 90 days past due or accruing interest (percent of total loans and leases).
- Other real estate owned (REO) assets: other REO assets (percent of total assets).
- Loan concentration in residential real estate: residential, 1-4 family, real estate loans (percent of total assets).

---

[159] We included community bank fixed-effects, which are bank-level characteristics unique to each bank that do not vary over time in the lending and pretax return on assets models, which used panel data.

- Geographic diversification: equals one if community bank has branches in multiple states and equals zero otherwise (an indicator).
- Subchapter S corporation (indicator): equals one if community bank is a subchapter S corporation and equals zero otherwise (an indicator).

Results of Analysis of Community Bank Outcomes

We analyzed community bank outcomes for mergers, new bank formations, small business lending, and pretax return on assets from 2010 through 2016. The analysis examined the relative contributions of nonregulatory factors—represented by macroeconomic conditions, local market conditions (consisting of local market demographics and local market competition), and bank characteristics—and all the factors not included in the models (other factors), which would include changes in the regulatory environment, to the community bank outcomes. We estimated our regression models using data from 2003 through 2009, the period before the post 2010 regulatory changes. Using the regression estimates from the model and the data for the factors that we were able to include in our models we forecasted community bank outcomes from 2010 through 2016. Our analysis indicated that for all the models the actual outcomes were within the 95 percent prediction intervals we constructed for the forecasted outcomes, except for 1 year in the mergers model and for 2 years in the return on assets model. This suggests that the net effect of factors that we included (i.e., macroeconomic, local market, bank characteristics) on community bank outcomes may not have fundamentally changed from the 2003–2009 period to the 2010– 2016 period, and the effect of other factors that we did not include, such as the regulatory changes, on community bank outcomes were likely small over the 2010-

2016 period.[160] It is important to note, our forecast of the influence of the other factors is combined and we could not decompose it to determine the cumulative effects of the changes in the regulatory environment since 2010.

Mergers

As shown in Figure 20, our model forecasted that the contribution of the other factors to acquisition of community banks ranged between 6 percent and 31 percent from 2010 through 2016, implying that macroeconomic, local market, and bank characteristics explain most (that is, 69 to 94 percent) of the mergers for this period. Our analysis indicates that the actual number of mergers was higher than forecasted by the macroeconomic, local market, and bank characteristics, and this higher number is attributable to the effects of other factors. The other factors could include regulatory changes since 2010, as well as factors such as the availability of failed banks that attracted banks seeking to grow, the opportunity to expand in their existing markets or enter new markets, and incentives to achieve scale economies to lower costs of increased regulatory compliance. New regulations required by the Dodd-Frank Act entail significant compliance costs for banks above the $10 billion asset threshold and could have made banks approaching or just above the threshold more likely to engage in acquisitions to reduce such costs.[161] The individual contributions of these other factors is unknown, which limits our ability to determine the cumulative effects of changes in the regulatory environment on the acquisitions of community banks.

---

[160] The regression estimates using data from 2003 to 2009 are provided in tables 6 and 7. The relationship between the actual outcomes and the predicted outcomes from 2003 to 2009 provide an indication of the extent to which the macroeconomic, local market, and bank characteristics predicted the outcomes. All the estimated models were statistically significant at the 1 percent level; however, the strength of the relationships between the community bank outcomes and the measured factors, represented by the R-squared or the area under the receiver operating characteristic (ROC) curve for the mergers and return on assets models, is moderate. We performed several robustness checks of the models, including using different sample data and estimation techniques, and obtained results similar to those we have reported. See tables 6 and 7 or more details.

[161] See the study by Ballew, Iselin, and Nicoletti (2017), who suggested that increased costs, which may not vary substantially with assets, could result from the requirement to perform annual stress tests and Bureau of Consumer Financial Protection oversight.

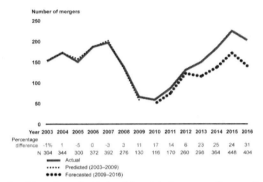

Source: GAO analysis of data from the Federal Deposit Insurance Corporation (FDIC), Board of Governors of the Federal Reserve System, Bureau of Economic Analysis, Bureau of Labor Statistics, Census Bureau, Federal Housing Finance Agency, and National Credit Union Administration. | GAO-18-312.

Notes: We defined community banks using FDIC's definition, which takes into account institutions' assets, foreign interests, specializations, and geographic characteristics. Community banks include banks with up to $39.5 billion in assets in 2017. The data consisted of acquired community banks, and community banks that were not acquired, randomly selected to match the acquired community banks for each year to create a matched-pairs data set. The solid line in this figure depicts the actual number of community banks acquired by other community banks or large banks for each year. The numbers do not include banks that were omitted due to missing data. The remaining data represented 83 percent of the total community banks that were acquired. The dotted line in this figure—the predicted or forecasted number of mergers in each year—is the mean of the product of the estimated coefficients of the macroeconomic, local market, and bank characteristics (including the constant term) from the regression model using 2003–2009 data and their levels from 2003 through 2016, multiplied by the total number of treatment and control banks we used in the model. From 2003 through 2009, the difference between the actual and predicted lines (given in percentage terms below the figure) represents the extent to which our model was a reasonable fit for the data; a smaller difference indicates a better fit. The forecasted outcomes from 2010 through 2016 are the counterfactuals since 2010 based on the regression model in the absence of the other factors, including regulatory changes. The forecasted—not actual—relative contributions of other factors, which include the regulatory environment, in explaining the acquisitions of community banks from 2010 through 2016, are measured by the percent of the difference between the actual number of mergers and the forecasted number of mergers for the factors included in the regression model to the actual number of mergers. With the exception of 1 year, the actual number of community bank mergers was within the 95 percent confidence intervals for the forecasted number of mergers. "N" refers to the number of community banks used in the model in each year.

Figure 20. Actual Number of Community Bank Mergers Compared to Number Expected Based on Macroeconomic, Local Market, and Bank Characteristics, 2003–2016.

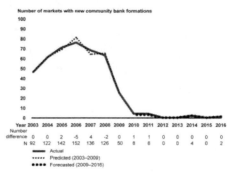

Source: GAO analysis of data from the Federal Deposit Insurance Corporation (FDIC), Board of Governors of the Federal Reserve System, Bureau of Economic Analysis, Bureau of Labor Statistics, Census Bureau, Federal Housing Finance Agency, and National Credit Union Administration. | GAO-18-312.

Notes: We defined community banks using FDIC's definition, which takes into account institutions' assets, foreign interests, specializations, and geographic characteristics. Community banks include banks with up to $39.5 billion in assets in 2017. The data consisted of markets with new community banks, and markets where no new community banks were formed, randomly selected to match the markets with new community banks for each year, creating a matched-pairs data set. The solid line in this figure depicts the actual number of markets with new community banks for each year. The numbers do not include markets that were omitted due to missing data. The remaining data represented 78 percent of the markets where new community banks were formed. The dotted line in this figure—the predicted or forecasted number of markets with new community banks in each year—is the mean of the product of the estimated coefficients of the macroeconomic and local market characteristics (including the constant term) from the regression model using 2003–2009 data and their levels from 2003 through 2016, multiplied by the total number of treatment and control markets we used in the model. From 2003 through 2009, the difference between the actual and predicted lines (given in number terms below the figure) represents the extent to which our model was a reasonable fit for the data; a smaller difference indicates a better fit. The forecasted outcomes from 2010 through 2016 are the counterfactuals since 2010 based on the regression model in the absence of the other factors, including regulatory changes. The forecasted—not actual—relative contributions of other factors, which include the regulatory environment, in explaining the formation of new community banks from 2010 through 2016, is measured by the difference between the actual number of markets with new community banks and the forecasted number of markets with new community banks for the factors included in the regression model. The actual number of new community bank formations was within the 95 percent confidence intervals for the forecasted number of formations. There were no new community bank formations in 2012, 2013, and 2015. "N" refers to the number of markets used in the model in each year.

Figure 21. Actual Number of Markets with New Community Bank Formations Compared to Number Expected Based on Macroeconomic and Local Market Characteristics, 2003–2016.

New Bank Formations

Although our model forecasted relatively few new community bank formations from 2010 through 2016, not exceeding 3 in any year, based on macroeconomic and local market conditions, the actual number of new community bank formations was only slightly higher, meaning that the difference that is attributable to the effects of other factors is small.[162] Furthermore, our model forecasted the sharp decline in the number of new community banks from 2010 through 2016, meaning that macroeconomic and local market conditions explained the majority of the decline in new bank formations.[163] Nonetheless, the other factors, which include regulatory changes since 2010, might have played a limited role. In particular, from 2009 through 2016, FDIC increased the required *de novo* period for newly organized, state nonmember institutions from 3 years to 7 years, which means new banks seeking deposit insurance are subject to a longer probationary period of examinations, capital requirements, and other requirements. Also, the low number of new bank formations from 2010 through 2016 could be because it was cheaper to buy a failed bank that had an existing charter than obtain a new charter for a bank. Again, the individual contributions of these other factors is unknown, which limits our ability to determine the cumulative effects of changes in the regulatory environment on the new community bank formations.

Small Business Lending

As shown in Figure 22 (left panel), our model forecasted that the contribution of the other factors to total small business loans held by community banks was 11 percent or less from 2010 through 2016, implying that macroeconomic conditions, local market, and bank characteristics explain most of total small business loans held by community banks for this period, using data for "survivor" community banks—community banks that existed or formed since 2001 and remained in existence through 2017, excluding banks that exited the population of

---

[162] This analysis does not include bank characteristics in the measured factors because it is for the formation of new community banks in a market.
[163] Adams and Gramlich (2014) obtained a similar result.

community banks at any time from 2001 through 2017.[164] Our analysis indicates that total small business loans were generally lower from 2010 through 2014 but higher in 2015 and 2016 than forecasted by the macroeconomic, local market, and bank characteristics, and the difference is attributable to the effects of other factors. The other factors could include regulatory changes since 2010, as well as factors such as low demand for small business loans, innovations in online banking and competition from nonbank lenders, technological changes, and tightened credit standards in the aftermath of the financial crisis, which more likely affected smaller loans. The right panel of Figure 22 shows our results for total business lending, which includes loans over the small business loan threshold that are excluded from the left panel of Figure 22. Our analysis indicates that total business loans were higher than forecasted by the macroeconomic, local market, and bank characteristics and the higher amount of loans is attributable to the effects of other factors, which is 23 percent or less. The difference between the results for the small business loans under the survivor community banks model and the total business loans model is likely because the small business loans model includes only loans under the $1 million threshold while the total business loans model includes loans of all sizes.[165] A possible reason is that after a merger (especially when a large bank acquired a small bank) the merged bank's small business lending would likely exceed the premerger lending of both the acquirer and the target resulting in more business lending postmerger.[166] The individual contributions of the other factors is unknown, which limits our ability to determine the cumulative effects of changes in the regulatory environment on business lending by community banks.

---

[164] We obtained similar results for the effects of the factors when we used data for small business loans for all community banks.

[165] We conducted a sensitivity analysis of the total business lending model using data for survivor banks only. We obtained similar results suggesting that the difference between the small and total business lending models is not likely due to using data for different community bank populations.

[166] See Jagtiani, Kotliar, and Maingi (2016), who studied the effect of community bank mergers on small business lending using data from 2000 through 2012.

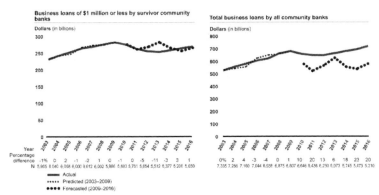

Source: GAO analysis of data from the Federal Deposit Insurance Corporation (FDIC), Board of Governors of the Federal Reserve System, Bureau of Economic Analysis, Bureau of Labor Statistics, Census Bureau, Federal Housing Finance Agency, and National Credit Union Administration. | GAO-18-312.

Notes: We defined community banks using FDIC's definition, which takes into account institutions' assets, foreign interests, specializations, and geographic characteristics. Community banks include banks with up to $39.5 billion in assets in 2017. The solid lines in each panel depict the actual total dollar amount of outstanding loans for the two measures of community bank small business lending we modeled: (1) survivor community banks' business loans of $1 million or less and (2) total business loans for all community banks for each year. The amounts do not include lending by banks that were omitted due to missing data. The data we used represented 70 percent of community banks for the model of survivor community banks' loans of $1 million or less and 80 percent of community banks for the model of all community banks' total business loans. The dotted lines in each panel—the predicted or forecasted total dollar amount outstanding of business loans of $1 million or less and total business loans in each year—is the mean of the product of the estimated coefficients of the macroeconomic, local market, and bank characteristics (including the constant term) from the regression model using 2003–2009 data and their levels from 2003 through 2016, multiplied by the number of community banks we used in the models. From 2003 through 2009, the difference between the actual and predicted lines (given in percentage terms below the panels) represents the extent to which our model was a reasonable fit for the data; a smaller difference indicates a better fit. The forecasted outcomes from 2010 through 2016 are the counterfactuals since 2010 based on the regression model in the absence of the other factors, including regulatory changes. The forecasted—not actual—relative contribution of other factors, which may include the regulatory environment, in explaining business lending by community banks from 2010 through 2016, is measured by the percent of the difference between actual business loans and the forecasted business loans for the factors included in the regression models to the actual business loans. The actual amounts of community bank business lending were within the 95 percent confidence intervals for the forecasted lending amounts. All dollar amounts are in constant 2016 dollars. "N" refers to the number of community banks used in the model in each year.

Figure 22. Actual Outstanding Amounts of Survivor Community Banks' Business Loans with Original Principal Balances of $1 Million or Less and All Community Banks' Total Business Loans Compared to Amounts Expected Based on Macroeconomic, Local Market, and Bank Characteristics, 2003–2016.

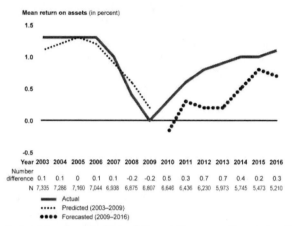

Source: GAO analysis of data from the Federal Deposit Insurance Corporation (FDIC), Board of Governors of the Federal Reserve System, Bureau of Economic Analysis, Bureau of Labor Statistics, Census Bureau, Federal Housing Finance Agency, and National Credit Union Administration. | GAO-18-312.

Notes: We defined community banks using FDIC's definition, which takes into account institutions' assets, foreign interests, specializations, and geographic characteristics. Community banks include banks with up to $39.5 billion in assets in 2017. The solid line in this figure depicts the actual pretax return on assets of community banks for each year. The returns do not include the performance of banks that were omitted due to missing data. The remaining data represented 80 percent of the community banks. The dotted line in this figure—the predicted or forecasted pretax return on assets in each year—is the mean of the product of the estimated coefficients of the macroeconomic, local market, and bank characteristics (including the constant term) from the regression model using 2003–2009 data and their levels from 2003 through 2016. From 2003 through 2009, the difference between the actual and predicted lines (given in number terms below the figure) represents the extent to which our model was a reasonable fit for the data; a smaller difference indicates a better fit. The forecasted outcomes from 2010 through 2016 are the counterfactuals since 2010 based on the regression model in the absence of the other factors, including regulatory changes. The forecasted—not actual—relative contribution of other factors, which include the regulatory environment, in explaining pretax return on assets of community banks from 2010 through 2016, is measured by the difference between actual pretax return on assets and the forecasted pretax return on assets for the factors included in the regression model. With the exception of 2 years, community banks' actual return on assets was within the 95 percent confidence intervals for the forecasted returns. "N" refers to the number of community banks used in the model in each year.

Figure 23. Actual Community Bank Return on Assets Compared to Returns Expected Based on Macroeconomic, Local Market, and Bank Characteristics, 2003–2016.

Pretax Return on Assets

As shown in Figure 23, the actual return on assets was higher than our model forecasted.[167] Our model forecasted that the contribution of the other factors to the pretax return on assets of community banks increased from 50 basis points to 70 basis points from 2010 through 2013, and fell below 50 basis points from 2014 through 2016. The other factors could include regulatory changes since 2010, the subsequent failure of numerous banks from 2009 through 2012 that eliminated many underperforming community banks with low pretax return on assets, and increased competition from other lenders that improved the performance of bank operations over time. The individual contributions of these other factors is unknown, which limits our ability to determine the cumulative effects of changes in the regulatory environment on the pretax return on assets of community banks.

Regression Estimates of Community Bank Outcomes

The regression estimates using data from 2003 through 2009 are provided in Tables 6 and 7. All the estimated models are highly significant based on the p-values of the tests of the models. We performed several robustness checks of the models, including using different sample data and estimation techniques. We obtained results similar to those we have reported.[168]

Mergers

In Table 6, the regression estimates, which used data from 2003 through 2009 to obtain counterfactual of the effects of macroeconomic, local market, and bank characteristics from 2010 through 2016 in the absence of the other factors, indicate that several factors were associated with an increased likelihood of a community bank being acquired. These acquired community banks had lower equity capital and higher

---

[167] The strength of relationship between return on assets and the factors we included in the model is consistent with previous studies; see, for example, Fronk (2016).
[168] See Tables 6 and 7 for more details.

nonperforming assets, suggesting they were more likely to be underperforming. Also, the acquired community banks had lower core deposits but higher brokered deposits (which suggests a lower proportion of funding from stable sources), were the smallest community banks, or were more likely to operate in multiple states but not likely to be subchapter S corporations. The acquisitions were also more likely to be in markets with higher unemployment, higher population growth, faster house price growth, and in MSA markets.[169]

New Bank Formations

In Table 6, the regression estimates, which used data from 2003 through 2009 to obtain counterfactual of the effects of macroeconomic and local market characteristics from 2010 through 2016 in the absence of the other factors, indicate that several factors were associated with an increased likelihood of new community bank formation in markets. They include markets with a high presence of credit unions. New bank formations were more likely in MSA areas and markets with high population growth. Also new bank formations were more likely when interest rates and the rate spread were high.[170]

Table 6. Logistic Regression Estimates of Community Bank Outcomes of Mergers and New Bank Formations, 2003–2009

Explanatory variables [a]	Mergers [b]	New bank formations [c]
Federal funds rate	1.2213	2.2440*
	(0.1698)	(0.9659)
Rate spread	1.2702	3.5768**
	(0.2356)	(1.9933)
Gross state product growth rate	1.0300	1.0873
	(0.0244)	(0.0660)
Market size: 2nd quartile (indicator)	n/a	0.8745
	n/a	(0.3436)
Market size: 3rd quartile (indicator)	n/a	0.8805
	n/a	(0.3521)

---

[169] See Table 6 for more details.
[170] See Table 6 for more details.

Explanatory variables [a]	Mergers [b]	New bank formations [c]
Market size: 4th quartile (indicator)	n/a	0.9624
	n/a	(0.3983)
Metropolitan statistical area markets (indicator)	1.9411***	8.4694***
	(0.2947)	(3.0204)
Income per capita growth rate in market	1.0194	1.0385
	(0.0165)	(0.0465)
Unemployment rate in market	1.0844**	1.0289
	(0.0407)	(0.0743)
Population growth rate in market	1.2123**	2.4351***
	(0.0971)	(0.4740)
Population density in market	1.0004***	1.0031**
	(0.0001)	(0.0013)
Explanatory variables [a]	Mergers [b]	New bank formations [c]
House price percentage change in market	1.0295***	1.0358
	(0.0112)	(0.0276)
Market concentration of bank deposits	0.9999	n/a
	(0.0001)	n/a
Market concentration of bank branches	n/a	0.9997*
	n/a	(0.0002)
Credit union total assets in market (in logs)	0.9988	n/a
	(0.0086)	n/a
Number of credit unions in market	n/a	1.0237**
	n/a	(0.0111)
Community bank size: small (indicator)	0.5793***	n/a
	(0.0640)	n/a
Community bank size: medium (indicator)	0.4943***	n/a
	(0.0693)	n/a
Community bank size: large (indicator)	0.9425	n/a
	(0.2454)	n/a
Equity capital	0.0086***	n/a
	(0.0138)	n/a
Nonperforming assets	1.3809***	n/a
	(0.1486)	n/a
Core deposits	0.9889**	n/a
	(0.0047)	n/a
Brokered deposits	1.0323***	n/a
	(0.0118)	n/a
Geographic diversification (indicator)	1.9969**	n/a
	(0.5957)	n/a
Subchapter S corporation (indicator)	0.5069***	n/a
	(0.0596)	n/a
Constant	0.6062	0.0012***
	(0.5395)	(0.0027)
Unit of analysis	Bank-year	Market-year

Table 6. (Continued)

Explanatory variables [a]	Mergers [b]	New bank formations [c]
Model p-value	0.0000	0.0000
Area under the receiver operating characteristic (ROC) curve	0.70	0.92
Number of unique banks or markets	Treatments: 1,059	Treatments: 227
	Controls: 1,059	Controls: 410
Number of observations	2,118	820

Legend: n/a=not applicable.

Source: GAO analysis of data from the Federal Deposit Insurance Corporation, Board of Governors of the Federal Reserve System, Bureau of Economic Analysis, Bureau of Labor Statistics, Census Bureau, Federal Housing Finance Agency, and National credit Union Administration. | GAO-18-312.

Notes: In this chapter, we define community bank using FDIC's definition, which takes into account institutions' assets, foreign interests, specializations, and geographic characteristics. Community banks include banks with up to $39.5 billion in assets in 2017. Community bank size (micro) is the omitted category for the community bank size variables. Market size (1st quartile) is the omitted category for the market size variable.

[a] The reported coefficients are odds ratios and robust standard errors are in parentheses. ***, **, and * represents coefficients that are statistically significant at 1 percent, 5 percent, or 10 percent or less, respectively. We could not use fixed-effects estimation because the banks and markets predicted the outcomes perfectly, respectively; however, we randomly selected control banks or markets to match the treatments to help minimize any potential bias in the selection of the controls. For both the mergers and new bank formations models, we also estimated the effects of only macroeconomic factors and local market demographics because local market competition and bank characteristics could be affected by regulatory changes. We obtained similar results.

[b] Mergers model: The mergers model is for community banks that are acquired (equals 1) and community banks that are not acquired (equals 0) in a year. The model used a random sample of nonacquired community banks as controls to match the number of acquired community banks for each year to create matched pairs of bank-year observations. We also estimated the model by market-year observations, and obtained similar results.

[c] New bank formations model: The new bank formations model is for markets where any number of new community banks are formed (equals 1) and markets with no new community banks formed (equals 0) in a year. The model used a random sample of markets with no new community banks formed as controls to match the number of markets where new community banks were formed for each year to create matched pairs of market-year observations. We also estimated the model using an ordered logistic technique—we obtained results for the markets where only one new community bank was formed, which represented 75 percent of the markets with new community bank formations. We obtained similar results. Although the ordered logistic estimation imposed the assumption of proportional odds, we could not relax this assumption using a generalized ordered logistic estimation because the estimation did not converge.

Lending

In Table 7, the regression estimates, which used data from 2003 through 2009 to obtain counterfactual of the effects of macroeconomic, local market, and bank characteristics from 2010 to 2016 in the absence of the other factors, indicate that several community bank characteristics were associated with small business lending. Lending was higher for community banks with lower equity capital, higher current loans, lower nonperforming loans, lower core deposits but higher brokered deposits, lower concentration of residential loans, geographically diversified banks with branches in multiple states, and larger banks. Also, lending was higher in markets with higher personal income growth and lower house prices, in states with lower economic growth, when interest rates were lower, and when the rate spread was smaller. In general, the direction of the effects is similar for total business lending, but with slightly larger impacts.[171]

Table 7. Ordinary Least Squares Regression Estimates of Community Bank Outcomes of Business Lending and Pretax Return on Assets, 2003–2009

Explanatory variables [a]	Small business lending [b]	Total business lending [c]	Pretax return on assets [d]
Federal funds rate	-0.0020***	-0.0076***	0.0219*
	(0.0002)	(0.0006)	(0.0126)
Rate spread	-0.0038***	-0.0137***	0.1382***
	(0.0003)	(0.0008)	(0.0170)
Gross state product growth rate	-0.0002***	-0.0005***	0.0547***
	(4.3e-05)	(0.0001)	(0.0026)
Metropolitan Statistical Area markets (indicator)	0.0072	0.0276	-0.5563
	(0.0082)	(0.0211)	(0.4524)
Income per capita growth rate in market	0.0001***	0.0004***	-0.0051***
	(2.0e-05)	(4.9e-05)	(0.0014)
Unemployment rate in market	-0.0001	-0.0037***	0.0301***
	(0.0002)	(0.0006)	(0.0106)
Population growth rate in market	0.0003*	0.0018***	-0.0902***
	(0.0002)	(0.0004)	(0.0100)
Population density in market	1.6e-06	1.9e-05	-0.0001
	(1.1e-05)	(4.2e-05)	(0.0002)

---

[171] See Table 7 for more details.

Table 7. (Continued)

Explanatory variables [a]	Small business lending [b]	Total business lending [c]	Pretax return on assets [d]
House price percentage change in market	-0.0002***	0.0011***	0.0452***
	(3.3e-05)	(0.0001)	(0.0017)
Market concentration of bank deposits	6.7e-07*	2.4e-06***	4.2e-05*
	(4.0e-07)	(8.1e-07)	(2.5e-05)
Credit union assets in market (in logs)	-2.0e-05	0.0003*	1.9e-05
	(0.0001)	(0.0002)	(0.0040)
Community bank size: small (indicator)	0.0070***	0.0073***	0.0343
	(0.0006)	(0.0010)	(0.0362)
Community bank size: medium (indicator)	0.0220***	0.0450***	-0.1418**
	(0.0018)	(0.0028)	(0.0568)
Community bank size: large (indicator)	0.0629***	0.1829***	-0.7980***
	(0.0081)	(0.0152)	(0.1189)
Equity capital	-0.0244***	-0.0356***	-3.1378***
	(0.0031)	(0.0114)	(0.2301)
Nonperforming loans	-0.0006***	-0.0022***	-0.0702***
	(0.0002)	(0.0005)	(0.0211)
Core deposits	-0.0001**	-0.0002**	0.0119***
	(2.8e-05)	(0.0001)	(0.0016)
Brokered deposits	0.0003***	0.0010***	-0.0334***
	(0.0001)	(0.0002)	(0.0034)
Current loans	0.0005***	0.0009***	0.2396***
	(0.0001)	(0.0003)	(0.0114)
Other Real Estate Owned loans in total	-0.0002	-0.0005	-0.4369***
	(0.0003)	(0.0007)	(0.0357)
Loan concentration in residential real estate	-0.0001***	-0.0005***	n/a
	(3.6e-05)	(0.0001)	n/a
Geographic diversification (indicator)	0.0165***	0.0497***	-0.2906***
	(0.0044)	(0.0080)	(0.1046)
Subchapter S corporation.(indicator)	0.0004	-0.0009	-0.0477
	(0.0006)	(0.0013)	(0.0368)
Constant	0.0009	0.0342	-23.6057***
	(0.0117)	(0.0310)	(1.1563)
Unit of analysis	Bank-year	Bank-year	Bank-year
Fixed effects	Banks, markets	Banks, markets	Banks, markets
Model p-value	0.0000[e]	0.0000[e]	0.0000[e]
R-squared	0.93	0.95	0.66
Number of unique banks	6,703	8,316	8,316

Explanatory variables [a]	Small business lending [b]	Total business lending [c]	Pretax return on assets [d]
Number of unique markets	1,587	1,644	1,644
Number of observations	42,003	49,445	49,445

Legend: n/a = not applicable. Source: GAO analysis of data from the Federal Deposit Insurance Corporation, Board of Governors of the Federal Reserve System, Bureau of Economic Analysis, Bureau of Labor Statistics, Census Bureau, Federal Housing Finance Agency, and National Credit Union Administration. | GAO-18-312.

Notes: In this chapter, we define community bank using FDIC's definition, which takes into account institutions' assets, foreign interests, specializations, and geographic characteristics. Community banks include banks with up to $39.5 billion in assets in 2017. Community bank size (micro) is the omitted category for the community bank size variables.

[a] The reported coefficients are marginal effects and the robust standard errors are in parentheses. ***, **, and * represent coefficients that are statistically significant at 1 percent, 5 percent, or 10 percent or less, respectively. We used bank and market fixed-effects estimation to control for possible unobserved heterogeneity across the banks and markets. For the small business lending and return on assets models, we also estimated the effects of only macroeconomic factors and local market demographics because local market competition and bank characteristics could be affected by regulatory changes. We obtained similar results.

[b] Small business lending model: The small business model is for total loans (in billions of 2016 dollars) with origination amounts of $1 million or less for commercial and industrial loans or commercial real estate loans, or $500,000 for farm loans, for "survivor" community banks—community banks that existed or formed since 2001 and remained in existence through 2017, and we excluded banks that exited the population of community banks at any time from 2001 through 2017. Survivor community banks include community banks that merged with another community bank such that the resulting bank remained a community bank. The model was estimated with robust standard errors clustered at the bank level using data for the "survivor" community banks. We also estimated lending that was within the thresholds of the business loans with outstanding principal balances of $1 million or less for all community banks. We obtained similar results.

[c] Total business lending model: The total business model is for total loans (in billions of 2016 dollars) for commercial and industrial loans, commercial real estate loans, or farm loans, for a community bank in a year. The model was estimated with robust standard errors clustered at the bank level. We also used a two-step Heckman selection procedure to account for the entry and exit of community banks over time, and estimated total business loans using data for only survivor community banks. We obtained similar results.

[d] Pretax return on assets model: The pretax return on assets model, in percent, is for a community bank in a year. The model was estimated with robust standard errors clustered at the bank level. We also used a two-step Heckman selection procedure to account for the entry and exit of community banks over time, and used data for only survivor community banks. We obtained similar results.

[e] The value is based on a model without the bank and market fixed-effects because the model F-value could not be computed due to lack of variation between some clusters in the model presented in the table, which is estimated with robust standard errors clustered at the bank level.

Pretax Return on Assets

In Table 7, the regression estimates, which used data from 2003 through 2009 to obtain counterfactual of the effects of macroeconomic, local market, and bank characteristics from 2010 through 2016 in the absence of the other factors, indicate that several community bank characteristics factors were associated with pretax return on assets. Performance was higher for community banks with lower equity capital, higher current loans, lower nonperforming loans, higher core deposits but lower brokered deposits, lower real estate owned loans, and community banks that were not diversified in multiple states and were smaller. Community bank performance was higher in markets with higher state economic growth, lower personal income growth, higher unemployment rate, lower population growth, and faster house price growth. Also, performance was higher when interest rates and rate spread were larger.[172]

Data Sources Used for Regression Analysis

1) Federal Deposit Insurance Corporation (FDIC) Community Banking Structure Reference Data: It contains data on the entrances and exits of banks (mergers and failed banks).
2) FDIC Statistics of Depository Institutions: These data come primarily from the Consolidated Reports of Condition and Income (Call Reports) of all FDIC-insured depository institutions. They are organized by subject, e.g., assets and liabilities, income and expense, loans, and performance and conditions ratios (data for bank characteristics).
3) FDIC Summary of Deposits: It is the annual survey of branch office deposits as of June 30 for all FDIC-insured institutions, including insured U.S. branches of foreign banks (data for bank branches).
4) Board of Governors of the Federal Reserve System National Information Center: It is a central repository of data about banks and

---

[172] See Table 7 for more details.

other institutions for which the Federal Reserve has a supervisory, regulatory, or research interest. It includes ownership relationships of the institution and changes to its structure over time (data for new bank formations).
5) Board of Governors of the Federal Reserve System: Data for effective federal funds rate.
6) National Credit Union Administration, Form 5300: Data for credit unions.
7) Bureau of Economic Analysis: Data for gross state product; state, metropolitan statistical area (MSA), and county personal incomes; and county population.
8) Bureau of Labor Statistics: Data for state, MSA, and county unemployment rates.
9) Census Bureau: Data for state and MSA populations; MSA and county land areas.
10) Federal Housing Finance Agency: Data for state, MSA, and county house price indexes.

Selected Previous Studies

To facilitate these analyses, we consulted the following prior studies.

General

1) Adam Levitin, *Fostering Economic Growth: The Role of Financial Institutions in Local Communities,* Testimony before the Senate Committee on Banking, Housing, and Urban Affairs, June 8, 2017.
2) Council of Economic Advisers, *The Performance of Community Banks Over Time*, Issue Brief, August 2016.
3) Drew Dahl, Andrew Meyer, and Michelle Neely, "Scale Matters: Community Banks and Compliance Costs," The Regional Economist, July 2016.

4) Federal Deposit Insurance Corporation (FDIC), *FDIC Community Banking Study*, December 2012.
5) Hester Peirce, Ian Robinson, and Thomas Stratmann, *How Are Small Banks Faring Under Dodd-Frank?* George Mason University, Mercatus Center Working Paper No. 14-05, February 2014.
6) James DiSalvo and Ryan Johnston, "How Dodd-Frank Affects Small Bank Costs: Do stricter regulations enacted since the financial crisis pose a significant burden?" Federal Reserve Bank of Philadelphia Research Department, *First Quarter* 2016.
7) James Heckman, "Sample Selection Bias as a Specification Error," *Econometrica*, vol. 47, no. 1 (1979), 153-161.
8) Marshall Lux and Robert Greene, *The State and Fate of Community Banking*, M-RCBG Associate Working Paper Series, No. 37 (Boston, Mass.: Mossavar-Rahmani Center for Business and Government, Harvard Kennedy School, Harvard University, February 2015).
9) Martin Baily and Nicholas Montalbano, *The Community Banks: The Evolution of the Financial Sector, Part III*, Economic Studies at Brookings, The Brookings Institution, December 2015.
10) Tanya Marsh and Joseph Norman, *The Impact of Dodd-Frank on Community Banks*, American Enterprise Institute, May 2013.
11) The Economist, *America's Community Banks Hope for Lighter Regulation* (Washington, D.C.: June 1, 2017), accessed on November 27, 2017, at https://www.economist.com/news/finance-and-economics/21722893-other-challenges-include-technology-staff-retention-succession-planning-and-thin.

Mergers

1) Aigbe Akhigbe, Jeff Madura, and Ann Marie Whyte, "Partial Anticipation and the Gains to Bank Merger Targets," *Journal of Financial Services Research*, vol. 26, no. 1 (2004) pp. 55-71.

2) Elena Becalli and Pascal Frantz, "The Determinants of Mergers and Acquisitions in Banking," *Journal of Financial Services Research*, vol. 43 (2013), pp. 265-291.
3) Hailey Ballew, Michael Iselin, and Allison Nicoletti, *Regulatory Asset Thresholds and Acquisition Activity in the Banking Industry* (June 16, 2017). Accessed from SSRN: https://ssrn.com/abstract=2910440 (2/1/2018).
4) Julapa Jagtiani, "Understanding the Effects of the Merger Boom on Community Banks," Federal Reserve Bank of Kansas City, *Economic Review*, Second Quarter, 2008, pp. 29-48.
5) Michal Kowalik, Troy Davig, Charles Morris, and Kristen Regehr, "Bank Consolidation and Merger Activity Following the Crisis," Federal Reserve Bank of Kansas City, *Economic Review*, First Quarter, 2015, pp. 31-49.
6) Robert Adams, "Consolidation and Merger Activity in the United States Banking Industry from 2000 through 2010," *Finance and Economics Discussion Series*, 2012-51, Federal Reserve Board, Washington, D.C.
7) Timothy Hannan and Steven Pilloff, "Acquisition Targets and Motives in the Banking Industry," *Journal of Money, Credit and Banking*, vol. 41, no. 6 (September 2009), pp. 1167-1187.

New Bank Formations

1) Allen Berger, Seth Bonime, Lawrence Goldberg, and Lawrence White, "The Dynamics of Market Entry: The Effects of Mergers and Acquisitions on Entry in the Banking Industry," *The Journal of Business*, vol. 77, no. 4 (October 2004), pp. 797-834.
2) Robert Adams and Dean Amel, "The Effects of Past Entry, Market Consolidation, and Expansion by Incumbents on the Probability of Entry," *Finance and Economics Discussion Series*, 2007-51, Federal Reserve Board, Washington, D.C.

3) Robert Adams and Jacob Gramlich, "Where Are All the New Banks? The Role of Regulatory Burden in New Charter Creation," *Finance and Economics Discussion Series*, 2014-113, Federal Reserve Board, Washington, D.C.
4) Steven Seelig and Tim Critchfield, *Merger Activity as a Determinant of De Novo Entry into Urban Banking Markets*, Working Paper 2003-01, April (2003).
5) Yan Lee and Chiwon Yom, "The Entry, Performance, and Risk Profile of De novo Banks," *FDIC CFR WP 2016-03*, Federal Deposit Insurance Corporation, April (2016).

Lending

1) Dean Amel and Traci Mach, "The Impact of the Small Business Lending Fund on Community Bank Lending to Small Businesses," *Finance and Economics Discussion Series, 2014-111*, Federal Reserve Board, Washington, D.C.
2) Elizabeth Kiser, Robin Prager, and Jason Scott, "Supervisor Ratings and the Contraction of Bank Lending to Small Businesses," *Finance and Economics Discussion Series*, 2012-59, Federal Reserve Board, Washington, D.C.
3) Elyas Elyasiani and Lawrence Goldberg, "Relationship Lending: A Survey of the Literature," *Journal of Economics and Business*, vol. 56 (2004), pp.315-330.
4) Jose Berrospide and Rochelle Edge, "The Effects of Bank Capital on Lending: What Do We Know, and What Does it Mean?" *Finance and Economics Discussion Series*, 2010-44, Federal Reserve Board, Washington, D.C.
5) Julapa Jagtiani, Ian Kotliar, and Raman Quinn Maingi, "Community Bank Mergers and the Impact on Small Business Lending," *Journal of Financial Stability*, vol. 27 (2016), pp. 106-121.

Return on Assets

1) Jared Fronk, "Core Profitability of Community Banks: 1985-2015," *FDIC Quarterly*, vol. 10, no. 4 (2016), pp. 37-46.
2) Panayiotis Athanasoglu, Sophocles Brissimis, and Matthaios Delis, "Bank-Specific, Industry-Specific and Macroeconomic Determinants of Bank Profitability," *Journal of International Financial Markets, Institutions, and Money* 18 (2008) pp. 121-136.
3) Dean Amel and Robin Prager, "Community Bank Performance: How Important Are Managers?" *Finance and Economics Discussion Series*, 2014-26, Federal Reserve Board, Washington, D.C.

APPENDIX III: RESULTS OF GAO'S SURVEY OF THE EFFECTS OF FEDERAL FINANCIAL REGULATIONS ON COMMUNITY BANKS AND THEIR SMALL BUSINESS AND RESIDENTIAL MORTGAGE LENDING

From July 2017 through August 2017, we administered a web-based survey to a nationally representative sample of community bank representatives.[173] We received valid responses from 68 percent of our sample. All survey results presented in this appendix are generalizable to the population of community banks, and we express our confidence in the precision of our estimates at 95 percent confidence intervals. For a more detailed discussion of our survey methodology, see appendix I.

---

[173] We define community banks using FDIC's definition, which takes into account institutions' assets, foreign interest, specializations, and geographic characteristics. Community banks include banks with up to $39.5 billion in assets in 2017.

Survey Results

The web-based survey consisted of three multiple–choice sections: (1) business lending activities, (2) management decisions, and (3) residential mortgage lending activities. Opportunities for respondents to voice additional comments were also provided.

Multiple-choice survey questions and their aggregate results are included in this appendix. Open-ended questions are not included in this appendix, but responses have been incorporated into the text of the report where relevant.

For multiple-choice questions, respondents were asked to report activities and decisions their institution implemented since January 2010 and then identify to what extent specific factors, which we identified and defined, affected those changes. Factors included the following:

- Competition from Other Financial Institutions or Alternative Lenders (Competition): Banks face competition from other institutions and increasingly from nonbank firms offering lending or payment services.
- Effect of Economic Conditions on Loan Demand (Economic conditions): Customer loan demand at banks varies based on local economic conditions, such as unemployment rates or housing prices.
- Low-Interest Rate Environment (Interest rate): Since the financial crisis interest rates have been at historic lows, making it less expensive to borrow money and finance investments, but lender profits may also have been affected.
- Technological Advances in the Finance Industry (Technological advances): The financial sector is experiencing rapid technological changes, including increased customer demand for online and mobile access to their financial institutions and electronic application and document submission.
- Compliance with Government Financial Regulations Implemented since 2010 (Regulatory environment): Changes to regulations and

uncertainty around their interpretation, enforcement, and future extension can affect staffing, lending, and time and resource allocation at banks.

The following sections present tables containing the survey questions and resulting response data.

Small Business Lending Activities

In our web-based survey, we instructed participants to consider the following definition of small business lending: "For community banks, small business loans, as defined by the Consolidated Reports of Condition and Income (Call Report), are commercial real estate or commercial and industrial loans with original amounts of $1 million or less, and farm loans with original amounts of $500,000 or less."[174] We asked participants to consider the small business lending activities of their institution since 2010. Tables 8–13 present the survey questions related to small business lending and resulting response data.

Management Decisions

In our web-based survey, we instructed participants to consider the following definition of management decisions: "Mergers, branch openings and closures, and decisions about time and resource allocation are management decisions that financial institutions make to strengthen and maintain their position in the market." We asked participants to consider management decisions made by their institution since 2010. Tables 14–21 present the survey questions related to management decisions and resulting response data.

---

[174] Call Reports are a primary source of financial data used for the supervision and regulation of banks. They are quarterly financial reports prepared by insured depository institutions for federal banking regulators and consist of a balance sheet, an income statement, and supporting schedules. Every national bank, state member bank, and insured state nonmember bank, is required to file a consolidated Call Report. The specific reporting requirements depend on the size of the institutions and whether they have any foreign offices.

Table 8. Reported Changes to the Time to Make Individual Small Business Loans and the Factors Affecting Those Changes, January 2010–August 2017

Since 2010, has your institution increased or decreased the time to make individual small business loans, or has it remained the same?			Since 2010, what effect have the following factors had on your institution's increase/decrease in the time to make individual small business loans?									
Response	Percentage of community banks by response		Factors affecting change	Extent to which factors affected change								
				Great		Moderate		Minor		None		
	E.P.	C.I.		E.P.	C.I.	E.P.	C.I.	E.P.	C.I.	E.P.	C.I.	
Increased	69	64, 74	Competition	12	8, 17	27	21, 34	33	27, 40	27	21, 33	
			Economic conditions	18	13, 24	39	32, 46	22	17, 28	20	15, 26	
			Low Interest rates	9	5, 14	28	22, 34	28	22, 35	35	28, 41	
			Technological advances	4	1, 7	22	16, 28	41	34, 48	33	27, 40	
			Regulatory environment	74	68, 80	23	18, 29	2	0, 4	1	0, 4	
Decreased	6	3, 9	Competition	—	—	—	—	—	—	—	—	
			Economic conditions	—	—	—	—	—	—	—	—	
			Low Interest rates	—	—	—	—	—	—	—	—	
			Technological advances	—	—	—	—	—	—	—	—	
			Regulatory environment	—	—	—	—	—	—	—	—	
Remained the same	25	20, 30	n/a	n/a	n/a	n/a	n/a	n/a	n/a	n/a	n/a	

Legend: E.P. = Estimated Percent, C.I. = Confidence Interval (Upper and lower bound 95 percent confidence intervals are provided for each point estimate), — = margin of error was greater than +/- 15 percentage points at the 95 percent level of confidence and deemed insufficiently reliable for this chapter, n/a = not applicable (data not collected or insufficient response for analysis).

Source: GAO analysis of community bank survey data. | GAO-18-312.

Note: The time to make a small business loan is measured as the time from application to disbursement of funds.

Table 9. Reported Changes to the Number of Small Business Lending Products or Services Offered and the Factors Affecting Those Changes, January 2010–August 2017

Since 2010, has your institution increased or decreased the number of small business lending products or services offered, or have they remained the same?

Since 2010, what effect have the following factors had on your institution's increase/decrease in the number of small business lending products or services offered?

Response	Percentage of community banks by response		Factors affecting change	Extent to which factors affected change							
				Great		Moderate		Minor		None	
	E.P.	C.I.		E.P.	C.I.	E.P.	C.I.	E.P.	C.I.	E.P.	C.I.
Increased	23	18, 28	Competition	27	17, 39	42	30, 54	26	17, 38	5	1, 13
			Economic conditions	22	13, 34	38	27, 50	28	18, 41	11	5, 21
			Low Interest rates	18	9, 29	41	29, 53	24	14, 36	18	9, 29
			Technological advances	13	6, 23	49	37, 61	27	17, 40	11	5, 22
			Regulatory environment	23	13, 35	29	19, 42	27	16, 39	21	12, 33
Decreased	8	5, 11	Competition	—	—	—	—	—	—	—	—
			Economic conditions	—	—	—	—	—	—	—	—
			Low Interest rates	—	—	—	—	—	—	—	—
			Technological advances	—	—	—	—	1	0, 18	0	0, 13
			Regulatory environment	—	—	—	—	—	—	—	—
Remained the same	69	64, 74	n/a	n/a	n/a	n/a	n/a	n/a	n/a	n/a	n/a

Legend: E.P. = Estimated Percent, C.I. = Confidence Interval (Upper and lower bound 95 percent confidence intervals are provided for each point estimate), — = margin of error was greater than +/- 15 percentage points at the 95 percent level of confidence and deemed insufficiently reliable for this chapter, n/a = not applicable (data not collected or insufficient response for analysis).
Source: GAO analysis of community bank survey data. | GAO-18-312.

Table 10. Reported Changes to the Minimum Credit Quality Criteria Needed to Qualify for Small Business Loans and the Factors Affecting Those Changes, January 2010– August 2017

Since 2010, has your institution increased or decreased the minimum credit quality criteria needed to qualify for small business loans, or has it remained the same?

Since 2010, what effect have the following factors had on your institution's increase/decrease in the minimum credit quality criteria needed to qualify for small business loans?

Response	Percentage of community banks by response		Factors affecting change	Extent to which factors affected change							
				Great		Moderate		Minor		None	
	E.P.	C.I.		E.P.	C.I.	E.P.	C.I.	E.P.	C.I.	E.P.	C.I.
Increased	45	39, 50	Competition	11	6, 18	15	9, 21	45	36, 53	30	22, 38
			Economic conditions	26	19, 33	41	33, 50	24	17, 32	9	4, 15
			Low Interest rates	13	8, 20	19	13, 26	45	36, 53	23	16, 32
			Technological advances	6	3, 12	19	13, 27	41	33, 50	33	25, 41
			Regulatory environment	60	52, 68	29	21, 37	9	4, 15	2	1, 7
Decreased	1	0, 3	Competition	—	—	—	—	—	—	—	—
			Economic conditions	—	—	—	—	—	—	—	—
			Low Interest rates	—	—	—	—	—	—	—	—
			Technological advances	—	—	—	—	—	—	—	—
			Regulatory environment	—	—	—	—	—	—	—	—
Remained the same	54	49, 60	n/a	n/a	n/a	n/a	n/a	n/a	n/a	n/a	n/a

Legend: E.P. = Estimated Percent, C.I. = Confidence Interval (Upper and lower bound 95 percent confidence intervals are provided for each point estimate, — = margin of error was greater than +/- 15 percentage points at the 95 percent level of confidence and deemed insufficiently reliable for this chapter, n/a = not applicable (data not collected or insufficient response for analysis).
Source: GAO analysis of community bank survey data.| GAO-18-312.

Table 11. Reported Changes to the Documentation Borrowers Are Required to Provide for Small Business Loans and the Factors Affecting Those Changes, January 2010– August 2017

Since 2010, has your institution increased or decreased the documentation you require borrowers to provide for small business loans, or has it remained the same?			Since 2010, what effect have the following factors had on your institution's increase/decrease in the documentation you require borrowers to provide for small business loans?								
Response	Percentage of community banks by response		Factors affecting change	Extent to which factors affected change							
				Great		Moderate		Minor		None	
	E.P.	C.I.		E.P.	C.I.	E.P.	C.I.	E.P.	C.I.	E.P.	C.I.
Increased	79	75, 84	Competition	6	3, 10	10	7, 15	35	29, 41	49	43, 55
			Economic conditions	15	11, 20	35	29, 41	27	21, 32	23	18, 29
			Low Interest rates	6	3, 9	10	7, 15	36	30, 42	48	42, 54
			Technological advances	3	1, 6	16	12, 22	37	31, 43	43	37, 50
			Regulatory environment	75	70, 81	22	17, 27	3	1, 6	0	0, 2
Decreased	1	0, 4	Competition	—	—	—	—	—	—	—	—
			Economic conditions	—	—	—	—	—	—	—	—
			Low Interest rates	—	—	—	—	—	—	—	—
			Technological advances	—	—	—	—	—	—	—	—
			Regulatory environment	—	—	—	—	—	—	—	—
Remained the same	19	15, 24	n/a	n/a	n/a	n/a	n/a	n/a	n/a	n/a	n/a

Legend: E.P. = Estimated Percent, C.I. = Confidence Interval (Upper and lower bound 95 percent confidence intervals are provided for each point estimate), — = margin of error was greater than +/- 15 percentage points at the 95 percent level of confidence and deemed insufficiently reliable for this chapter, n/a = not applicable (data not collected or insufficient response for analysis).

Source: GAO analysis of community bank survey data. | GAO-18-312.

Table 12. Reported Changes to the Availability of Small Business Loans to Individual Borrowers with Atypical Financial Characteristics and the Factors Affecting Those Changes, January 2010–August 2017

Since 2010, has your institution increased or decreased the availability of small business loans to individual borrowers with atypical financial characteristics, or has it remained the same?			Since 2010, what effect have the following factors had on your institution's increase/decrease in the availability of small business loans to individual borrowers with atypical financial characteristic?	Extent to which factors affected change							
Response	Percentage of community banks by response		Factors affecting change	Great		Moderate		Minor		None	
	E.P.	C.I.		E.P.	C.I.	E.P.	C.I.	E.P.	C.I.	E.P.	C.I.
Increased	8	5, 11	Competition	—	—	—	—	—	—	—	—
			Economic conditions	—	—	—	—	—	—	—	—
			Low Interest rates	—	—	—	—	—	—	—	—
			Technological advances	—	—	—	—	—	—	—	—
			Regulatory environment	—	—	—	—	—	—	—	—
Decreased	26	21, 31	Competition	6	2, 14	15	8, 25	41	30, 52	38	27, 49
			Economic conditions	17	10, 27	34	23, 45	26	16, 37	23	14, 35
			Low Interest rates	5	2, 13	12	6, 21	35	24, 46	48	36, 59
			Technological advances	6	2, 14	7	3, 16	33	23, 44	54	42, 65
			Regulatory environment	86	76, 93	11	5, 20	2	0, 8	1	0, 5
Remained the same	66	61, 72	n/a	n/a	n/a	n/a	n/a	n/a	n/a	n/a	n/a

Legend: E.P. = Estimated Percent, C.I. = Confidence Interval (Upper and lower bound 95 percent confidence intervals are provided for each point estimate), — = margin of error was greater than +/- 15 percentage points at the 95 percent level of confidence and deemed insufficiently reliable for this chapter, n/a = not applicable (data not collected or insufficient response for analysis).

Source: GAO analysis of community bank survey data. | GAO-18-312.

Note: "Borrowers with atypical financial characteristics" are defined as the following: (i) borrowers generating income from self-employment (including working as "contract" or "1099" employees); (ii) borrowers anticipated to rely on income from assets to repay the loan; (iii) borrowers who rely on intermittent, supplemental, part-time, seasonal, bonus, or overtime income.

Table 13. Reported Changes to Product or Service Fees for Small Business Loans and the Factors Affecting Those Changes, January 2010–August 2017

Since 2010, has your institution increased or decreased product or service fees for small business loans, or have they remained the same?			Since 2010, what effect have the following factors had on your institution's increase/decrease in product or service fees for small business loans?								
Response	Percentage of community banks by response		Factors affecting change	Extent to which factors affected change							
				Great		Moderate		Minor		None	
	E.P.	C.I.		E.P.	C.I.	E.P.	C.I.	E.P.	C.I.	E.P.	C.I.
Increased	38	33, 44	Competition	10	5, 17	25	18, 35	34	25, 43	31	22, 39
			Economic conditions	5	2, 11	35	26, 44	29	20, 37	31	22, 40
			Low Interest rates	18	11, 26	34	25, 43	30	22, 39	18	11, 26
			Technological advances	4	1, 9	26	19, 36	27	19, 37	42	33, 51
			Regulatory environment	45	35, 54	33	24, 41	14	8, 23	8	4, 15
Decreased	3	1, 5	Competition	—	—	—	—	—	—	—	—
			Economic conditions	—	—	—	—	—	—	—	—
			Low Interest rates	—	—	—	—	—	—	—	—
			Technological advances	—	—	—	—	—	—	—	—
			Regulatory environment	—	—	—	—	—	—	—	—
Remained the same	59	54, 65	n/a	n/a	n/a	n/a	n/a	n/a	n/a	n/a	n/a

Legend: E.P. = Estimated Percent, C.I. = Confidence Interval (Upper and lower bound 95 percent confidence intervals are provided for each point estimate), — = margin of error was greater than +/- 15 percentage points at the 95 percent level of confidence and deemed insufficiently reliable for this chapter, n/a = not applicable (data not collected or insufficient response for analysis). Source: GAO analysis of community bank survey data. | GAO-18-312.

Table 14. Reported Decisions Related to Opening One or More Branches and the Factors Affecting Those Decisions, January 2010–August 2017

Since 2010, has your institution completed, started, or seriously considered opening one or more branches? (Please check all that apply.)			Since 2010, what effect have the following factors had on your institution's decision to open/seriously consider, but not move forward on opening one or more branches?								
Decision	Percentage of community banks by decision		Factors affecting decision	Extent to which factors affected the decision							
				Great		Moderate		Minor		None	
	E.P.	C.I.		E.P.	C.I.	E.P.	C.I.	E.P.	C.I.	E.P.	C.I.
Opened or were in the process of opening a branch	35	30, 40	Competition	24	17, 34	53	43, 62	15	9, 23	8	4, 15
			Economic conditions	21	13, 30	42	33, 52	20	13, 29	17	10, 25
			Low Interest rates	6	2, 12	15	8, 23	40	30, 49	40	31, 49
			Technological advances	13	7, 21	26	18, 36	33	24, 42	28	20, 37
			Regulatory environment	15	9, 24	17	10, 26	24	16, 34	43	34, 53
Seriously considered, but did not open a branch	10	7, 13	Competition	—	—	—	—	—	—	—	—
			Economic conditions	—	—	—	—	—	—	—	—
			Low Interest rates	—	—	—	—	—	—	—	—
			Technological advances	—	—	—	—	—	—	—	—
			Regulatory environment	—	—	—	—	—	—	—	—
Had not seriously considered opening a branch	55	50, 60	n/a	n/a	n/a	n/a	n/a	n/a	n/a	n/a	n/a

Legend: E.P. = Estimated Percent, C.I. = Confidence Interval (Upper and lower bound 95 percent confidence intervals are provided for each point estimate), — = margin of error was greater than +/- 15 percentage points at the 95 percent level of confidence and deemed insufficiently reliable for this chapter, n/a = not applicable (data not collected or insufficient response for analysis).
Source: GAO analysis of community bank survey data. | GAO-18-312.

Table 15. Reported Decisions Related to Closing One or More Branches and the Factors Affecting Those Decisions, January 2010–August 2017

Decision	Percentage of community banks by decision		Since 2010, what effect have the following factors had on your institution's decision to close/seriously consider, but not move forward on closing one or more branches?									
			Factors affecting decision	Extent to which factors affected the decision								
				Great		Moderate		Minor		None		
	E.P.	C.I.		E.P.	C.I.	E.P.	C.I.	E.P.	C.I.	E.P.	C.I.	
Closed or were in the process of closing a branch	20	16, 25	Competition	8	3, 18	30	19, 43	26	16, 39	36	24, 49	
			Economic conditions	19	31	30	19, 43	15	26	36	24, 48	
			Low Interest rates	2	0, 10	6	2, 15	29	18, 43	63	50, 75	
			Technological advances	19	10, 31	23	14, 36	17	29	41	28, 53	
			Regulatory environment	29	18, 42	22	13, 33	17	28	33	21, 46	
Seriously considered, but did not close a branch	10	7, 14	Competition	—	—	—	—	—	—	—	—	
			Economic conditions	—	—	—	—	—	—	—	—	
			Low Interest rates	—	—	—	—	—	—	—	—	
			Technological advances	—	—	—	—	—	—	—	—	
			Regulatory environment	—	—	—	—	—	—	—	—	
Had not seriously considered closing a branch	68	63, 73	n/a	n/a	n/a	n/a	n/a	n/a	n/a	n/a	n/a	

Legend: E.P. = Estimated Percent, C.I. = Confidence Interval (Upper and lower bound 95 percent confidence intervals are provided for each point estimate), — = margin of error was greater than +/- 15 percentage points at the 95 percent level of confidence and deemed insufficiently reliable for this chapter, n/a = not applicable (data not collected or insufficient response for analysis).

Source: GAO analysis of community bank survey data. | GAO-18-312.

Table 16. Reported Decisions Related to Acquiring Another Institution through a Merger and the Factors Affecting Those Decisions, January 2010–August 2017

Decision	Percentage of community banks by decision		Since 2010, what effect have the following factors had on your institution's decision to acquire/seriously consider, but not move forward on acquiring another institution through a merger?								
			Factors affecting decision	Extent to which factors affected the decision							
				Great		Moderate		Minor		None	
	E.P.	C.I.		E.P.	C.I.	E.P.	C.I.	E.P.	C.I.	E.P.	C.I.
Acquired or were in the process of acquiring another institution	12	9, 16	Competition	11	3, 26	—	—	—	—	10	3, 24
			Economic conditions	—	—	—	—	—	—	13	5, 28
			Low Interest rates	—	—	11	3, 25	—	—	—	—
			Technological advances	—	—	—	—	—	—	—	—
			Regulatory environment	—	—	—	—	—	—	—	—
Seriously considered, but did not acquire another institution	26	22, 31	Competition	21	13, 31	37	27, 47	24	15, 34	18	11, 28
			Economic conditions	16	9, 26	35	25, 45	22	13, 32	27	38
			Low Interest rates	13	6, 22	23	14, 33	30	40	35	24, 45
			Technological advances	11	5, 20	30	40	30	20, 40	28	39
			Regulatory environment	52	41, 63	17	10, 26	18	10, 28	14	7, 23
Had not seriously considered acquiring another institution	61	56, 66	n/a	n/a	n/a	n/a	n/a	n/a	n/a	n/a	n/a

Legend: E.P. = Estimated Percent, C.I. = Confidence Interval (Upper and lower bound 95 percent confidence intervals are provided for each point estimate), — = margin of error was greater than +/- 15 percentage points at the 95 percent level of confidence and deemed insufficiently reliable for this chapter, n/a = not applicable (data not collected or insufficient response for analysis).
Source: GAO analysis of community bank survey data. | GAO-18-312.

Table 17. Reported Decisions Related to Being Acquired by Another Institution and the Factors Affecting Those Decisions, January 2010–August 2017

Since 2010, has your institution completed, started, or seriously considered being acquired by another institution through a merger? (Please check all that apply.)			Since 2010, what effect have the following factors had on your institution's decision to be acquired/seriously consider, but not move forward on being acquired by another institution through a merger?									
Decision	Percentage of community banks by decision		Factors affecting decision	Extent to which factors affected the decision								
				Great		Moderate		Minor		None		
	E.P.	C.I.		E.P.	C.I.	E.P.	C.I.	E.P.	C.I.	E.P.	C.I.	
In the process of being acquired by another institution	4	2, 6	Competition	—	—	—	—	—	—	—	—	
			Economic conditions	—	—	—	—	—	—	—	—	
			Interest rates	—	—	—	—	—	—	—	—	
			Technological advances	—	—	—	—	—	—	—	—	
			Regulatory environment	—	—	—	—	—	—	—	—	
Seriously considered, but were not acquired by another institution	16	12, 21	Competition	21	11, 34	32	20, 46	31	19, 46	17	8, 29	
			Economic conditions	21	11, 34	32	20, 46	21	11, 34	26	15, 40	
			Low Interest rates	11	4, 22	19	9, 32	38	25, 51	33	20, 47	
			Technological advances	11	4, 23	24	13, 37	38	25, 53	26	15, 40	
			Regulatory environment	76	63, 87	12	5, 24	9	3, 20	2	0, 11	
Had not seriously considered being acquired by another institution	80	76, 84	n/a	n/a	n/a	n/a	n/a	n/a	n/a	n/a	n/a	

Legend: E.P. = Estimated Percent, C.I. = Confidence Interval (Upper and lower bound 95 percent confidence intervals are provided for each point estimate), — = margin of error was greater than +/- 15 percentage points at the 95 percent level of confidence and deemed insufficiently reliable for this chapter, n/a = not applicable (data not collected or insufficient response for analysis). | GAO-18-312.

Source: GAO analysis of community bank survey data. | GAO-18-312.

Table 18. Reported Changes to Customer-Facing Technology and the Factors Affecting Those Changes, January 2010–August 2017

Since 2010, has your institution increased or decreased your investment in customer-facing technology, such as online or mobile banking, or has your investment remained the same?	Since 2010, what effect have the following factors had on your institution's decision to increase/decrease your investment in customer-facing technology?									
Response	Percentage of community banks by response		Factors affecting change	Extent to which factors affected change						
				Great		Moderate		Minor		None	
	E.P.	C.I.		E.P.	C.I.	E.P.	C.I.	E.P.	C.I.	E.P.	C.I.
Increased	89	85, 92	Competition	61	55, 67	32	38	5	3, 8	2	1, 5
			Economic conditions	11	7, 15	14	10, 18	31	25, 36	45	39, 51
			Low Interest rates	5	3, 8	11	7, 15	32	37	53	47, 59
			Technological advances	68	63, 73	27	22, 32	3	1, 6	2	1, 4
			Regulatory environment	24	19, 30	26	21, 31	26	21, 31	24	19, 28
Decreased	0	0, 2	Competition	n/a	n/a	n/a	n/a	n/a	n/a	n/a	n/a
			Economic conditions	n/a	n/a	n/a	n/a	n/a	n/a	n/a	n/a
			Low Interest rates	n/a	n/a	n/a	n/a	n/a	n/a	n/a	n/a
			Technological advances	n/a	n/a	n/a	n/a	n/a	n/a	n/a	n/a
			Regulatory environment	n/a	n/a	n/a	n/a	n/a	n/a	n/a	n/a
Remained the same	11	8, 14	n/a	n/a	n/a	n/a	n/a	n/a	n/a	n/a	n/a

Legend: E.P. = Estimated Percent, C.I. = Confidence Interval (Upper and lower bound 95 percent confidence intervals are provided for each point estimate), — = margin of error was greater than +/- 15 percentage points at the 95 percent level of confidence and deemed insufficiently reliable for this chapter, n/a = not applicable (data not collected or insufficient response for analysis).
Source: GAO analysis of community bank survey data. | GAO-18-312.

Table 19. Reported Changes to Time Staff Spend Engaging Directly with Individual Customers and the Factors Affecting Those Changes, January 2010–August 2017

Since 2010, has your institution increased or decreased the time your staff spend engaging directly with individual customers, or has it remained the same?			Since 2010, what effect have the following factors had on your institution's decision to increase/decrease the time your staff spend engaging directly with individual customers?									
Response	Percentage of community banks by response		Factors affecting change	Extent to which factors affected change								
				Great		Moderate		Minor		None		
	E.P.	C.I.		E.P.	C.I.	E.P.	C.I.	E.P.	C.I.	E.P.	C.I.	
Increased	35	30, 40	Competition	23	15, 32	24	17, 34	30	21, 39	23	16, 32	
			Economic conditions	14	8, 22	22	15, 31	31	22, 40	32	23, 41	
			Low Interest rates	9	4, 16	18	11, 26	31	22, 39	43	33, 52	
			Technological advances	15	9, 24	35	26, 44	30	21, 38	20	13, 28	
			Regulatory environment	64	55, 73	20	13, 29	8	4, 15	8	4, 15	
Decreased	18	13, 22	Competition	9	3, 20	25	14, 38	28	17, 42	38	25, 51	
			Economic conditions	1	0, 8	20	10, 32	24	14, 37	55	42, 68	
			Low Interest rates	1	0, 8	8	3, 18	26	15, 40	64	50, 76	
			Technological advances	57	44, 70	30	18, 44	8	2, 18	5	1, 14	
			Regulatory environment	45	32, 58	10	3, 21	21	11, 33	25	14, 38	
Remained the same	48	42, 53	n/a	n/a	n/a	n/a	n/a	n/a	n/a	n/a	n/a	

Legend: E.P. = Estimated Percent, C.I. = Confidence Interval (Upper and lower bound 95 percent confidence intervals are provided for each point estimate), — = margin of error was greater than +/- 15 percentage points at the 95 percent level of confidence and deemed insufficiently reliable for this chapter, n/a = not applicable (data not collected or insufficient response for analysis). | GAO-18-312.

Source: GAO analysis of community bank survey data.

Table 20. Reported Changes to Time Staff Spend Identifying New or Innovative Products and the Factors Affecting Those Changes, January 2010–August 2017

Since 2010, has your institution increased or decreased the time your staff spends identifying new or innovative products, or has it remained the same?

Since 2010, what effect have the following factors had on your institution's decision to increase/decrease the time your staff spends identifying new or innovative products?

Response	Percentage of community banks by response		Factors affecting change	Extent to which factors affected change						
				Great		Moderate		Minor		None	
	E.P.	C.I.		E.P.	C.I.	E.P.	C.I.	E.P.	C.I.	E.P.	C.I.
Increased	51	46, 57	Competition	62	54, 69	32	25, 39	4	2, 9	2	0, 5
			Economic conditions	14	9, 20	28	21, 35	29	22, 36	30	— 37
			Low Interest rates	10	6, 16	16	11, 23	34	26, 41	40	32, 47
			Technological advances	65	58, 72	26	— 33	7	3, 12	2	0, 5
			Regulatory environment	33	26, 40	28	— 35	29	— 36	10	6, 15
Decreased	9	6, 13	Competition	3	0, 17	—	—	—	—	—	—
			Economic conditions	—	—	—	—	—	—	—	—
			Low Interest rates	—	—	—	—	—	—	—	—
			Technological advances	—	—	—	—	—	—	—	—
			Regulatory environment	97	86, 100	3	0, 14	0	0, 11	0	0, 11
Remained the same	40	34, 45	n/a	n/a	n/a	n/a	n/a	n/a	n/a	n/a	n/a

Legend: E.P. = Estimated Percent, C.I. = Confidence Interval (Upper and lower bound 95 percent confidence intervals are provided for each point estimate), — = margin of error was greater than +/- 15 percentage points at the 95 percent level of confidence and deemed insufficiently reliable for this chapter, n/a = not applicable (data not collected or insufficient response for analysis).

Source: GAO analysis of community bank survey data. | GAO-18-312.

Table 21. Reported Actions by Community Banks to Comply with Federal Regulations, January 2010–August 2017

In order to comply with federal financial regulations, since 2010, has your institution taken any of the following actions:	Yes		No	
	E.P.	C.I.	E.P.	C.I.
Hired additional staff for compliance purposes	73	68, 77	27	23, 32
Relocated existing staff to compliance-related positions	86	82, 90	14	10, 18
Hired a third party to assist with compliance	85	81, 89	15	11, 19
Increased staff time for compliance-related activities	96	93, 98	4	2, 7
Purchased additional software or automated systems to aid in compliance activities	89	85, 92	11	8, 15

Legend: E.P. = Estimated Percent, C.I. = Confidence Interval (Upper and lower bound 95 percent confidence intervals are provided for each point estimate.
Source: GAO analysis of community bank survey data. | GAO-18-312.

Table 22. Reported Changes to the Time to Make Individual Residential Mortgage Loans and the Factors Affecting Those Changes, January 2010–August 2017

Since 2010, has your institution increased or decreased the time to make individual residential mortgage loans, or has it remained the same?			Since 2010, what effect have the following factors had on your institution's increase/decrease in the time to make individual residential mortgage loans?									
Response	Percentage of community banks by response		Factors affecting change	Extent to which factors affected change								
				Great		Moderate		Minor		None		
	E.P.	C.I.		E.P.	C.I.	E.P.	C.I.	E.P.	C.I.	E.P.	C.I.	
Increased	91	87, 94	Competition	8	5, 12	13	10, 18	33	27, 39	45	39, 51	
			Economic conditions	11	8, 16	21	16, 26	35	30, 41	33	27, 38	
			Low Interest rates	12	8, 16	14	10, 19	32	26, 37	42	36, 48	
			Technological advances	7	5, 11	19	15, 24	40	34, 46	33	28, 39	
			Regulatory environment	96	94, 98	2	1, 5	1	0, 3	0	0, 2	
Decreased	3	2, 6	Competition	—	—	—	—	—	—	—	—	
			Economic conditions	—	—	—	—	—	—	—	—	
			Low Interest rates	—	—	—	—	—	—	—	—	
			Technological advances	—	—	—	—	—	—	—	—	
			Regulatory environment	—	—	—	—	—	—	—	—	
Remained the same	5	3, 9	n/a	n/a	n/a	n/a	n/a	n/a	n/a	n/a	n/a	

Legend: E.P. = Estimated Percent, C.I. = Confidence Interval (Upper and lower bound 95 percent confidence intervals are provided for each point estimate), — = margin of error was greater than +/- 15 percentage points at the 95 percent level of confidence and deemed insufficiently reliable for this chapter, n/a = not applicable (data not collected or insufficient response for analysis).

Source: GAO analysis of community bank survey data. | GAO-18-312.

Note: The time to make a residential mortgage loan is measured as the time from application to disbursement of funds.

Table 23. Reported Changes to the Number of Individual Residential Mortgage Lending Products or Services Offered and the Factors Affecting Those Changes, January 2010–August 2017

Since 2010, has your institution increased or decreased the number of residential mortgage lending products or services offered, or have they remained the same?	Percentage of community banks by response		Since 2010, what effect have the following factors had on your institution's increase/decrease in the number of residential mortgage lending products or services offered?	Extent to which factors affected the reported change							
Direction of change			Factors affecting change	Great		Moderate		Minor		None	
	E.P.	C.I.		E.P.	C.I.	E.P.	C.I.	E.P.	C.I.	E.P.	C.I.
Increased	31	25, 36	Competition	39	29, 49	38	28, 48	14	8, 23	9	4, 17
			Economic conditions	16	9, 25	52	41, 62	18	11, 27	14	8, 23
			Low Interest rates	26	17, 36	39	29, 49	14	8, 23	21	13, 30
			Technological advances	18	10, 27	35	25, 44	34	24, 44	13	7, 22
			Regulatory environment	48	38, 59	13	7, 22	19	11, 29	20	13, 30
Decreased	29	24, 34	Competition	12	6, 20	10	5, 18	23	15, 33	55	45, 65
			Economic conditions	7	2, 14	11	6, 20	35	25, 45	47	37, 57
			Low Interest rates	4	1, 10	14	8, 23	28	19, 38	54	44, 64
			Technological advances	8	3, 15	10	5, 18	28	19, 38	54	44, 65
			Regulatory environment	96	90, 99	3	1, 9	0	0, 3	1	0, 6
Remained the same	40	35, 46	n/a	n/a	n/a	n/a	n/a	n/a	n/a	n/a	n/a

Legend: E.P. = Estimated Percent, C.I. = Confidence Interval (Upper and lower bound 95 percent confidence intervals are provided for each point estimate), — = margin of error was greater than +/- 15 percentage points at the 95 percent level of confidence and deemed insufficiently reliable for this chapter, n/a = not applicable (data not collected or insufficient response for analysis).

Source: GAO analysis of community bank survey data. | GAO-18-312.

Table 24. Reported Changes to the Minimum Credit Quality Criteria Needed to Qualify for Individual Residential Mortgage Loans and the Factors Affecting Those Changes, January 2010–August 2017

Since 2010, has your institution increased or decreased the minimum credit quality criteria needed to qualify for residential mortgage loans, or has it remained the same?

Since 2010, what effect have the following factors had on your institution's increase/decrease in the minimum credit quality criteria needed to qualify for residential mortgage loans?

Response	Percentage of community banks by response		Factors affecting change	Extent to which factors affected change							
				Great		Moderate		Minor		None	
	E.P.	C.I.		E.P.	C.I.	E.P.	C.I.	E.P.	C.I.	E.P.	C.I.
Increased	59	53, 64	Competition	8	4, 13	13	8, 19	26	19, 32	53	46, 61
			Economic conditions	18	12, 24	25	18, 31	31	24, 37	27	20, 33
			Low Interest rates	10	6, 16	15	10, 21	26	19, 32	48	41, 56
			Technological advances	3	1, 7	15	10, 21	25	19, 32	56	49, 64
			Regulatory environment	88	82, 93	9	5, 14	2	0, 5	1	0, 4
Decreased	2	1, 4	Competition	—	—	—	—	—	—	—	—
			Economic conditions	—	—	—	—	—	—	—	—
			Low Interest rates	—	—	—	—	—	—	—	—
			Technological advances	—	—	—	—	—	—	—	—
			Regulatory environment	—	—	—	—	—	—	—	—
Remained the same	39	34, 45	n/a	n/a	n/a	n/a	n/a	n/a	n/a	n/a	n/a

Legend: E.P. = Estimated Percent, C.I. = Confidence Interval (Upper and lower bound 95 percent confidence intervals are provided for each point estimate), — = margin of error was greater than +/- 15 percentage points at the 95 percent level of confidence and deemed insufficiently reliable for this chapter, n/a = not applicable (data not collected or insufficient response for analysis).

Source: GAO analysis of community bank survey data. | GAO-18-312.

Table 25. Reported Changes to the Documentation Borrowers Are Required to Provide for Individual Residential Mortgage Loans and the Factors Affecting Those Changes, January 2010–August 2017

Since 2010, has your institution increased or decreased the documentation you require borrowers to provide for residential mortgage loans, or has it remained the same?

Since 2010, what effect have the following factors had on your institution's increase/decrease in the documentation you require borrowers to provide for residential mortgage loans?

Response	Percentage of community banks by response		Factors affecting change	Extent to which factors affected change							
				Great		Moderate		Minor		None	
	E.P.	C.I.		E.P.	C.I.	E.P.	C.I.	E.P.	C.I.	E.P.	C.I.
Increased	93	90, 96	Competition	5	3, 8	9	6, 13	25	30	61	55, 67
			Economic conditions	7	4, 11	17	13, 22	27	32	49	43, 55
			Low Interest rates	6	4, 10	7	4, 11	23	18, 28	63	57, 69
			Technological advances	4	2, 7	13	9, 17	29	24, 34	54	48, 60
			Regulatory environment	96	94, 98	3	2, 6	0	0, 2	0	0, 1
Decreased	0	0, 1	Competition	—	—	—	—	—	—	—	—
			Economic conditions	—	—	—	—	—	—	—	—
			Low Interest rates	—	—	—	—	—	—	—	—
			Technological advances	—	—	—	—	—	—	—	—
			Regulatory environment	—	—	—	—	—	—	—	—
Remained the same	6	4, 10	n/a	n/a	n/a	n/a	n/a	n/a	n/a	n/a	n/a

Legend: E.P. = Estimated Percent, C.I. = Confidence Interval (Upper and lower bound 95 percent confidence intervals are provided for each point estimate), — = margin of error was greater than +/- 15 percentage points at the 95 percent level of confidence and deemed insufficiently reliable for this chapter, n/a = not applicable (data not collected or insufficient response for analysis).
Source: GAO analysis of community bank survey data. | GAO-18-312.

Table 26. Reported Changes to the Availability of Individual Residential Mortgage Loans to Individual Borrowers with Atypical Financial Characteristics and the Factors Affecting Those Changes, January 2010–August 2017

Since 2010, has your institution increased or decreased the availability of residential mortgage loans to individual borrowers with atypical financial characteristics, or has it remained the same?			Since 2010, what effect have the following factors had on your institution's increase/decrease in the availability of residential mortgage loans to individual borrowers with atypical financial characteristic?										
Response	Percentage of community banks by response		Factors affecting change	Extent to which factors affected the reported change									
				Great		Moderate		Minor		None			
	E.P.	C.I.		E.P.	C.I.	E.P.	C.I.	E.P.	C.I.	E.P.	C.I.		
Increased	10	7, 14	Competition	—	—	—	—	—	—	—	—		
			Economic conditions	—	—	—	—	—	—	—	—		
			Low Interest rates	—	—	—	—	—	—	—	—		
			Technological advances	6	1, 20	—	—	—	—	—	—		
			Regulatory environment	—	—	—	—	—	—	—	—		
Decreased	49	43, 55	Competition	5	2, 10	5	2, 10	24	18, 32	65	58, 73		
			Economic conditions	6	3, 11	17	11, 24	26	19, 33	51	43, 59		
			Low Interest rates	5	2, 10	6	3, 11	24	17, 31	65	57, 73		
			Technological advances	5	2, 9	4	1, 8	25	18, 32	67	59, 74		
			Regulatory environment	94	88, 97	6	3, 12	0	0, 2	0	0, 2		
Remained the same	41	36, 47	n/a	n/a	n/a	n/a	n/a	n/a	n/a	n/a	n/a		

Legend: E.P. = Estimated Percent, C.I. = Confidence Interval (Upper and lower bound 95 percent confidence intervals are provided for each point estimate), — = margin of error was greater than +/- 15 percentage points at the 95 percent level of confidence and deemed insufficiently reliable for this chapter, n/a = not applicable (data not collected or insufficient response for analysis). Source: GAO analysis of community bank survey data. | GAO-18-312.

Note: "Borrowers with atypical financial characteristics" are defined as the following: (i) borrowers generating income from self-employment (including working as "contract" or "1099" employees); (ii) borrowers anticipated to rely on income from assets to repay the loan; (iii) borrowers who rely on intermittent, supplemental, part-time, seasonal, bonus, or overtime income.

Table 27. Reported Changes to Product or Service Fees for Individual Residential Mortgage Loans and the Factors Affecting Those Changes, January 2010–August 2017

Since 2010, has your institution increased or decreased product or service fees for residential mortgage loans, or have they remained the same?			Since 2010, what effect have the following factors had on your institution's increase/decrease in product or service fees for residential mortgage loans?	Extent to which factors affected change							
Response	Percentage of community banks by response		Factors affecting change	Great		Moderate		Minor		None	
	E.P.	C.I.		E.P.	C.I.	E.P.	C.I.	E.P.	C.I.	E.P.	C.I.
Increased	48	42, 53	Competition	8	4, 14	22	15, 30	32	25, 40	38	30, 46
			Economic conditions	7	3, 12	19	13, 27	29	21, 36	45	37, 54
			Low Interest rates	13	8, 20	23	17, 31	23	16, 31	40	31, 48
			Technological advances	6	3, 12	19	13, 27	22	15, 29	53	44, 61
			Regulatory environment	82	74, 88	13	8, 20	3	1, 7	2	1, 7
Decreased	5	3, 8	Competition	—	—	—	—	—	—	—	—
			Economic conditions	—	—	—	—	—	—	—	—
			Low Interest rates	—	—	—	—	—	—	—	—
			Technological advances	—	—	—	—	—	—	—	—
			Regulatory environment	—	—	—	—	—	—	—	—
Remained the same	47	42, 53	n/a	n/a	n/a	n/a	n/a	n/a	n/a	n/a	n/a

Legend: E.P. = Estimated Percent, C.I. = Confidence Interval (Upper and lower bound 95 percent confidence intervals are provided for each point estimate), — = margin of error was greater than +/- 15 percentage points at the 95 percent level of confidence and deemed insufficiently reliable for this chapter, n/a = not applicable (data not collected or insufficient response for analysis).

Source: GAO analysis of community bank survey data. | GAO-18-312.

For the multiple-choice question, respondents were asked what actions they had taken in order to comply with federal regulations. Respondents were not asked to identify the extent to which the factors had affected these actions.

Residential Mortgage Lending Activities

In our web-based survey, we instructed participants to consider the following definition of residential mortgage lending: "Residential mortgage lending includes new mortgage loans, refinancing, and home equity lines of credit or home equity loans." We asked participants to consider the residential mortgage lending activities of their institution since 2010. Tables 22–27 present the survey questions related to residential mortgage lending and resulting response data.

APPENDIX IV: RESULTS OF GAO'S SURVEY OF THE EFFECTS OF FEDERAL FINANCIAL REGULATIONS ON CREDIT UNIONS AND THEIR MEMBER BUSINESS AND RESIDENTIAL MORTGAGE LENDING

From July 2017 through August 2017, we administered a web-based survey to a nationally representative sample of credit union representatives. We received valid responses from 61 percent of our sample. All survey results presented in this appendix are generalizable to the population of small and medium credit unions, and we express our confidence in the precision of our estimates as 95 percent confidence intervals.[175] For a more detailed discussion of survey methodology, see appendix I.

---

[175] Our analysis considered only small and medium credit unions, which accounted for about 95 percent of all credit unions in June 2017. We excluded large credit unions with total assets above an annual threshold (equal to $201 million in 2001 and $994 million in 2017).

Survey Results

The web-based survey consisted of three multiple choice sections: (1) member business lending activities, (2) management decisions, and (3) residential mortgage lending activities. Opportunities for respondents to voice additional comments were also provided. Multiple-choice survey questions and their aggregate results are included in this appendix. Open-ended questions are not included in this appendix, but responses have been incorporated into the text of the report where relevant.

For multiple-choice questions, respondents were asked to report activities and decisions their institution implemented since January 2010 and then identify to what extent specific factors, which we identified and defined, affected those changes. Factors included the following:

- Competition from Other Financial Institutions or Alternative Lenders (Competition): Credit unions face competition from other institutions and increasingly from nonbank firms offering lending or payment services.
- Effect of Economic Conditions on Loan Demand (Economic conditions): Member loan demand at credit unions varies based on local economic conditions, such as unemployment rates or housing prices.
- Low-Interest Rate Environment (Low interest rates): Since the financial crisis interest rates have been at historic lows, making it less expensive to borrow money and finance investments, but lender profits may also have been affected.
- Technological Advances in the Finance Industry (Technological advances): The financial sector is experiencing rapid technological changes, including increased member demand for online and mobile access to their financial institutions and electronic application and document submission.

- Compliance with Government Financial Regulations Implemented since 2010 (Regulatory environment): Changes to regulations and uncertainty around their interpretation, enforcement, and future extension can affect staffing, lending, and time and resource allocation at credit unions.

The following sections present tables containing the survey questions and resulting response data.

Member Business Lending Activities

In our web-based survey, we instructed participants to consider the following definition of member business lending: "Member business loans (as defined by the National Credit Union Administration) include any loan, line of credit, or letter of credit where the proceeds will be used for a commercial, corporate, or agricultural purpose and the total net member business loan balances are $50,000 or greater. Participation loans should not be included." We asked participants to consider the member business lending activities of their institution since 2010. Tables 28–33 present the survey questions related to member business lending and resulting response data.

Management Decisions

In our web-based survey, we instructed participants to consider the following definition of management decisions: "Mergers, branch openings and closures, and decisions about time and resource allocation are management decisions that financial institutions make to strengthen and maintain their position in the market." We asked participants to consider management decisions made by their institution since 2010. Tables 34–41 present the survey questions related to management decisions and resulting response data.

Table 28. Reported Changes to the Time to Make Individual Member Business Loans and the Factors Affecting Those Changes, January 2010–August 2017

Since 2010, has your institution increased or decreased the time to make individual member business loans, or has it remained the same?	Percentage of credit unions by response		Since 2010, what effect have the following factors had on your institution's increase/decrease in the time to make individual member business loans?	Extent to which factors affected change							
Response			Factors affecting change	Great		Moderate		Minor		None	
	E.P.	C.I.		E.P.	C.I.	E.P.	C.I.	E.P.	C.I.	E.P.	C.I.
Increased	47	38, 55	Competition	13	6, 23	26	16, 37	31	20, 43	30	20, 43
			Economic conditions	16	8, 27	44	32, 55	29	19, 41	12	6, 21
			Low interest rates	17	9, 28	37	25, 48	21	12, 32	25	16, 37
			Technological advances	4	2, 9	28	18, 40	43	31, 55	24	15, 37
			Regulatory environment	59	47, 70	38	29, 49	4	1, 12	0	0, 3
Decreased	4	1, 10	Competition	—	—	—	—	—	—	—	—
			Economic conditions	—	—	—	—	—	—	—	—
			Low interest rates	—	—	—	—	—	—	—	—
			Technological advances	—	—	—	—	—	—	—	—
			Regulatory environment	—	—	—	—	—	—	—	—
Remained the same	49	41, 58	n/a	n/a	n/a	n/a	n/a	n/a	n/a	n/a	n/a

Legend: E.P. = Estimated Percent, C.I. = Confidence Interval (Upper and lower bound 95 percent confidence intervals are provided for each point estimate), — = margin of error was greater than +/- 15 percentage points at the 95 percent level of confidence and deemed insufficiently reliable for this chapter, n/a = not applicable (data not collected or insufficient response for analysis).

Source: GAO analysis of credit union survey data. | GAO-18-312.

Note: The time to make a member business loans is measured as the date of application to disbursement of funds.

Table 29. Reported Changes to the Number of Member Business Lending Products or Services Offered and the Factors Affecting Those Changes, January 2010–August 2017

Response	Percentage of credit unions by response		Since 2010, what effect have the following factors had on your institution's increase/decrease in the number of member business lending products or services offered?								
			Factors affecting change	Extent to which factors affected change							
				Great		Moderate		Minor		None	
	E.P.	C.I.		E.P.	C.I.	E.P.	C.I.	E.P.	C.I.	E.P.	C.I.
Increased	34	26, 42	Competition	24	13, 38	51	36, 65	19	9, 34	6	2, 16
			Economic conditions	25	14, 39	—	—	—	—	4	0, 13
			Low interest rates	—	—	—	—	—	—	4	1, 15
			Technological advances	—	—	—	—	—	—	16	7, 30
			Regulatory environment	19	10, 33	—	—	—	—	—	—
Decreased	22	15, 31	Competition	8	2, 22	—	—	—	—	—	—
			Economic conditions	—	—	—	—	—	—	—	—
			Low interest rates	—	—	—	—	—	—	—	—
			Technological advances	—	—	8	2, 21	—	—	—	—
			Regulatory environment	—	—	—	—	7	1, 21	5	0, 19
Remained the same	44	36, 53	n/a	n/a	n/a	n/a	n/a	n/a	n/a	n/a	n/a

Legend: E.P. = Estimated Percent, C.I. = Confidence Interval (Upper and lower bound 95 percent confidence intervals are provided for each point estimate), — = margin of error was greater than +/- 15 percentage points at the 95 percent level of confidence and deemed insufficiently reliable for this chapter, n/a = not applicable (data not collected or insufficient response for analysis).

Source: GAO analysis of credit union survey data. | GAO-18-312.

Table 30. Reported Changes to the Minimum Credit Quality Criteria Needed to Qualify for Member Business Loans and the Factors Affecting Those Changes, January 2010–August 2017

Response	Percentage of credit unions by response		Factors affecting change	Extent to which factors affected change							
				Great		Moderate		Minor		None	
	E.P.	C.I.		E.P.	C.I.	E.P.	C.I.	E.P.	C.I.	E.P.	C.I.
Increased	31	24, 39	Competition	6	2, 13	—	—	—	—	40	26, 55
			Economic conditions	18	9, 31	—	—	—	—	11	5, 21
			Low interest rates	13	6, 24	44	29, 58	29	17, 44	15	7, 25
			Technological advances	—	—	10	3, 22	—	—	47	33, 61
			Regulatory environment	56	42, 70	29	17, 43	9	3, 21	6	1, 17
Decreased	2	0, 6	Competition	—	—	—	—	—	—	—	—
			Economic conditions	—	—	—	—	—	—	—	—
			Low interest rates	—	—	—	—	—	—	—	—
			Technological advances	—	—	—	—	—	—	—	—
			Regulatory environment	—	—	—	—	—	—	—	—
Remained the same	67	59, 75	n/a	n/a	n/a	n/a	n/a	n/a	n/a	n/a	n/a

Legend: E.P. = Estimated Percent, C.I. = Confidence Interval (Upper and lower bound 95 percent confidence intervals are provided for each point estimate), — = margin of error was greater than +/- 15 percentage points at the 95 percent level of confidence and deemed insufficiently reliable for this chapter, n/a = not applicable (data not collected or insufficient response for analysis).

Source: GAO analysis of credit union survey data. | GAO-18-312.

Table 31. Reported Changes to the Documentation Borrowers Are Required to Provide for Member Business Loans and the Factors Affecting Those Changes, January 2010–August 2017

Since 2010, has your institution increased or decreased the documentation you require borrowers to provide for member business loans, or has it remained the same?			Since 2010, what effect have the following factors had on your institution's increase/decrease in the documentation you require borrowers to provide for member business loans?									
Response	Percentage of credit unions by response		Factors affecting change	Extent to which factors affected change								
				Great		Moderate		Minor		None		
	E.P.	C.I.		E.P.	C.I.	E.P.	C.I.	E.P.	C.I.	E.P.	C.I.	
Increased	66	57, 74	Competition	2	1, 4	16	8, 26	24	15, 35	58	48, 69	
			Economic conditions	17	9, 27	24	16, 34	30	20, 41	29	20, 39	
			Low interest rates	6	2, 15	19	11, 30	24	15, 34	51	40, 62	
			Technological advances	4	1, 13	19	11, 29	28	19, 38	49	38, 59	
			Regulatory environment	71	60, 80	25	16, 35	4	1, 11	0	0, 3	
Decreased	0	0, 2	Competition	n/a	n/a	n/a	n/a	n/a	n/a	n/a	n/a	
			Economic conditions	n/a	n/a	n/a	n/a	n/a	n/a	n/a	n/a	
			Low interest rates	n/a	n/a	n/a	n/a	n/a	n/a	n/a	n/a	
			Technological advances	n/a	n/a	n/a	n/a	n/a	n/a	n/a	n/a	
			Regulatory environment	n/a	n/a	n/a	n/a	n/a	n/a	n/a	n/a	
Remained the same	34	26, 43	n/a	n/a	n/a	n/a	n/a	n/a	n/a	n/a	n/a	

Legend: E.P. = Estimated Percent, C.I. = Confidence Interval (Upper and lower bound 95 percent confidence intervals are provided for each point estimate), — = margin of error was greater than +/- 15 percentage points at the 95 percent level of confidence and deemed insufficiently reliable for this chapter, n/a = not applicable (data not collected or insufficient response for analysis).

Source: GAO analysis of credit union survey data. | GAO-18-312.

Table 32. Reported Changes to the Availability of Member Business Loans to Individual Borrowers with Atypical Financial Characteristics and the Factors Affecting Those Changes, January 2010–August 2017

Since 2010, has your institution increased or decreased the availability of member business loans to individual borrowers with atypical financial characteristics, or has it remained the same?			Since 2010, what effect have the following factors had on your institution's increase/decrease in the availability of member business loans to individual borrowers with atypical financial characteristic?									
Response	Percentage of credit unions by response		Factors affecting change	Extent to which factors affected change								
				Great		Moderate		Minor		None		
	E.P.	C.I.		E.P.	C.I.	E.P.	C.I.	E.P.	C.I.	E.P.	C.I.	
Increased	16	10, 24	Competition	4	0, 17	—	—	—	—	—	—	
			Economic conditions	—	—	—	—	—	—	—	—	
			Low interest rates	—	—	—	—	—	—	—	—	
			Technological advances	0	0, 13	—	—	—	—	—	—	
			Regulatory environment	—	—	—	—	—	—	—	—	
Decreased	28	20, 37	Competition	8	2, 20	—	—	11	3, 25	—	—	
			Economic conditions	—	—	—	—	15	6, 30	—	—	
			Low interest rates	—	—	7	3, 13	—	—	—	—	
			Technological advances	—	—	2	1, 6	—	—	—	—	
			Regulatory environment	—	—	—	—	0	0, 6	3	0, 17	
Remained the same	56	47, 65	n/a	n/a	n/a	n/a	n/a	n/a	n/a	n/a	n/a	

Legend: E.P. = Estimated Percent, C.I. = Confidence Interval (Upper and lower bound 95 percent confidence intervals are provided for each point estimate), — = margin of error was greater than +/- 15 percentage points at the 95 percent level of confidence and deemed insufficiently reliable for this chapter, n/a = not applicable (data not collected or insufficient response for analysis).

Source: GAO analysis of credit union survey data. | GAO-18-312.

Note: "Borrowers with atypical financial characteristics" are defined as the following: (i) borrowers generating income from self-employment (including working as "contract" or "1099" employees); (ii) borrowers anticipated to rely on income from assets to repay the loan; (iii) borrowers who rely on intermittent, supplemental, part-time, seasonal, bonus, or overtime income.

Table 33. Reported Changes to Product or Service Fees for Member Business Loans and the Factors Affecting Those Changes, January 2010–August 2017

Since 2010, has your institution increased or decreased product or service fees for member business loans, or have they remained the same?			Since 2010, what effect have the following factors had on your institution's increase/decrease in product or service fees for member business loans?								
Response	Percentage of credit unions by response		Factors affecting change	Extent to which factors affected change							
				Great		Moderate		Minor		None	
	E.P.	C.I.		E.P.	C.I.	E.P.	C.I.	E.P.	C.I.	E.P.	C.I.
Increased	24	17, 33	Competition	—	—	—	—	—	—	—	—
			Economic conditions	—	—	—	—	—	—	—	—
			Low interest rates	—	—	—	—	—	—	16	7, 31
			Technological advances	—	—	—	—	—	—	—	—
			Regulatory environment	—	—	—	—	4	1, 13	—	—
Decreased	8	4, 16	Competition	—	—	—	—	—	—	—	—
			Economic conditions	—	—	—	—	—	—	—	—
			Low interest rates	—	—	—	—	—	—	—	—
			Technological advances	—	—	—	—	—	—	—	—
			Regulatory environment	—	—	—	—	—	—	—	—
Remained the same	67	59, 76	n/a	n/a	n/a	n/a	n/a	n/a	n/a	n/a	n/a

Legend: E.P. = Estimated Percent, C.I. = Confidence Interval (Upper and lower bound 95 percent confidence intervals are provided for each point estimate), — = margin of error was greater than +/- 15 percentage points at the 95 percent level of confidence and deemed insufficiently reliable for this chapter, n/a = not applicable (data not collected or insufficient response for analysis).

Source: GAO analysis of credit union survey data. | GAO-18-312.

Table 34. Reported Decisions Related to Opening One or More Branches and the Factors Affecting Those Decisions, January 2010–August 2017

Decision	Percentage of credit unions by decision		Since 2010, to what extent have the following factors affected your institution's decision to open/seriously consider, but not move forward on opening one or more branches?	Extent to which factors affected the decision							
				Great		Moderate		Minor		None	
	E.P.	C.I.	Factors affecting decision	E.P.	C.I.	E.P.	C.I.	E.P.	C.I.	E.P.	C.I.
Opened or were in the process of opening a branch	29	24, 35	Competition	31	21, 44	46	34, 58	14	7, 25	8	4, 16
			Economic conditions	19	10, 31	31	20, 43	26	15, 39	25	16, 37
			Low interest rates	14	6, 25	18	10, 28	27	16, 40	42	30, 54
			Technological advances	18	9, 31	31	20, 44	25	15, 37	25	16, 36
			Regulatory environment	17	8, 29	10	4, 20	24	14, 36	49	37, 61
Seriously considered, but did not open a branch	14	10, 19	Competition	—	—	—	—	—	—	—	—
			Economic conditions	—	—	—	—	—	—	16	7, 30
			Low interest rates	—	—	—	—	—	—	14	6, 27
			Technological advances	—	—	—	—	19	9, 34	—	—
			Regulatory environment	—	—	19	9, 33	—	—	—	—
Had not seriously considered opening a branch	56	49, 62	n/a	n/a	n/a	n/a	n/a	n/a	n/a	n/a	n/a

Legend: E.P. = Estimated Percent, C.I. = Confidence Interval (Upper and lower bound 95 percent confidence intervals are provided for each point estimate), — = margin of error was greater than +/- 15 percentage points at the 95 percent level of confidence and deemed insufficiently reliable for this chapter, n/a = not applicable (data not collected or insufficient response for analysis).

Source: GAO analysis of credit union survey data. | GAO-18-312.

Table 35. Reported Decisions Related to Closing One or More Branches and the Factors Affecting Those Decisions, January 2010–August 2017

Since 2010, has your institution completed, started, or seriously considered closing one or more branches? (Please check all that apply.)			Since 2010, what effect have the following factors had on your institution's decision to close/seriously consider, but not move forward on closing one or more branches?									
Decision	Percentage of credit unions by decision		Factors affecting decision	Extent to which factors affected the decision								
				Great		Moderate		Minor		None		
	E.P.	C.I.		E.P.	C.I.	E.P.	C.I.	E.P.	C.I.	E.P.	C.I.	
Closed or were in the process of closing a branch	22	16, 27	Competition	15	6, 28	25	14, 40	14	6, 27	46	32, 60	
			Economic conditions	29	17, 43	—	—	—	—	23	12, 38	
			Low interest rates	21	11, 34	—	—	—	—	34	21, 48	
			Technological advances	15	6, 29	—	—	—	—	38	25, 53	
			Regulatory environment	13	5, 26	—	—	—	—	—	—	
Seriously considered, but did not close a branch	10	6, 14	Competition	—	—	—	—	—	—	—	—	
			Economic conditions	—	—	—	—	—	—	—	—	
			Low interest rates	—	—	5	0, 19	—	—	—	—	
			Technological advances	—	—	—	—	—	—	—	—	
			Regulatory environment	—	—	—	—	—	—	—	—	
Had not seriously considered closing a branch	67	61, 73	n/a	n/a	n/a	n/a	n/a	n/a	n/a	n/a	n/a	

Legend: E.P. = Estimated Percent, C.I. = Confidence Interval (Upper and lower bound 95 percent confidence intervals are provided for each point estimate), — = margin of error was greater than +/- 15 percentage points at the 95 percent level of confidence and deemed insufficiently reliable for this chapter, n/a = not applicable (data not collected or insufficient response for analysis).
Source: GAO analysis of credit union survey data. | GAO-18-312.

Table 36. Reported Decisions Related to Acquiring Another Institution through a Merger and the Factors Affecting Those Decisions, January 2010–August 2017

Decision	Percentage of credit unions by decision		Factors affecting decision	Extent to which factors affected the decision							
				Great		Moderate		Minor		None	
	E.P.	C.I.		E.P.	C.I.	E.P.	C.I.	E.P.	C.I.	E.P.	C.I.
Since 2010, has your institution completed, started, or seriously considered acquiring another institution through a merger? (Please check all that apply.)			Since 2010, what effect have the following factors had on your institution's decision to acquire/seriously consider, but not move forward on acquiring another institution through a merger?								
Acquired or were in the process of acquiring another institution	21	15, 26	Competition	—	—	35	22, 49	19	9, 33	—	—
			Economic conditions	—	—	—	—	23	11, 37	18	8, 32
			Low interest rates	18	8, 33	23	12, 37	—	—	—	—
			Technological advances	—	—	21	11, 35	23	12, 37	—	—
			Regulatory environment	—	—	23	38	7	2, 19	—	—
Seriously considered, but did not acquire another institution	23	17, 28	Competition	23	37	—	—	14	6, 26	—	—
			Economic conditions	20	10, 33	19	10, 31	17	7, 31	45	31, 59
			Low interest rates	11	5, 21	8	2, 18	20	10, 34	61	47, 75
			Technological advances	8	3, 16	23	12, 37	19	9, 33	50	36, 64
			Regulatory environment	26	15, 41	22	11, 36	18	10, 31	—	—
Had not seriously considered acquiring another institution	55	48, 62	n/a	n/a	n/a	n/a	n/a	n/a	n/a	n/a	n/a

Legend: E.P. = Estimated Percent, C.I. = Confidence Interval (Upper and lower bound 95 percent confidence intervals are provided for each point estimate), — = margin of error was greater than +/- 15 percentage points at the 95 percent level of confidence and deemed insufficiently reliable for this chapter, n/a = not applicable (data not collected or insufficient response for analysis).

Source: GAO analysis of credit union survey data. | GAO-18-312.

Table 37. Reported Decisions Related to Being Acquired by Another Institution and the Factors Affecting Those Decisions, January 2010–August 2017

Since 2010, has your institution started, or seriously considered being acquired by another institution through a merger? (Please check all that apply.)			Since 2010, what effect have the following factors had on your institution's decision to be acquired/seriously consider, but not move forward on being acquired by another institution through a merger?									
Decision	Percentage of credit unions by decision		Factors affecting decision	Extent to which factors affected the decision								
				Great		Moderate		Minor		None	
	E.P.	C.I.		E.P.	C.I.	E.P.	C.I.	E.P.	C.I.	E.P.	C.I.
In the process of being acquired by another institution	1	0, 3	Competition	—	—	—	—	—	—	—	—
			Economic conditions	—	—	—	—	—	—	—	—
			Low interest rates	—	—	—	—	—	—	—	—
			Technological advances	—	—	—	—	—	—	—	—
			Regulatory environment	—	—	—	—	—	—	—	—
Seriously considered, but did not move forward on being acquired by another institution	9	5, 13	Competition	—	—	—	—	—	—	—	—
			Economic conditions	—	—	—	—	—	—	—	—
			Low interest rates	—	—	8	2, 22	—	—	—	—
			Technological advances	—	—	—	—	—	—	—	—
			Regulatory environment	—	—	—	—	3	0, 13	—	—
Had not seriously considered being acquired by another institution	90	85, 94	n/a	n/a	n/a	n/a	n/a	n/a	n/a	n/a	n/a

Legend: E.P. = Estimated Percent, C.I. = Confidence Interval (Upper and lower bound 95 percent confidence intervals are provided for each point estimate), — = margin of error was greater than +/- 15 percentage points at the 95 percent level of confidence and deemed insufficiently reliable for this chapter, n/a = not applicable (data not collected or insufficient response for analysis).

Source: GAO analysis of credit union survey data. | GAO-18-312.

Table 38. Reported Changes to Customer-Facing Technology and the Factors Affecting Those Changes, January 2010–August 2017

Since 2010, has your institution increased or decreased your investment in customer-facing technology, such as online or mobile banking, or has your investment remained the same?

Since 2010, what effect have the following factors had on your institution's decision to increase/decrease your investment in customer-facing technology?

Response	Percentage of credit unions by response		Factors affecting change	Extent to which factors affected change							
				Great		Moderate		Minor		None	
	E.P.	C.I.		E.P.	C.I.	E.P.	C.I.	E.P.	C.I.	E.P.	C.I.
Increased	92	88, 95	Competition	65	58, 71	32	25, 38	2	1, 3	2	1, 6
			Economic conditions	18	13, 24	28	22, 35	23	17, 29	31	24, 38
			Low interest rates	8	5, 13	17	11, 23	30	24, 37	45	38, 52
			Technological advances	74	67, 80	20	15, 27	3	1, 7	3	1, 6
			Regulatory environment	22	16, 28	24	18, 30	27	21, 33	28	21, 34
Decreased	0	0, 2	Competition	n/a	n/a	n/a	n/a	n/a	n/a	n/a	n/a
			Economic conditions	n/a	n/a	n/a	n/a	n/a	n/a	n/a	n/a
			Low interest rates	n/a	n/a	n/a	n/a	n/a	n/a	n/a	n/a
			Technological advances	n/a	n/a	n/a	n/a	n/a	n/a	n/a	n/a
			Regulatory environment	n/a	n/a	n/a	n/a	n/a	n/a	n/a	n/a
Remained the same	7	4, 12	n/a	n/a	n/a	n/a	n/a	n/a	n/a	n/a	n/a

Legend: E.P. = Estimated Percent, C.I. = Confidence Interval (Upper and lower bound 95 percent confidence intervals are provided for each point estimate), — = margin of error was greater than +/- 15 percentage points at the 95 percent level of confidence and deemed insufficiently reliable for this chapter, n/a = not applicable (data not collected or insufficient response for analysis).

Source: GAO analysis of credit union survey data. | GAO-18-312.

Table 39. Reported Changes to Time Staff Spend Engaging Directly with Individual Customers and the Factors Affecting Those Changes, January 2010–August 2017

Since 2010, has your institution increased or decreased the time your staff spend engaging directly with individual customers, or has it remained the same?

Since 2010, what effect have the following factors had on your institution's decision to increase/decrease the time your staff spend engaging directly with individual customers?

Response	Percentage of credit unions by response		Factors affecting change	Extent to which factors affected change							
				Great		Moderate		Minor		None	
	E.P.	C.I.		E.P.	C.I.	E.P.	C.I.	E.P.	C.I.	E.P.	C.I.
Increased	27	21, 32	Competition	35	23, 48	34	22, 48	17	9, 29	14	6, 25
			Economic conditions	24	14, 37	30	18, 43	23	14, 34	24	13, 37
			Low interest rates	16	8, 28	23	12, 37	22	13, 33	39	27, 52
			Technological advances	34	22, 47	33	21, 46	18	9, 29	16	8, 28
			Regulatory environment	38	26, 50	35	23, 49	6	2, 14	21	12, 33
Decreased	19	13, 25	Competition	—	—	—	—	—	—	—	—
			Economic conditions	—	—	16	6, 31	—	—	—	—
			Low interest rates	7	1, 22	—	—	—	—	—	—
			Technological advances	—	—	—	—	5	0, 18	2	0, 10
			Regulatory environment	9	2, 23	—	—	—	—	—	—
Remained the same	55	48, 61	n/a	n/a	n/a	n/a	n/a	n/a	n/a	n/a	n/a

Legend: E.P. = Estimated Percent, C.I. = Confidence Interval (Upper and lower bound 95 percent confidence intervals are provided for each point estimate), — = margin of error was greater than +/- 15 percentage points at the 95 percent level of confidence and deemed insufficiently reliable for this chapter, n/a = not applicable (data not collected or insufficient response for analysis). | GAO-18-312.

Source: GAO analysis of credit union survey data. | GAO-18-312.

Table 40. Reported Changes to Time Staff Spend Identifying New or Innovative Products and the Factors Affecting Those Changes, January 2010–August 2017

Since 2010, has your institution increased or decreased the time your staff spends identifying new or innovative products, or has it remained the same?			Since 2010, what effect have the following factors had on your institution's decision to increase/decrease the time your staff spends identifying new or innovative products?								
Response	Percentage of credit unions by response		Factors affecting change	Extent to which factors affected change							
				Great		Moderate		Minor		None	
	E.P.	C.I.		E.P.	C.I.	E.P.	C.I.	E.P.	C.I.	E.P.	C.I.
Increased	56	49, 62	Competition	68	60, 77	24	17, 33	5	2, 10	2	0, 7
			Economic conditions	24	17, 33	38	29, 46	20	13, 28	18	12, 26
			Low interest rates	13	8, 20	24	17, 33	32	23, 40	30	22, 39
			Technological advances	71	63, 79	20	13, 28	5	2, 10	4	1, 10
			Regulatory environment	23	16, 32	32	24, 40	22	15, 30	24	16, 32
Decreased	3	1, 7	Competition	—	—	—	—	—	—	—	—
			Economic conditions	—	—	—	—	—	—	—	—
			Low interest rates	—	—	—	—	—	—	—	—
			Technological advances	—	—	—	—	—	—	4	0, 14
			Regulatory environment	—	—	—	—	—	—	—	—
Remained the same	41	35, 48	n/a	n/a	n/a	n/a	n/a	n/a	n/a	n/a	n/a

Legend: E.P. = Estimated Percent, C.I. = Confidence Interval (Upper and lower bound 95 percent confidence intervals are provided for each point estimate), — = margin of error was greater than +/- 15 percentage points at the 95 percent level of confidence and deemed insufficiently reliable for this chapter, n/a = not applicable (data not collected or insufficient response for analysis).

Source: GAO analysis of credit union survey data. | GAO-18-312.

Table 41. Reported Actions by Credit Unions to Comply with Federal Regulations, January 2010- August 2017

In order to comply with federal financial regulations, since 2010, has your institution taken any of the following actions:	Yes		No	
	E.P.	C.I.	E.P.	C.I.
Hired additional staff for compliance purposes	39	32, 45	61	55, 68
Reallocated existing staff to compliance-related positions	61	54, 68	39	32, 46
Hired a third party to assist with compliance	65	59, 72	35	28, 41
Increased staff time for compliance-related activities	82	76, 88	18	12, 24
Purchased additional software or automated systems to aid in compliance activities	69	63, 76	31	24, 37

Legend: E.P. = Estimated Percent, C.I. = Confidence Interval (Upper and lower bound 95 percent confidence intervals are provided for each point estimate).

Source: GAO analysis of credit union survey data. | GAO-18-312.

Table 42. Reported Changes to the Time to Make Individual Residential Mortgage Loans and the Factors Affecting Those Changes, January 2010–August 2017

Response	Since 2010, has your institution increased or decreased the time to make individual residential mortgage loans, or has it remained the same? Percentage of credit unions by response		Since 2010, what effect have the following factors had on your institution's increase/decrease in the time to make individual residential mortgage loans?	Extent to which factors affected change							
				Great		Moderate		Minor		None	
	E.P.	C.I.	Factors affecting change	E.P.	C.I.	E.P.	C.I.	E.P.	C.I.	E.P.	C.I.
Increased	68	62, 75	Competition	9	5, 15	22	15, 29	30	23, 37	39	31, 47
			Economic conditions	12	7, 18	30	22, 37	30	23, 38	28	21, 35
			Low interest rates	16	10, 22	27	19, 34	22	15, 29	36	29, 44
			Technological advances	8	4, 15	25	18, 32	29	22, 36	37	29, 45
			Regulatory environment	82	75, 88	16	10, 23	2	0, 6	1	0, 3
Decreased	6	3, 11	Competition	—	—	—	—	—	—	—	—
			Economic conditions	—	—	—	—	—	—	—	—
			Low interest rates	—	—	—	—	—	—	—	—
			Technological advances	—	—	—	—	—	—	1	0, 4
			Regulatory environment	—	—	—	—	—	—	—	—
Remained the same	25	19, 31	n/a	n/a	n/a	n/a	n/a	n/a	n/a	n/a	n/a

Legend: E.P. = Estimated Percent, C.I. = Confidence Interval (Upper and lower bound 95 percent confidence intervals are provided for each point estimate), — = margin of error was greater than +/- 15 percentage points at the 95 percent level of confidence and deemed insufficiently reliable for this chapter, n/a = not applicable (data not collected or insufficient response for analysis).

Source: GAO analysis of credit union survey data. | GAO-18-312.

Note: The time to make a residential mortgage loan is measured as the date of application to disbursement of funds.

Table 43. Reported Changes to the Number of Individual Residential Mortgage Lending Products or Services Offered and the Factors Affecting Those Changes, January 2010–August 2017

Since 2010, has your institution increased or decreased the number of residential mortgage lending products or services offered, or have they remained the same?			Since 2010, what effect have the following factors had on your institution's increase/decrease in the number of residential mortgage lending products or services offered?								
Response	Percentage of credit unions by response		Factors affecting change	Extent to which factors affected change							
				Great		Moderate		Minor		None	
	E.P.	C.I.		E.P.	C.I.	E.P.	C.I.	E.P.	C.I.	E.P.	C.I.
Increased	29	23, 35	Competition	34	23, 46	40	28, 51	17	9, 28	9	16
			Economic conditions	17	9, 28	51	39, 63	21	12, 32	11	19
			Low interest rates	33	22, 45	37	25, 48	16	8, 26	15	7, 26
			Technological advances	22	12, 34	35	24, 46	25	16, 37	18	28
			Regulatory environment	38	27, 50	22	14, 34	17	28	22	13, 33
Decreased	17	12, 23	Competition	—	—	—	—	—	—	—	—
			Economic conditions	—	—	—	—	—	—	—	—
			Low interest rates	—	—	—	—	—	—	—	—
			Technological advances	—	—	—	—	0	0, 6	1	0, 4
			Regulatory environment	n/a	n/a	n/a	n/a	n/a	n/a	n/a	n/a
Remained the same	54	47, 60	n/a	n/a							

Legend: E.P. = Estimated Percent, C.I. = Confidence Interval (Upper and lower bound 95 percent confidence intervals are provided for each point estimate), — = margin of error was greater than +/- 15 percentage points at the 95 percent level of confidence and deemed insufficiently reliable for this chapter, n/a = not applicable (data not collected or insufficient response for analysis).

Source: GAO analysis of credit union survey data. | GAO-18-312.

Table 44. Reported Changes to the Minimum Credit Quality Criteria Needed to Qualify for Individual Residential Mortgage Loans and the Factors Affecting Those Changes, January 2010–August 2017

Since 2010, has your institution increased or decreased the minimum credit quality criteria needed to qualify for residential mortgage loans, or has it remained the same?

Since 2010, what effect have the following factors had on your institution's increase/decrease in the minimum credit quality criteria needed to qualify for residential mortgage loans?

Response	Percentage of credit unions by response		Factors affecting change	Extent to which factors affected change							
				Great		Moderate		Minor		None	
	E.P.	C.I.		E.P.	C.I.	E.P.	C.I.	E.P.	C.I.	E.P.	C.I.
Increased	31	25, 37	Competition	6	2, 15	15	7, 26	33	22, 44	46	35, 58
			Economic conditions	13	7, 22	37	25, 48	30	20, 42	20	12, 30
			Low interest rates	11	5, 21	32	21, 44	19	11, 29	39	28, 50
			Technological advances	4	1, 12	19	10, 31	30	20, 42	46	35, 58
			Regulatory environment	72	59, 82	25	15, 37	2	0, 7	1	0, 5
Decreased	3	1, 6	Competition	—	—	—	—	—	—	—	—
			Economic conditions	—	—	—	—	—	—	—	—
			Low interest rates	—	—	—	—	5	0, 17	—	—
			Technological advances	—	—	5	0, 17	—	—	—	—
			Regulatory environment	—	—	2	0, 9	—	—	—	—
Remained the same	66	60, 72	n/a	n/a	n/a	n/a	n/a	n/a	n/a	n/a	n/a

Legend: E.P. = Estimated Percent, C.I. = Confidence Interval (Upper and lower bound 95 percent confidence intervals are provided for each point estimate), — = margin of error was greater than +/- 15 percentage points at the 95 percent level of confidence and deemed insufficiently reliable for this chapter, n/a = not applicable (data not collected or insufficient response for analysis).

Source: GAO analysis of credit union survey data. | GAO-18-312.

Table 45. Reported Changes to the Documentation Borrowers Are Required to Provide for Individual Residential Mortgage Loans and the Factors Affecting Those Changes, January 2010–August 2017

Since 2010, has your institution increased or decreased the documentation you require borrowers to provide for residential mortgage loans, or has it remained the same?

Since 2010, what effect have the following factors had on your institution's increase/decrease in the documentation you require borrowers to provide for residential mortgage loans?

Response	Percentage of credit unions by response		Factors affecting change	Extent to which factors affected change							
				Great		Moderate		Minor		None	
	E.P.	C.I.		E.P.	C.I.	E.P.	C.I.	E.P.	C.I.	E.P.	C.I.
Increased	74	68, 80	Competition	5	2, 10	10	6, 16	23	16, 30	62	54, 70
			Economic conditions	11	6, 17	20	14, 27	25	18, 32	44	36, 51
			Low interest rates	8	4, 14	10	6, 16	26	19, 33	56	49, 64
			Technological advances	7	3, 13	17	11, 24	25	18, 32	51	44, 59
			Regulatory environment	86	79, 91	12	8, 19	1	0, 3	1	0, 5
Decreased	1	0, 4	Competition	n/a	n/a	n/a	n/a	n/a	n/a	n/a	n/a
			Economic conditions	n/a	n/a	n/a	n/a	n/a	n/a	n/a	n/a
			Low interest rates	n/a	n/a	n/a	n/a	n/a	n/a	n/a	n/a
			Technological advances	n/a	n/a	n/a	n/a	n/a	n/a	n/a	n/a
			Regulatory environment	n/a	n/a	n/a	n/a	n/a	n/a	n/a	n/a
Remained the same	25	19, 31	n/a								

Legend: E.P. = Estimated Percent, C.I. = Confidence Interval (Upper and lower bound 95 percent confidence intervals are provided for each point estimate), — = margin of error was greater than +/- 15 percentage points at the 95 percent level of confidence and deemed insufficiently reliable for this chapter, n/a = not applicable (data not collected or insufficient response for analysis).
Source: GAO analysis of credit union survey data. | GAO-18-312.

Table 46. Reported Changes to the Availability of Individual Residential Mortgage Loans to Individual Borrowers with Atypical Financial Characteristics and the Factors Affecting Those Changes, January 2010–August 2017

Since 2010, has your institution increased or decreased the availability of residential mortgage loans to individual borrowers with atypical financial characteristics, or has it remained the same?

Since 2010, what effect have the following factors had on your institution's increase/decrease in the availability of residential mortgage loans to individual borrowers with atypical financial characteristic?

Response	Percentage of credit unions by response		Factors affecting change	Extent to which factors affected change								
				Great		Moderate		Minor		None	
	E.P.	C.I.		E.P.	C.I.	E.P.	C.I.	E.P.	C.I.	E.P.	C.I.
Increased	11	7, 17	Competition	—	—	—	—	—	—	—	—
			Economic conditions	—	—	—	—	—	—	—	—
			Low interest rates	—	—	—	—	—	—	—	—
			Technological advances	—	—	—	—	—	—	—	—
			Regulatory environment	—	—	—	—	—	—	—	—
Decreased	28	21, 34	Competition	4	1, 15	11	4, 22	25	13, 39	60	45, 74
			Economic conditions	16	7, 29	33	20, 48	21	11, 35	31	19, 45
			Low interest rates	14	5, 27	16	8, 29	22	11, 36	48	35, 62
			Technological advances	7	2, 20	7	2, 14	28	16, 43	58	44, 72
			Regulatory environment	79	65, 89	15	7, 28	5	1, 15	1	0, 4
Remained the same	61	54, 68	n/a	n/a	n/a	n/a	n/a	n/a	n/a	n/a	n/

Legend: E.P. = Estimated Percent, C.I. = Confidence Interval (Upper and lower bound 95 percent confidence intervals are provided for each point estimate), — = margin of error was greater than +/- 15 percentage points at the 95 percent level of confidence and deemed insufficiently reliable for this chapter, n/a = not applicable (data not collected or insufficient response for analysis). Source: GAO analysis of credit union survey data. | GAO-18-312.

Note: "Borrowers with atypical financial characteristics" are defined as the following: (i) borrowers generating income from self-employment (including working as "contract" or "1099" employees); (ii) borrowers anticipated to rely on income from assets to repay the loan; (iii) borrowers who rely on intermittent, supplemental, part-time, seasonal, bonus, or overtime income.

Table 47. Reported Changes to Product or Service Fees for Individual Residential Mortgage Loans and the Factors Affecting Those Changes, January 2010–August 2017

Since 2010, has your institution increased or decreased product or service fees for residential mortgage loans, or have they remained the same?			Since 2010, what effect have the following factors had on your institution's increase/decrease in product or service fees for residential mortgage loans?							
Response	Percentage of credit unions by response		Factors affecting change	Extent to which factors affected change						
				Great		Moderate		Minor		None
	E.P	C.I.		E.P.	C.I.	E.P.	C.I.	E.P.	C.I.	E.P.	C.I.
Increased	32	26, 39	Competition	7	2, 17	21	12, 32	36	24, 47	37	25, 48
			Economic conditions	7	2, 17	32	21, 45	27	17, 39	34	23, 47
			Low interest rates	12	5, 21	28	18, 40	28	17, 41	33	22, 44
			Technological advances	10	5, 18	23	13, 35	30	20, 43	37	26, 48
			Regulatory environment	74	62, 84	17	9, 28	5	2, 10	5	1, 14
Decreased	4	2, 8	Competition	—	—	—	—	—	—	—	—
			Economic conditions	—	—	—	—	—	—	—	—
			Low interest rates	—	—	—	—	—	—	—	—
			Technological advances	—	—	—	—	—	—	—	—
			Regulatory environment	—	—	—	—	—	—	—	—
Remained the same	63	57, 70	n/a	n/a	n/a	n/a	n/a	n/a	n/a	n/a	n/a

Legend: E.P. = Estimated Percent, C.I. = Confidence Interval (Upper and lower bound 95 percent confidence intervals are provided for each point estimate), — = margin of error was greater than +/- 15 percentage points at the 95 percent level of confidence and deemed insufficiently reliable for this chapter, n/a = not applicable (data not collected or insufficient response for analysis)
Source: GAO analysis of credit union survey data. | GAO-18-312.

For the multiple-choice question, respondents were asked what actions they had taken in order to comply with federal regulations. Respondents were not asked to identify the extent to which the factors had affected these actions.

Residential Mortgage Lending Activities

In our web-based survey, we instructed participants to consider the following definition of residential mortgage lending: "Residential mortgage lending includes new mortgage loans, refinancing, and home equity lines of credit or home equity loans." We asked participants to consider the residential mortgage lending activities of their institution since 2010. Tables 42–47 present the survey questions related to residential mortgage lending and resulting response data.

APPENDIX V: COMMENTS FROM THE BOARD OF GOVERNORS OF THE FEDERAL RESERVE SYSTEM

BOARD OF GOVERNORS OF THE FEDERAL RESERVE SYSTEM
WASHINGTON, DC 20551

Division of Supervision
and Regulation

June 27, 2018

Lawrance Evans, Jr.
Managing Director
Financial Markets and Community Investment
United States Government Accountability Office
441 G Street, NW
Washington, DC 20548

United States Government Accountability Office

Dear Mr. Evans:

Thank you for providing the Board of Governors of the Federal Reserve System ("Federal Reserve" or "Board") with an opportunity to review the final draft of the Government Accountability Office ("GAO") report entitled: *Community Banks: Effect of Regulations on Small Business Lending and Institutions Appears Modest, but Lending Data Could Be Improved* (GAO-18-312). The GAO's report reviews the effects of regulatory changes since 2010 on community banks and small business lending. We appreciate the report's recognition of the Federal Reserve's efforts, in conjunction with the Office of the Comptroller of the Currency ("OCC") and the Federal Deposit Insurance Corporation ("FDIC"), to identify and mitigate the effects of changes in the regulatory environment on community banks and small business lending and ensure that financial institutions, including community banks, continue to make credit available to small businesses.

The GAO's report makes one recommendation to the Federal Reserve:

> The Chairman of the Board of Governors of the Federal Reserve System should collaborate with FDIC and OCC to
>
> reevaluate, and modify as needed, the requirements for the data banks report in the Consolidated Reports of Condition and Income to better reflect lending to small businesses.

With respect to the GAO's recommendation about data collected on the Consolidated Reports of Condition and Income (commonly referred to as the Call Reports), the Federal Reserve recognizes the importance of maximizing the utility of information collected, while minimizing, to the extent practicable and appropriate, the reporting burden on financial institutions. Consequently, the Federal Reserve will coordinate with the FDIC and OCC, through the Federal Financial Institution Examination Council ("FFIEC"[1]) Task Force on Reports,[2] to reassess and potentially modify the requirements for the data financial institutions report in the Call Reports on lending to small businesses.

We appreciate the GAO's review of the effects of regulatory changes on small business lending, their professional approach to the review, and the opportunity to comment.

Sincerely,

Michael S. Gibson

Director

---

[1] The Board, FDIC, and OCC are members of the FFIEC.
[2] The law establishing the FFIEC and defining its functions requires the FFIEC to develop uniform reporting systems for federally supervised financial institutions. To meet this objective, the FFIEC established the Task Force on Reports to develop interagency uniform reports, such as the Call Reports, to collect periodic information needed for effective supervision and other public policy purposes.

APPENDIX VI: COMMENTS FROM THE FEDERAL DEPOSIT INSURANCE CORPORATION

Federal Deposit Insurance Corporation
550 17th Street NW, Washington, D.C. 20429-9990

July 2, 2018

Mr. Lawrance L. Evans Jr., Managing Director
Financial Markets and Community Investment
U.S. Government Accountability Office
441 G Street, NW
Washington, DC 20548

Dear Mr. Evans:

    Thank you for the opportunity to review and comment on the Government Accountability Office's ("GAO") draft report entitled "*Community Banks: Effect of Regulations on Small Business Lending and Institutions Appears Modest, but Lending Data Could Be Improved* (GAO-18-312) ("Report"). The Report reviewed, among other things, potential effects of changes in the regulatory environment on community bank outcomes from 2010 through 2016, measures of small business lending, and the extent to which regulatory changes or characteristics of insured depository institutions ("IDIs") could potentially explain changes in small business lending measures.

    The FDIC recognizes the important role small businesses play in the U.S. economy and the vital support that lending by community banks provides to small business activity in general. In 2016 the FDIC conducted a Small Business Lending Survey to obtain a more accurate picture of trends in small business lending by community banks. We expect to make the results of the survey available to the public later this year. Additionally, the FDIC continually evaluates the factors that affect the performance and activities of community banks, including regulatory changes. We did so most recently in a paper titled *Core Profitability of Community Banks: 1985 – 2015* (Fronk, 2016).

    The Report includes a recommendation to assist the FDIC in enhancing its analytical capabilities with regard to small business lending by community banks. Specifically, the Report recommends that the FDIC:

1. Collaborate with the Federal Reserve and OCC to reevaluate, and modify as needed, the requirements for the data banks report in the Consolidated Reports of Condition and Income to better reflect lending to small businesses.

    We appreciate the GAO's recommendation and will consider it as we continually evaluate the data we collect from IDIs and the ability of these data to provide insights on vital aspects of the health and performance of community banks to the FDIC and the public.

The Federal Financial Institutions Examination Council ("FFIEC"), of which the FDIC is a member, establishes the reporting requirements for the Consolidated Reports of Condition and Income ("Call Report"), including the data items for loans to small businesses. The FDIC, in coordination with the Federal Reserve and the OCC, will assess the feasibility and merits of modifications to the reporting of loans to small businesses in the Call Report through the FFIEC's Task Force on Reports.[1] The FDIC also understands the resource constraints that small IDIs face and will continue to tailor regulations and reporting requirements in a manner commensurate with those constraints.

Again, thank you for your efforts. If you have any questions or need additional follow-up information, please do not hesitate to contact us.

Sincerely,

Doreen R. Eberley
Director, Division of Risk Management Supervision

Diane Ellis
Director, Division of Insurance and Research

---

[1] The law establishing the FFIEC and defining its functions requires the FFIEC to develop uniform reporting systems for federally supervised financial institutions. To meet this objective, the FFIEC established the Task Force on Reports to develop uniform interagency reports, such as the Call Report, to collect periodic information that is needed for effective supervision and other public policy purposes.

Appendix VII: Comments from the Office of the Comptroller of the Currency

 Office of the Comptroller of the Currency

Washington, DC 20219

July 2, 2018

Mr. Lawrance L. Evans, Jr.
Director, Financial Markets and Community Investment
U.S. Government Accountability Office
Washington, DC 20548

Dear Mr. Evans:

The Office of the Comptroller of the Currency (OCC) has received and reviewed the U.S. Government Accountability Office's (GAO) draft report titled "Community Banks: Effect of Regulations on Small Business Lending and Institutions Appears Modest, but Lending Data Could Be Improved (GAO-18-312)." The report examined, for the period 2010 through 2017, the effect of the regulatory environment on banks and credit unions, including: (1) the data regulators use to measure the volume of small business lending and how and why small business lending volumes changed, (2) how and why small business lending processes changed among these institutions, (3) how and why the number of institutions and their financial performances changed, and (4) actions regulators took to identify and mitigate the effects of changes on the regulatory environment on these institutions and their small business customers.

As part of this review, the GAO makes one recommendation for the OCC. The GAO recommends that the Comptroller of the Currency should collaborate with the Board of Governors of the Federal Reserve System and the Federal Deposit Insurance Corporation to reevaluate, and modify as needed, the requirements for the data banks report in the Consolidated Reports of Condition and Income (Call Report) to better reflect lending to small businesses.

The OCC appreciates the concerns raised by the GAO and understands the importance of the recommendation. As a result, the OCC will raise this matter to the Federal Financial Institutions Examination Council's (FFIEC) Task Force on Reports (TFOR) during the third quarter of 2018.[1] The TFOR includes representatives from the Board of Governors of the Federal Reserve System and the Federal Deposit Insurance Corporation.[2] The OCC will discuss with the TFOR

---

[1] By law, the FFIEC is responsible for developing uniform reporting systems for federally supervised financial institutions, including the Call Report, and has assigned that responsibility to the TFOR working group. See 12 U.S.C. § 3305(c).

[2] The FFIEC comprises the principals of the following agencies: OCC, Board of Governors of the Federal Reserve System, Federal Deposit Insurance Corporation, National Credit Union Administration, Bureau of Consumer Financial Protection, and State Liaison Committee. Each agency is represented on the TFOR.

the concerns raised by the GAO and potential modifications to existing data items that could result in collecting data to better reflect lending to small businesses while minimizing any additional burden on financial institutions. Any potential revisions agreed to by the TFOR would then be issued for public comment and require approval from the Office of Management and Budget, consistent with the requirements of the Paperwork Reduction Act,[3] before any revisions could be implemented.

Sincerely,

Toney M. Bland
Senior Deputy Comptroller
Midsize and Community Bank Supervision

---

[3] 44 U.S.C. § 3501 *et seq.*

In: Community Banks and Credit Unions
Editor: Richard L. Mizelle

ISBN: 978-1-53616-066-6
© 2019 Nova Science Publishers, Inc.

Chapter 2

COMMUNITY BANKS AND CREDIT UNIONS: REGULATORS COULD TAKE ADDITIONAL STEPS TO ADDRESS COMPLIANCE BURDENS[*]

United States Government Accountability Office

ABBREVIATIONS

AML	anti-money laundering
BSA	Bank Secrecy Act
Call Reports	Consolidated Report of Condition and Income
CFPB	Consumer Financial Protection Bureau
CTR	Currency Transaction Reports
Dodd-Frank Act	Dodd-Frank Wall Street Reform and Consumer Protection Act of 2010
EGRPRA	Economic Growth and Regulatory Paperwork Reduction Act of 1996

---

[*] This is an edited, reformatted and augmented version of the United States Government Accountability Office Report to the Chairman, Committee onSmall Business, House of Representatives, Publication No. GAO-18-213, dated February 2018.

FDIC	Federal Deposit Insurance Corporation
Federal Reserve	Board of Governors of the Federal Reserve System
FFIEC	Federal Financial Institutions Examination Council
FinCEN	Financial Crimes Enforcement Network
HMDA	Home Mortgage Disclosure Act of 1975
NCUA	National Credit Union Administration
OCC	Office of the Comptroller of the Currency
RESPA	Real Estate Settlement Procedures Act
RFA	Regulatory Flexibility Act
SAR	Suspicious Activity Reports
TILA	Truth-in-Lending Act
TRID	TILA-RESPA Integrated Disclosure
USA PATRIOT ACT	Uniting and Strengthening America by Providing Appropriate Tools Required to Intercept and Obstruct Terrorism Act of 2001

WHY GAO DID THIS STUDY

In recent decades, many new regulations intended to strengthen financial soundness, improve consumer protections, and aid anti-money laundering efforts were implemented for financial institutions. Smaller community banks and credit unions must comply with some of the regulations, but compliance can be more challenging and costly for these institutions. GAO examined (1) the regulations community banks and credit unions viewed as most burdensome and why, and (2) efforts by depository institution regulators to reduce any regulatory burden. GAO analyzed regulations and interviewed more than 60 community banks and credit unions (selected based on asset size and financial activities), regulators, and industry associations and consumer groups. GAO also analyzed letters and transcripts commenting on regulatory burden that regulators prepared responding to the comments.

WHAT GAO RECOMMENDS

GAO makes a total of 10 recommendations to CFPB and the depository institution regulators. CFPB should assess the effectiveness of guidance on mortgage disclosure regulations and publicly issue its plans for the scope and timing of its regulation reviews and coordinate these with the other regulators' review process. As part of their burden reviews, the depository institution regulators should develop plans to report quantitative rationales for their actions and addressing the cumulative burden of regulations. In written comments, CFPB and the four depository institution regulators generally agreed with the recommendations.

WHAT GAO FOUND

Interviews and focus groups GAO conducted with representatives of over 60 community banks and credit unions indicated regulations for reporting mortgage characteristics, reviewing transactions for potentially illicit activity, and disclosing mortgage terms and costs to consumers were the most burdensome. Institution representatives said these regulations were time-consuming and costly to comply with, in part because the requirements were complex, required individual reports that had to be reviewed for accuracy, or mandated actions within specific timeframes. However, regulators and others noted that the regulations were essential to preventing lending discrimination and use of the banking system for illicit activity, and they were acting to reduce compliance burdens. Institution representatives also said that the new mortgage disclosure regulations increased compliance costs, added significant time· to loan closings, and resulted in institutions absorbing costs when others, such as appraisers and inspectors, changed disclosed fees. The Consumer Financial Protection Bureau (CFPB) issued guidance and conducted other outreach to educate institutions after issuing these regulations in 2013. But GAO found that some compliance burdens arose from misunderstanding the disclosure regulations—which in turn may have led institutions to take actions not actually required. Assessing the effectiveness of the guidance for the disclosure regulations could help mitigate the misunderstandings and thus also reduce compliance burdens.

Regulators of community banks and credit unions—the Board of Governors of the Federal Reserve, the Federal Deposit Insurance Corporation, the Office of the Comptroller of the Currency, and the National Credit Union Administration— conduct decennial reviews to obtain industry comments on regulatory burden. But the reviews, conducted under the Economic Growth and Regulatory Paperwork Reduction Act of 1996 (EGRPRA), had the following limitations:

- CFPB and the consumer financial regulations for which it is responsible were not included.
- Unlike executive branch agencies, the depository institution regulators are not required to analyze and report quantitative-based rationales for their responses to comments.
- Regulators do not assess the cumulative burden of the regulations they administer.

CFPB has formed an internal group that will be tasked with reviewing regulations it administers, but the agency has not publicly announced the scope of regulations included, the timing and frequency of the reviews, and the extent to which they will be coordinated with the other federal banking and credit union regulators as part of their periodic EGRPRA reviews. Congressional intent in mandating that these regulators review their regulations was that the cumulative effect of all federal financial regulations be considered. In addition, sound practices required of other federal agencies require them to analyze and report their assessments when reviewing regulations. Documenting in plans how the depository institution regulators would address these EGRPRA limitations would better ensure that all regulations relevant to community banks and credit unions were reviewed, likely improve the analyses the regulators perform, and potentially result in additional burden reduction.

February 13, 2018

The Honorable Steve Chabot Chairman
Committee on Small Business House of Representatives

Dear Mr. Chairman:

Within the past two decades, financial regulators have implemented many new regulations in the aftermath of events such as the September 2001 terrorist attacks and the financial crisis in 2007–2009, These regulations were intended to address the risks and problematic practices that contributed or led to the events, and included provisions that ranged from strengthening financial institutions' anti-money laundering (AML) programs to prevent terrorism financing to creating additional protections for mortgage lending. For example, in 2010 Congress passed the Dodd-Frank Wall Street Reform and Consumer Protection Act (Dodd-Frank Act), which includes numerous reforms to strengthen oversight of financial institutions.[1] As a result of this act and other actions taken by financial regulators, additional regulatory requirements were placed on financial institutions, including community banks and credit unions. These institutions historically have played an important role in serving their local customers, including providing credit to small businesses.

We previously reported that representatives of community banks and credit unions expressed concerns about the burden that additional regulations create for them.[2] For example, some credit union, community

---

[1] Pub. L. No. 111-203, 124 Stat. 1376 (2010). We identified 236 provisions of the act that require regulators to issue rules. See GAO, *Financial Regulatory Reform: Regulators Have Faced Challenges Finalizing Key Reforms and Unaddressed Areas Pose Potential Risks*, GAO-13-195 (Washington, D.C.: Jan. 23, 2013).

[2] GAO, *Community Banks and Credit Unions: Impact of the Dodd-Frank Act Depends Largely on Future Rule Makings*, GAO-12-881 (Washington, D.C: Sep. 13, 2012); *Bank Capital*

bank, and industry association representatives told us in 2015 that several mortgage-related rules increased their overall compliance burden. In turn, some said this had begun to adversely affect some lending activities, such as mortgage lending to customers not typically served by larger financial institutions, although the regulations provided exemptions or other provisions to reduce such impacts. But surveys conducted by regulators, industry associations, and academics on the impact of the Dodd-Frank Act on small banks suggested that credit availability had been reduced by moderate to minimal amounts among those responding to the various surveys, and regulatory data up to that point had not confirmed a negative impact on mortgage lending.

You asked us to examine the impact of regulation on community banks and credit unions. This chapter examines (1) what regulations institutions regarded as most burdensome and why, and (2) what actions the regulators of these institutions have taken to address any burdens associated with financial regulations. In addition to this chapter, we will provide a separate report that addresses the effect of regulatory burden on lending activities by community banks and credit unions, the rate of formation of new institutions, and potential impacts of regulations that we expect to issue to you in spring 2018.

To identify regulations that community banks and credit unions viewed as most burdensome, we obtained opinions from a non-probability selection of selected community banks and credit unions. We drew our sample from institutions whose characteristics (such as asset size and activities) were typical of traditional community banking activities. The asset thresholds we used for our sample were $1.2 billion for banks (which represented 90 percent of banks as of March 2016) and $860 million for credit unions (which represented 95 percent of credit unions as of March 2016). We excluded institutions that were primarily conducting activities that were not typical of community banking, including institutions functioning primarily as credit card banks or institutions with headquarters outside the United

Reforms: Initial Effects of Basel III on Capital, Credit, and International Competitiveness, GAO-15-67 (Washington, D.C: Nov. 20, 2014); and *Dodd-Frank Regulations: Impacts on Community Banks, Credit Unions and Systemically Important Institutions*, GAO-16-169 (Washington, D.C: Dec. 30, 2015).

States. From this group, we used additional criteria to select institutions that were located in various regions of the country and whose lending asset levels indicated they would have experience with complying with relevant regulations. The sample also included institutions overseen by each of the depository institution regulators—the Board of Governors of the Federal Reserve (Federal Reserve), the Federal Deposit Insurance Corporation (FDIC), the Office of the Comptroller of the Currency (OCC), and the National Credit Union Administration (NCUA).

Using this sample, we obtained opinions from representatives 64 institutions during individual interviews, focus groups, and a site visit.

- More specifically, we interviewed 10 community banks and 7 credit unions.
- After the interviews demonstrated considerable consensus existed among institutions about the most burdensome regulations, we held six focus groups with an additional 46 banks and credit unions to identify the characteristics of the regulations that made them burdensome.
- We also reviewed 28 reports of examinations conducted by the regulators of banks and credit unions we selected for our interviews to identify the extent to which these examinations addressed regulations from which the banks were exempted.

To determine what actions regulators took to address regulatory burden, we reviewed the reports the depository institution regulators issued for the 2007 and 2017 Economic Growth and Regulatory Paperwork Reduction Act of 1996 (EGRPRA) reviews. We analyzed over 200 comment letters that the regulators received from community banks, credit unions, their trade associations, and others; and reviewed transcripts of all six public forums regulators held as part of the 2017 EGRPRA regulatory review they conducted. We analyzed the extent to which they addressed the issues raised in comments received for the reviews. We also interviewed the depository institution regulators and the Consumer Financial Protection Bureau (CFPB) about their actions to address burden when creating rules and thereafter. We discussed issues that banks and credit unions identified with specific regulations with the depository institution regulators, CFPB, and the Financial Crimes Enforcement Network (FinCEN), which has delegated authority from the Secretary of the Treasury to implement, administer, and enforce compliance with anti-money laundering and terrorist financing regulations. We also interviewed associations representing consumers with knowledge of relevant activities to understand the benefits of these regulations and the Small Business Administration's Office of Advocacy, which reviews and comments on burdens of regulations, including those issued by banking regulators.

For more information on our scope and methodology, see appendix I. We conducted this performance audit from March 2016 to February 2018 in accordance with generally accepted government auditing standards. Those standards require that we plan and perform the audit to obtain sufficient, appropriate evidence to provide a reasonable basis for our findings and conclusions based on our audit objectives. We believe that the evidence obtained provides a reasonable basis for our findings and conclusions based on our audit objectives.

BACKGROUND

While no commonly accepted definition of a community bank exists, they are generally smaller banks that provide banking services to the local community and have management and board members who reside in the local community. In some of our past reports, we often defined community banks as those with under $10 billion in total assets.[3] However, many banks have assets well below $10 billion as data from the financial condition reports that institutions submit to regulators (Call Reports) indicated that of the more than 6,100 banks in the United States, about 90 percent had assets below about $1.2 billion as of March 2016.

---

[3] See GAO-12-881, GAO-15-67, and GAO-16-169.

Based on our prior interviews and reviews of documents, regulators and others have observed that small banks tend to differ from larger banks in their relationships with customers.[4] Large banks are more likely to engage in transactional banking, which focuses on the provision of highly standardized products that require little human input to manage and are underwritten using statistical information. Small banks are more likely to engage in what is known as relationship banking in which banks consider not only data models but also information acquired by working with the banking customer over time. Using this banking model, small banks may be able to extend credit to customers such as small business owners who might not receive a loan from a larger bank.

Small business lending appears to be an important activity for community banks. As of June 2017, community banks had almost $300 billion outstanding in loans with an original principal balance of under $1 million (which banking regulators define as small business lending), or about 20 percent of these institutions' total lending. In that same month, non-community banks had about $390 billion outstanding in business loans under $1 million representing 5 percent of their total lending.

Credit unions are nonprofit member-owned institutions that take deposits and make loans. Unlike banks, credit unions are subject to limits on their membership because members must have a "common bond"—for example, working for the same employer or living in the same community. Financial reports submitted to NCUA (the regulator that oversees federally-insured credit unions) indicated that of the more than 6,000 credit unions in the United States, 90 percent had assets below about $393 million as of March 2016.

In addition to providing consumer products to their members, credit unions are also allowed to make loans for business activities subject to certain restrictions. These member business loans are defined as a loan, line of credit, or letter of credit that a credit union extends to a borrower for a commercial, industrial, agricultural, or professional purpose, subject to

---

[4] GAO, *Financial Institutions: Causes and Consequences of Recent Bank Failures*, GAO-13-71 (Washington, D.C.: Jan. 3, 2013).

certain exclusions.[5] In accordance with rules effective January 2017, the total amount of business lending credit unions can do is not to generally exceed 1.75 times the actual net worth of the credit union.[6]

Overview of Federal Financial Regulators for Community Banks and Credit Unions

Federal banking and credit union regulators have responsibility for ensuring the safety and soundness of the institutions they oversee, protecting federal deposit insurance funds, promoting stability in financial markets, and enforcing compliance with applicable consumer protection laws. All depository institutions that have federal deposit insurance have a federal prudential regulator. The regulator responsible for overseeing a community bank or credit union varies depending on how the institution is chartered, whether it is federally insured, and whether it is a Federal Reserve member (see table 1).

Other federal agencies also impose regulatory requirements on banks and credit unions. These include rules issued by CFPB, which has supervision and enforcement authority for various federal consumer protection laws for depository institutions with more than $10 billion in assets and their affiliates. The Federal Reserve, OCC, FDIC, and NCUA continue to supervise for consumer protection compliance at institutions that have $10 billion or less in assets. Although community banks and credit unions with less than $10 billion in assets typically would not be subject to CFPB examinations, they generally are required to comply with CFPB rules related to consumer protection.

---

[5] *See* 12 U.S.C. § 1757a(c)(1)(A).

[6] *See* 12 U.S.C. § 1757a(a). The statutory cap on outstanding member business loans does not apply in the case of an insured credit union that is chartered for the purpose of making, or that has a history of primarily making, member business loans to its members, that serves predominantly low-income members, or is a community development financial institution as defined by the Community Development Banking and Financial Institutions Act of 1994. 12 U.S.C. § 1757a(b). The net worth ratio is the total of a credit union's regular reserves, any secondary capital, its undivided earnings, and its net income or loss divided by its total assets. See 12 C.F.R. § 702.2(g).

provisions they identified as likely to affect these institutions included some of the act's mortgage reforms, such as those requiring institutions to

- ensure that a consumer obtaining a residential mortgage loan has the reasonable ability to repay the loan at the time the loan is consummated;
- comply with a new CFPB rule that combines two different mortgage loan disclosures that had been required by the Truth-in-Lending Act and the Real Estate Settlement Procedures Act of 1974; and
- ensure that property appraisers are sufficiently independent.

In addition to the regulations that have arisen from provisions in the Dodd-Frank Act, we reported that other regulations have created potential burdens for community banks. For example, the depository institution regulators also issued changes to the capital requirements applicable to these institutions.[10] Many of these changes were consistent with the Basel III framework, which is a comprehensive set of reforms to strengthen global capital and liquidity standards issued by an international body consisting of representatives of many nations' central banks and regulators. These new requirements significantly changed the risk-based capital standards for banks and bank holding companies. As we reported in November 2014, officials interviewed from community banks did not anticipate any difficulties in meeting the U.S. Basel III capital requirements but expected to incur additional compliance costs.[11]

In addition to regulatory changes that could increase burden or costs on community banks, some of the Dodd-Frank Act provisions have likely

---

[10] Regulatory Capital Rules: Regulatory Capital, Implementation of Basel III, Capital Adequacy, Transition Provisions, Prompt Corrective Action, Standardized Approach for Risk-weighted Assets, Market Discipline and Disclosure Requirements, Advanced Approaches Risk-Based Capital Rule, and Market Risk Capital Rule, 78 Fed. Reg. 62018 (Oct. 11, 2013) (Federal Reserve and OCC) and 78 Fed. Reg. 55340 (Sept. 10, 2013) (FDIC Interim Final Rule). With minor changes, the September 2013 FDIC interim final rule became a final rule in April 2014. See 79 Fed. Reg. 20754 (Apr. 14, 2014). The Basel III framework has no legal force but was issued by the agreement of the Basel Committee members with the expectation that individual national authorities would implement the standards.

[11] GAO-15-67.

resulted in reduced costs for these institutions. For example, revisions to the way that deposit insurance premiums are calculated reduced the amount paid by banks with less than $10 billion in assets by $342 million or 33 percent from the first to second quarter of 2011 after the change became effective. Another change reduced the audit-related costs that some banks were incurring in complying with provisions of the SarbanesOxley Act.

Prior Studies on Regulatory Burden Generally Focused on Costs

A literature search indicated that prior studies by other entities, including regulators, trade associations or others, which examined how to measure regulatory burden generally focused on direct costs resulting from compliance with regulations, and our analysis of them identified various limitations that restrict their usefulness in assessing regulatory burden. For example, researchers commissioned by the Credit Union National Association, which advocates for credit unions, found costs attributable to regulations totaled a median of 0.54 percent of assets in 2014 for a non-random sample of the 53 small, medium, and large credit unions responding to a nationwide survey.[12] However, one of the study's limitations was its use of a small, non-random sample of credit unions. In addition, the research was not designed to conclusively link changes in regulatory costs for the sampled credit unions to any one regulation or set of regulations.

CFPB also conducted a study of regulatory costs associated with specific regulations applicable to checking accounts, traditional savings accounts, debit cards, and overdraft programs.[13] Through case studies involving 200 interviews with staff at seven commercial banks with assets

---

[12] See Vincent Hui, Ryan Myers, and Kaleb Seymour, Credit Union National Association, *Regulatory Burden Financial Impact Study*, report prepared for the Credit Union National Association (February 2016).

[13] See Consumer Financial Protection Bureau, Understanding the Effects of Certain Deposit Regulations on Financial Institutions' Operations (Washington, D.C.: November 2013). The regulations were: Regulations DD (Truth-in-Savings Act), E (Electronic Fund Transfer Act), P (Gramm-Leach-Bliley Act), and V (Fair Credit Reporting Act).

over $1 billion, the agency's staff determined that the banks' costs related to ongoing regulatory compliance were concentrated in operations, information technology, human resources, and compliance and retail functions, with operations and information technology contributing the highest costs. While providing detailed information about the case study institutions, reliance on a small sample of mostly large commercial banks limits the conclusions that can be drawn about banks' regulatory costs generally. In addition, the study notes several challenges to quantifying compliance costs that made their cost estimates subject to some measurement error, and the study's design limits the extent to which a causal relationship between financial regulations and costs could be fully established. Researchers from the Mercatus Center at George Mason University used a nongeneralizable survey of banks to find that respondents believed they were spending more money and staff time on compliance than before due to Dodd-Frank regulations.[14] From a universe of banks with less than $10 billion of assets, the center's researchers used a non-random sample to collect 200 responses to a survey sent to 500 banks with assets less than $10 billion about the burden of complying with regulations arising from the Dodd-Frank Act. The survey sought information on the respondents' characteristics, products, and services and the effects various regulatory and compliance activities had on operations and decisions, including those related to bank profitability, staffing, and products. About 83 percent of the respondents reported increased compliance costs of greater than or equal to 5 percent due to regulatory requirements stemming from the Dodd-Frank Act. The study's limitations include use of a non-random sample selection, small response rate, and use of questions that

---

[14] Hester Peirce, Ian Robinson, and Thomas Stratmann, *How Are Small Banks Faring Under Dodd-Frank?* (Arlington, VA, February 2014). The Mercatus Center survey was based on convenience nonprobability sampling (sampling respondents who are easy to reach) and was conducted between July and September 2013, before the effective dates of some of the rules covered in the survey. The survey was distributed by national and state-level banking associations to their members and to 500 additional small banks. The survey had about 200 respondents with less than $10 billion in assets, although the number of respondents differed for each section of the survey. A majority of respondents fell in the asset-size range from $10 million to $1 billion. Because the survey relied on a nonprobability, convenience sample, it is not possible to use the results to draw inferences about the population of small banks.

asked about the Dodd-Frank Act in general. In addition, the self-reported survey items used to capture regulatory burden—compliance costs and profitability—have an increased risk of measurement error and the causal relationship between Dodd-Frank Act requirements and changes in these indicators is not well-established.

INSTITUTIONS CITED MORTGAGE AND ANTI-MONEY LAUNDERING REGULATIONS AS MOST BURDENSOME, ALTHOUGH OTHERS NOTED THEIR SIGNIFICANT PUBLIC BENEFITS

Community bank and credit union representatives that we interviewed identified three sets of regulations as most burdensome to their institutions: (1) data reporting requirements related to loan applicants and loan terms under the Home Mortgage Disclosure Act of 1975 (HMDA); (2) transaction reporting and customer due diligence requirements as part of the Bank Secrecy Act and related anti-money laundering laws and regulations (collectively, BSA/AML); and (3) disclosures of mortgage loan fees and terms to consumers under the TILA-RESPA Integrated Disclosure (TRID) regulations.[15] In focus groups and interviews, many of the institution representatives said these regulations were time-consuming and costly to comply with, in part because the requirements were complex, required preparation of individual reports that had to be reviewed for accuracy, or mandated actions within specific timeframes. However,

---

[15] To identify regulations deemed most burdensome, we interviewed institutions and reviewed comments made to regulators in letters or public forums. We selected a non-generalizable sample of 10 community banks and 7 credit unions to include institutions with certain asset levels, loan activity characteristics, and geographic locations. After the interviews demonstrated that considerable consensus existed among institutions about the most burdensome regulations, we conducted six focus groups with 46 banks and credit unions to identify the characteristics of the regulations that made them burdensome. Where possible, we corroborated these findings by reviewing the comment letters regulators received from banks, credit unions, their trade associations and other parties as part of regulatory review efforts conducted under EGRPRA in 2014–2016.

federal regulators and consumer advocacy groups said that benefits from these regulations were significant.

HMDA Requirements Deemed Time Consuming by Institutions but Critical to Others

Representatives of community banks and credit unions in all our focus groups and in most of our interviews told us that HMDA's data collection and reporting requirements were burdensome. Under HMDA and its implementing Regulation C, banks and credit unions with more than $45 million in assets that do not meet regulatory exemptions must collect, record, and report to the appropriate federal regulator, data about applicable mortgage lending activity.[16] For every covered mortgage application, origination, or purchase of a covered loan, lenders must collect information such as the loan's principal amount, the property location, the income relied on in making the credit decision, and the applicants' race, ethnicity, and sex. Institutions record this on a form called the loan/application register, compile these data each calendar year, and submit them to CFPB.[17] Institutions have also been required to make these data available to the public upon request, after modifying them to protect the privacy of applicants and borrowers.[18]

Representatives of many community banks and credit unions with whom we spoke said that complying with HMDA regulations was time consuming. For example, representatives from one community bank we

---

[16] *See* 12 U.S.C. §§ 2801-2810 and 12 C.F.R. pt. 1003. Effective July 2011, the Dodd-Frank Act transferred HMDA rulemaking authority to CFPB. *See* 12 U.S.C. § 2804(a) and 12 U.S.C. § 5481(12)(K).

[17] Through December 2017, institutions were required to submit their HMDA data to the Federal Reserve, which administered the data for all Federal Financial Institution Examination Council (FFIEC) agencies. As of January 2018, institutions submit their HMDA data to CFPB.

[18] See 12 C.F.R. § 1003.5(c). CFPB will modify submitted HMDA data for public disclosure on the CFPB website for HMDA data reported on or after January 1, 2018. In response to a request for HMDA data from a member of the public, a covered institution will be required to provide a notice that its disclosure statement and modified data are available on the CFPB's website.

interviewed said it completed about 1,100 transactions that required HMDA reporting in 2016, and that its staff spent about 16 hours per week complying with Regulation C. In one focus group, participants discussed how HMDA compliance was time consuming because the regulations were complex, which made determining whether a loan was covered and should be reported difficult. As a part of that discussion, one bank representative told us that it was not always clear whether a residence that was used as collateral for a commercial loan was a reportable mortgage under HMDA. In addition, representatives in all of our focus groups in which HMDA was discussed and in some interviews said that they had to provide additional staff training for HMDA compliance. Among the 28 community banks and credit unions whose representatives commented on HMDA in our focus groups, 61 percent noted having to conduct additional HMDA-related training.

In most of our focus groups and three of our interviews, representatives of community banks and credit unions also expressed concerns about how federal bank examiners review HMDA data for errors. When regulatory examiners conducting compliance examinations determine that an institution's HMDA data has errors above prescribed thresholds, the institution has to correct and resubmit its data, further adding to the time required for compliance. While regulators have revised their procedures for assessing errors as discussed later, prior to 2018, if 10 percent or more of the loan/application registers that examiners reviewed had errors, an institution was required to review all of their data, correct any errors, and resubmit them. If 5 percent or more of the reviewed loan/application registers had errors in a single data field, an institution had to review all other registers and correct the data in that field.[19] Participants in one focus group discussed how HMDA's requirements left them little room for error and that they were concerned that examiners weigh all HMDA fields

---

[19] Subsequent to our focus groups, FFIEC member agencies issued revised data resubmission guidelines effective for the 2018 data collection year. Among other things, under the revised guidelines, testing will be divided into two stages, there will be tolerances for certain data fields, and the revised guidelines eliminate the file error resubmission threshold under which a financial institution would be directed to correct and resubmit its entire Loan Application Register (LAR) if the total number of sample files with one or more errors equaled or exceeded a certain threshold.

equally when assessing errors. For example, representatives of one institution noted that for purposes of fair lending enforcement, errors in fields such as race and ethnicity can be more important than errors in the action taken date (the field for the date when a loan was originated or when an application not resulting in an origination was received). Representatives of one institution also noted that they no longer have access to data submission software that allowed them to verify the accuracy of some HMDA data, and this has led to more errors in their submissions. Representatives of another institution told us that they had to have staff conduct multiple checks of HMDA data to ensure the data met accuracy standards, which added to the time needed for compliance.

Representatives of many community banks and credit unions with whom we spoke also expressed concerns that compliance requirements for HMDA were increasing. The Dodd-Frank Act included provisions to expand the information institutions must collect and submit under HMDA, and CFPB issued rules implementing these new requirements that mostly became effective January 2018.[20] In addition to certain new data requirements specified in the act, such as age and the total points and fees payable at origination, CFPB's amendments to the HMDA reporting requirements also added additional data points, including some intended to collect more information about borrowers such as credit scores, as well as more information about the features of loans, such as fees and terms.[21] In the final rule implementing the new requirements, CFPB also expanded the types of loans on which some institutions must report HMDA data to include open-ended lines of credit and reverse mortgages. Participants in two of our focus groups with credit unions said reporting this expanded

---

[20] *See* Pub. L. No. 111-203, § 1094, 124 Stat. 2097 (2010) (codified as amended at 12 U.S.C. § 2803(b)) and Home Mortgage Disclosure (Regulation C), 80 Fed. Reg. 66128 (Oct. 28, 2015).

[21] The new fields that will be required to be included in HMDA reports after January 2018 include applicant or borrower age, credit score, automated underwriting system information, unique loan identifier, property value, application channel, points and fees, borrower-paid origination charges, discount points, lender credits, loan term, prepayment penalty, nonamortizing loan features, interest rate, and loan originator identifier as well as other data. *See* Home Mortgage Disclosure (Regulation C), 80 Fed. Reg. 66128 (Oct. 28, 2015).

information will require more staff time and training and cause them to purchase new or upgraded computer software.

In most of our focus groups, participants said that changes should be made to reduce the burdens associated with reporting HMDA data. For example, in some focus groups, participants suggested raising the threshold for institutions that have to file HMDA reports above the then current $44 million in assets, which would reduce the number of small banks and credit unions that are required to comply. Representatives of two institutions noted that because small institutions make very few loans compared to large ones, their contribution to the overall HMDA data was of limited value in contrast to the significant costs to the institutions to collect and report the data. Another participant said their institution sometimes make as few as three loans per month. In most of our focus groups, participants also suggested that regulators could collect mortgage data in other ways. For example, one participant discussed how it would be less burdensome for lenders if federal examiners collected data on loan characteristics during compliance examinations.

However, staff of federal regulators and consumer groups said that HMDA data are essential for enforcement of fair lending laws and regulations.[22] Representatives of CFPB, FDIC, NCUA, and OCC and groups that advocate for consumer protection issues said that HMDA data has helped address discriminatory practices. For example, some representatives noted a decrease in "redlining" (refusing to make loans to certain neighborhoods or communities). CFPB staff noted that HMDA data provides transparency about lending markets, and that HMDA data from community banks and credit unions is critical for this purpose, especially in some rural parts of the country where they make the majority of mortgage loans. While any individual institution's HMDA reporting might not make up a large portion of HMDA data for an area, CFPB staff told us that if all smaller institutions were exempted from HMDA requirements,

---

[22] Among other things, the act is intended to provide data that can help the public and policymakers determine whether financial institutions are serving the housing needs of their communities and to assist in identifying possible discriminatory lending patterns and enforcing antidiscrimination statutes. *See* 12 U.S.C. § 2801(b) and 12 C.F.R. 1003.1(b)(1).

regulators would have little or no data on the types of mortgages or on lending patterns in some areas.

Agency officials also told us that few good alternatives to HMDA data exist and that the current collection regime is the most effective available option for collecting the data. NCUA officials noted that collecting mortgage data directly from credit unions during examinations to enforce fair lending rules likely would be more burdensome for the institutions. CFPB staff and consumer advocates we spoke with also said that HMDA provides a low-cost data source for researchers and local policy makers, which leads to other benefits that cannot be directly measured but are included in HMDA's statutory goals—such as allowing local policymakers to target community investments to areas with housing needs.[23]

While representatives of some community banks and credit unions argued that HMDA data were no longer necessary because practices such as redlining have been reduced and they receive few requests for HMDA data from the public, representatives of some consumer advocate groups responded that eliminating the transparency that HMDA data creates could allow discriminatory practices to become more common. CFPB staff and representatives of one of these consumer groups also said that before the financial crisis of 2007–2009, some groups were not being denied credit outright but instead were given mortgages with terms, such as high interest rates, which made them more likely to default. The expanded HMDA data will allow regulators to detect such problematic lending practices for mortgage terms. CFPB and FDIC staff also told us that while lenders will have to collect and report more information, the new fields will add context to lending practices and should reduce the likelihood of incorrectly flagging institutions for potential discrimination. For example, with current data, a lender may appear to be denying mortgage applications to a particular racial or ethnic group, but with expanded data that includes applicant credit scores, regulators may determine that the denials were appropriate based on credit score underwriting.

---

[23] One of HMDA's purposes is to assist public officials in distributing public-sector investment to attract private investment to areas in which it is needed. *See* 12 U.S.C. § 2801(b).

CFPB staff acknowledged that HMDA data collection and reporting may be time consuming, and said they have taken steps to reduce the associated burdens for community banks and credit unions.

- First, in its final rule implementing the Dodd-Frank Act's expanded HMDA data requirements, CFPB added exclusions for banks and credit unions that make very few mortgage loans. Effective January 2018, an institution will be subject to HMDA requirements only if it has originated at least 25 closed-end mortgage loans or at least 100 covered open-end lines of credit in each of the 2 preceding calendar years and also has met other applicable requirements. In response to concerns about the burden associated with the new requirement for reporting open-end lines of credit, in 2017. CFPB temporarily increased the threshold for collecting and reporting data for open-end lines of credit from 100 to 500 for the 2018 and 2019 calendar years.[24] CFPB estimated that roughly 25 percent of covered depository institutions will no longer be subject to HMDA as a result of these exclusions.
- Second, the Federal Financial Institutions Examination Council (FFIEC), which includes CFPB, announced the new *FFIEC HMDA Examiner Transaction Testing Guidelines* that specify when agency examiners should direct an institution to correct and resubmit its HMDA data due to errors found during supervisory examinations.[25] CFPB said these revisions should greatly reduce the burden associated with resubmissions. Under the revised standards, institutions will no longer be directed to resubmit all their HMDA data if they exceeded the threshold for HMDA files with errors, but will still be directed to correct specific data fields that have errors

---

[24] Financial institutions originating fewer than 500 open-end lines of credit in either of the 2 preceding years will not be required to begin collecting such data until January 1, 2020. *See* Home Mortgage Disclosure (Regulation C), 82 Fed. Reg. 43088 (Sept. 13, 2017).

[25] Federal Financial Institutions Examination Council, *FFIEC HMDA Examiner Transaction Testing Guidelines* (Washington, D.C.: Aug. 22, 2017) for accessed October 6, 2017 at https://www.consumerfinance.gov/about-us/blog/heres-what-you-need-know-about-new-ffiec-hmda-examiner-transaction-testing-guidelines/.

Community Banks and Credit Unions 199

- exceeding the specified threshold.[26] The revised guidelines also include new tolerances for some data fields, such as application date and loan amount.
- Third, CFPB also introduced a new online system for submitting HMDA data in November 2017. CFPB staff said that the new system, the HMDA Platform, will reduce errors by including features to allow institutions to validate the accuracy and correct the formatting of their data before submitting.[27] They also noted that this platform will reduce burdens associated with the previous system for submitting HMDA data. For example, institutions no longer will have to regularly download software, and multiple users within an institution will be able to access the platform. NCUA officials added that some credit unions had tested the system and reported that it reduced their reporting burden.
- Finally, on December 21, 2017, CFPB issued a public statement announcing that, for HMDA data collected in 2018, CFPB does not intend to require resubmission of HMDA data unless errors are material, and does not intend to assess penalties for errors in submitted data. CFPB also announced that it intends to open a rule making to reconsider various aspects of the 2015 HMDA rule, such as the thresholds for compliance and data points that are not required by statute.

Institutions Found BSA/AML Regulations Burdensome and Regulators Have Been Considering Steps to Reduce Burden

In all our focus groups and many of our interviews, participants said they found BSA/AML requirements to be burdensome due to the staff time

---

[26] The thresholds for data resubmission in a single HMDA data field are based on the number of loans that an institution made in the previous year, and range from 2.5 percent for banks that made more than 100,000 loans to 10 percent for institutions that made 100 loans or fewer.

[27] This software is available at https://www.consumerfinance.gov/data-research/hmda/forfilers.

and other costs associated with their compliance efforts.[28] To provide regulators and law enforcement with information that can aid in pursuing criminal, tax, and regulatory investigations, BSA/AML statutes and regulations require covered financial institutions to

- file Currency Transaction Reports (CTR) for cash transactions conducted by a customer for aggregate amounts of more than $10,000 per day and Suspicious Activity Reports (SAR) for activity that might signal criminal activity (such as money laundering or tax evasion); and
- establish BSA/AML compliance programs that include efforts to identify and verify customers' identities and monitor transactions to report, for example, transactions that appear to violate federal law.[29]

Participants in all of our focus groups discussed how BSA/AML compliance was time-consuming, and in most focus groups participants said this took time away from serving customers. For example, representatives of one institution we interviewed told us that completing a

---

[28] The Currency and Foreign Transactions Reporting Act, commonly known as the Bank Secrecy Act (BSA), as amended by the Uniting and Strengthening America by Providing Appropriate Tools Required to Intercept and Obstruct Terrorism Act of 2001 (USA PATRIOT Act), establishes reporting, recordkeeping, and other anti-money laundering requirements for financial institutions, including a customer identification program and performance of customer due diligence or enhanced due diligence in certain situations, unless they are exempted by regulation. Pub. L. No. 91-508, tits. I and II, 84 Stat. 1114 (1970) (codified as amended at 12 U.S.C. §§ 1829b, 1951-1959; 18 U.S.C. §§ 1956-1957 and 1960; and 31 U.S.C. §§ 5311-5314 and 5316-5332); Pub. L. No. 107-506, § 352, 115 Stat. 272, 322 (codified at 31 U.S.C. § 5318(h)). Additionally, during BSA/AML examinations, regulators evaluate institutions' programs for identifying and reporting transactions that involve sanctioned countries and persons to ensure they comply with the economic sanctions administered and enforced by the Office of Foreign Assets Control.

[29] Financial institutions are required to have AML compliance programs that incorporate (1) compliance policies, procedures, and controls; (2) an independent audit review; (3) the designation of an individual to assure day-to-day compliance; and (4) ongoing training for appropriate personnel. See 31 U.S.C. § 5318(h)(1). Financial institutions also must satisfy the elements of the customer identification and customer due diligence programs—collectively, the Know Your Customer process—which includes having written risk-based procedures for verifying the identity of each customer, verifying the identify of "beneficial owners" of legal-entity customers, and conducting ongoing monitoring to maintain customer identification and identify suspicious transactions. See 31 C.F.R. § 1020.220(a)(2) and § 1010.230.

single SAR could take 4 hours, and that they might complete 2 to 5 SARs per month. However, representatives of another institution said that at some times of the year it has filed more than 300 SARs per month. In a few cases, representatives of institutions saw BSA/AML compliance as burdensome because they had to take actions that seemed unnecessary based on the nature of the transactions. For example, one institution's representatives said that filing a CTR because a high school band deposited more than $10,000 after a fundraising activity seemed unnecessary, while another's said that it did not see the need to file SARs for charitable organizations that are well known in their community. Representatives of institutions in most of our focus groups also noted that BSA/AML regulations required additional staff training. Some of these representatives noted that the requirements are complex and the activities, such as identifying transactions potentially associated with terrorism, are outside of their frontline staff's core competencies.

Representatives in all focus groups and a majority of interviews said BSA imposes financial costs on community banks and credit unions that must be absorbed by those institutions or passed along to customers. In most of our focus groups, representatives said that they had to purchase or upgrade software systems to comply with BSA/AML requirements, which can be expensive. Some representatives also said they had to hire third parties to comply with BSA/AML regulations. Representatives of some institutions also noted that the compliance requirements do not produce any material benefits for their institutions.

In most of our focus groups, participants were particularly concerned that the compliance burden associated with BSA/AML regulations was increasing. In 2016, FinCEN—the bureau in the Department of the Treasury that administers BSA/AML rules—issued a final rule that expanded due-diligence requirements for customer identification. The final rule was intended to strengthen customer identification programs by requiring institutions to obtain information about the identities of the beneficial owners of businesses opening accounts at their institutions.[30] The

---

[30] Under the final rule, the beneficial owners of a legal entity include each individual, if any, who directly or indirectly owns 25 percent or more of the legal entity; and a single individual

institutions covered by the rule are expected to be in compliance by May 11, 2018. Some representatives of community banks and credit unions that we spoke with said that this new requirement will be burdensome. For example, one community bank's representatives said the new due-diligence requirements will require more staff time and training and cause them to purchase new or upgraded computer systems. Representatives of some institutions also noted that accessing beneficial ownership information about companies can be difficult, and that entities that issue business licenses or tax identification numbers could perform this task more easily than financial institutions.

In some of our focus groups, and in some comment letters that we reviewed that community banks and credit unions submitted to bank regulators and NCUA as part of the EGRPRA process, representatives of community banks and credit unions said regulators should take steps to reduce the burdens associated with BSA/AML. Participants in two of our focus groups and representatives of two institutions we interviewed said that the $10,000 CTR threshold, which was established in 1972, should be increased, noting it had not been adjusted for inflation. One participant told us that if this threshold had been adjusted for inflation over time, it likely would be filing about half of the number of CTRs that it currently files. In several focus groups, participants also indicated that transactions that must be checked against the Office of Foreign Assets Control list also should be subject to a threshold amount. Representatives of one institution noted that they have to complete time-consuming compliance work for even very small transactions (such as less than $1). Representatives of some institutions suggested that the BSA/AML requirements be streamlined to make it easier for community banks and credit unions to comply. For example, representatives of one institution that participated in the EGRPRA review suggested that institutions could provide regulators with data on all cash transactions in the format in which they keep these records rather than filing CTRs. Finally, participants in one focus group said that

---

with significant responsibility to control, manage, or direct the legal entity, such as an executive officer or senior manager. Customer Due Diligence Requirements for Financial Institutions, 81 Fed. Reg. 29398 (May 11, 2016) (codified at 31 C.F.R. pts. 1010, 1020, 1023, 1024, and 1026).

regulators should better communicate how the information that institutions submit contributes to law enforcement successes in preventing or prosecuting crimes.

Staff from FinCEN told us that the reports and due-diligence programs required in BSA/AML rules are critical to safeguarding the U.S. financial sector from illicit activity, including illegal narcotics and terrorist financing activities. They said they rely on CTRs and SARs that financial institutions file for the financial intelligence they disseminate to law enforcement agencies, and noted that they saw all BSA/AML requirements as essential because activities are designed to complement each other. Officials also pointed out that entities conducting terrorism, human trafficking, or fraud all rely heavily on cash, and reporting frequently made deposits makes tracking criminals easier. They said that significant reductions in BSA/AML reporting requirements would hinder law enforcement, especially because depositing cash through ATMs has become very easy.

FinCEN staff said they utilize a continuous evaluation process to look for ways to reduce burden associated with BSA/AML requirements, and noted actions taken as a result. They said that FinCEN has several means of soliciting feedback about potential burdens, including through its Bank Secrecy Act Advisory Group that consists of industry, regulatory, and law enforcement representatives who meet twice a year, and also through public reporting and comments received through FinCEN's regulatory process. FinCEN officials said that based on this advisory group's recommendations, the agency provided SAR filing relief by reducing the frequency of submission for written SAR summaries on ongoing activity from 90 days to 120 days. FinCEN also has recognized that financial institutions do not generally see the beneficial impacts of their BSA/AML efforts, and officials said they have begun several different feedback programs to address this issue.

FinCEN staff said they have been discussing ways to improve the CTR filing process, but in response to comments obtained as part of a recent review of regulatory burden they noted that the staff of law enforcement agencies do not support changing the $10,000 threshold for CTR reporting.[31] FinCEN officials said that they have taken some steps to reduce the burden related to CTR reporting, such as by expanding the ability of institutions to seek CTR filing exemptions, especially for low-risk customers. FinCEN is also utilizing its advisory group to examine aspects of the CTR reporting obligations to assess ways to reduce reporting burden, but officials said it is too early to know the outcomes of the effort. However, FinCEN officials said that while evaluation of certain reporting thresholds may be appropriate, any changes to them or other CTR requirements to reduce burden on financial institutions, must still meet the needs of regulators and law enforcement, and prevent misuse of the financial system.

FinCEN staff also said that some of the concerns raised about the upcoming requirements on beneficial ownership may be based on misunderstandings of the rule. FinCEN officials told us that under the final rule, financial institutions can rely on the beneficial ownership information provided to them by the entity seeking to open the account. Under the final rule, the party opening an account on behalf of the legal entity customer is responsible for providing beneficial ownership information, and the financial institution may rely on the representations of the customer unless it has information that calls into question the accuracy of those representations. The financial institution does not have to confirm ownership; rather, it has to verify the identity of the beneficial owners as reported by the individual seeking to open the account, which can be done with photocopies of identifying documents such as a driver's license. FinCEN issued guidance explaining this aspect of the final rule in 2016.[32]

---

[31] We discuss this regulatory review process (EGRPRA) in the next section of this report. FinCEN officials said that the law enforcement agencies they spoke with included the Federal Bureau of Investigation, the Internal Revenue Service, and the Drug Enforcement Agency.

[32] Financial Crimes Enforcement Network, *Frequently Asked Questions Regarding Customer Due Diligence Requirements for Financial Institutions*, FIN-2016-G003 (Washington, D.C.: July 19, 2016), accessed September 28, 2017 at https://www.fincen.gov/ sites/default/ files/2016-09/FAQs_for_CDD_Final_Rule_%287_15_16%29.pdf.

Institutions Found New Mortgage Term Disclosure Rules Burdensome, but Some May Be Misinterpreting Requirements

In all of our focus groups and many of our interviews, representatives of community banks and credit unions said that new requirements mandating consolidated disclosures to consumers for mortgage terms and fees have increased the time their staff spend on compliance, increased the cost of providing mortgage lending services, and delayed the completion of mortgages for customers. The Dodd Frank Act directed CFPB to issue new requirements to integrate mortgage loan disclosures that previously had been separately required by the Truth-in-Lending Act (TILA) and the Real Estate Settlement Procedures Act (RESPA), and their implementing regulations, Regulation Z and X, respectively.[33] Effective in October 2015, the combined TILA-RESPA Integrated Disclosure (known as TRID) requires mortgage lenders to disclose certain mortgage terms, conditions, and fees to loan applicants during the origination process for certain mortgage loans and prescribe how the disclosures should be made.[34] The disclosure provisions also require lenders, in the absence of specified exceptions, to reimburse or refund to borrowers portions of certain fees that exceed the estimates previously provided in order to comply with the revised regulations.

Under TRID, lenders generally must provide residential mortgage loan applicants with two forms, and deliver these documents within specified time frames (as shown in fig. 1).

- Within 3 business days of an application and at least 7 business days before a loan is consummated, lenders must provide the applicant with the loan estimate, which includes estimates for all

---

[33] *See* Pub. L. No. 111-203, § 1032(f), 124 Stat. 1376, 2007 (2010) (codified at 12 U.S.C. § 5532(f)); *see also* 15 U.S.C. § 1604.

[34] *See* Integrated Mortgage Disclosures Under the Real Estate Settlement Procedures Act (Regulation X) and the Truth-in-Lending Act (Regulation Z), 78 Fed. Reg. 79730 (Dec. 31, 2013). TRID stands for TILA-RESPA Integrated Disclosure, which combined previously separate disclosures required under the Truth-in-Lending Act and the Real Estate Settlement Procedures Act.

financing costs and fees and other terms and conditions associated with the potential loan.[35] If circumstances change after the loan estimate has been provided (for example, if a borrower needs to change the loan amount), a new loan estimate may be required.

- At least 3 days before a loan is consummated, lenders must provide the applicant with the closing disclosure, which has the loan's actual terms, conditions, and associated fees. If the closing disclosure is mailed to an applicant, lenders must wait an additional 3 days for the applicant to receive it before they can execute the loan, unless they can demonstrate that the applicant has received the closing disclosure.
- If the annual percentage rate or the type of loan change after the closing disclosure is provided, or if a prepayment penalty is added, a new closing disclosure must be provided and a new 3-day waiting period is required. Other changes made to the closing disclosure require the provision of a revised closing disclosure, but a new 3-day waiting period is not required.

If the fees in the closing disclosure are more than the fees in the loan estimate (subject to some exceptions and tolerances discussed later in this section), the lender must reimburse the applicant for the amount of the increase in order to comply with the applicable regulations.

In all of our focus groups and most of our interviews, representatives of community banks and credit unions said that TRID has increased the time required to comply with mortgage disclosure requirements and increased the cost of mortgage lending. In half of our focus groups, participants discussed how they have had to spend additional time ensuring the accuracy of their initial estimates of mortgage costs, including fees

---

[35] Consummation occurs when the borrower becomes contractually obligated to the creditor on the loan. Consummation may commonly occur at the same time as closing or settlement, but it is a legally distinct event. The point in time when a borrower becomes contractually obligated to the creditor on the loan depends on applicable state law. CFPB instructs creditors and settlement agents to verify the applicable state laws to determine when consummation will occur and make sure delivery of the closing disclosure occurs at least 3 days before that event. For additional information, see *CFPB TILA-RESPA Integrated Disclosure Rule Small Entity Compliance Guide* (Washington, D.C.: March 2014).

charged by third parties, in part because they are now financially responsible for changes in fees during the closing process. Some participants also discussed how they have had to hire additional staff to meet TRID's requirements.

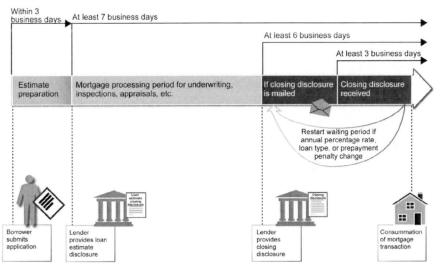

Source: GAO analysis of applicable statutes and regulations. | GAO-18-213.
Note: TILA = Truth-in-Lending Act and RESPA = the Real Estate Settlement Procedures Act.

Figure 1. Timeline of TILA-RESPA Integrated Disclosure Requirements.

In one focus group of community banks, participants described how mortgage loans frequently involve the use of multiple third parties, such as appraisers and inspectors, and obtaining accurate estimates of the amounts these parties will charge for their services within the 3-day period prescribed by TRID can be difficult. The community banks we spoke with also discussed how fees from these parties often change at closing, and ensuring an accurate estimate at the beginning of the process was not always possible. As a result, some representatives said that community banks and credit unions have had to pay to cure or correct the difference in changed third-party fees that are outside their control. In most of our focus groups and some of our interviews, representatives told us that this TRID requirement has made originating a mortgage more costly for community banks and credit unions.

Community banks and credit unions in half of our focus groups and some of our interviews also told us that TRID's requirements are complex and difficult to understand, which adds to their compliance burden. Participants in one focus group noted that CFPB's final rule implementing TRID was very long—the rule available on CFPB's website is more than 1,800 pages including the rule's preamble—and has many scenarios that require different actions by mortgage lenders or trigger different responsibilities as the following examples illustrate.

- Some fees in the loan estimate, such as prepaid interest, may be subsequently changed provided that the estimates were in good faith.
- Other fees, such as for third-party services where the charge is not paid to the lender or the lender's affiliate, may be changed by as much as 10 percent in aggregate before the lender becomes liable for the difference.
- However, for some charges the lender must reimburse or refund to the borrower portions of subsequent increases, such as fees paid to the creditor, mortgage broker, or a lender affiliate, without any percentage tolerance.

Based on a poll we conducted in all six focus groups, 40 of 43 participants said that they had to provide additional training to staff to ensure that TRID's requirements were understood, which takes additional time from serving customers.

In all of our focus groups and most of our interviews, community banks and credit unions also said that TRID's mandatory waiting periods and disclosure schedules increased the time required to close mortgage loans, which created burdens for the institutions and their customers. Several representatives we interviewed told us that TRID's waiting periods led to delays in closings of about 15 days. The regulation mandates that mortgage loans generally cannot be consummated sooner than 7 business days after the loan estimate is provided to an applicant, and no sooner than 3 business days after the closing disclosure is received by the applicant. If the closing disclosure is mailed, the lender must add another 3 business days to the closing period to allow for delivery. Representatives in some of our focus groups said that when changes needed to be made to a loan during the closing period, TRID requires them to restart the waiting periods, which can increase delays. For example, if the closing disclosure had been provided, and the loan product needed to be changed, a new closing disclosure would have to be provided and the applicant given at least 3 days to review it. Some representatives we interviewed said that their customers are frustrated by these delays and would like to close their mortgages sooner than TRID allows. Others said that TRID's waiting periods decreased flexibility in scheduling the closing date, which caused problems for homebuyers and sellers (for instance, because transactions frequently have to occur on the same day).

However, CFPB officials and staff of a consumer group said that TRID has streamlined previous disclosure requirements and is important for ensuring that consumers obtaining mortgages are protected. CFPB reported that for more than 30 years lenders have been required by law to provide mortgage disclosures to borrowers, and CFPB staff noted that prior time frames were similar to those required by TRID and Regulation Z. CFPB also noted that information on the disclosure forms that TRID replaced was sometimes overlapping, used inconsistent terminology, and could confuse consumers. In addition, CFPB staff and staff of a consumer group said that the previous disclosures allowed some mortgage-related fees to be combined, which prevented borrowers from knowing what charges for specific services were. They said that TRID disclosures better highlight important items for home buyers, allowing them to more readily compare loan options. Furthermore, CFPB staff told us that before TRID, lenders and other parties commonly increased a mortgage loan's fees during the closing process, and then gave borrowers a "take it or leave it" choice just before closing. As a result, borrowers often just accepted the increased costs. CFPB representatives said that TRID protects consumers from this practice by shifting the responsibility for most fee increases to lenders, and increases transparency in the lending process.

CFPB staff told us that it is too early to definitively identify what impact TRID has had on borrowers' understanding of mortgage terms, but told us that some information they have seen indicated that it has been helpful.[36] For example, CFPB staff said that preliminary results from the National Survey of Mortgage Originations conducted in 2017 found that consumer confidence in mortgage lending increased.[37] While CFPB staff said that this may indicate that TRID, which became effective in October 2015, has helped consumers better understand mortgage terms, they noted that the complete survey results are not expected to be released until 2018. CFPB staff said that these results should provide valuable information on how well consumers generally understood mortgage terms and whether borrowers were comparison shopping for loans that could be used to analyze TRID's effects on consumer understanding of mortgage products.

CFPB staff also told us that complying with TRID should not result in significant time being added to the mortgage closing process. Based on the final rule, they noted that TRID's waiting periods should not lead to delays of more than 3 days. CFPB staff also pointed out that the overall 7-day waiting period and the 3-day waiting period can be modified or waived if the consumer has a bona fide personal financial emergency, and thus should not be creating delays for those consumers. To waive the waiting period, consumers have to provide the lender with a written statement that describes the emergency. CFPB staff also said that closing times are affected by a variety of factors and can vary substantially, and that the delays that community banks and credit unions we spoke with reported may not be representative of the experiences of other lenders. A preliminary CFPB analysis of industry-published mortgage closing data found that closing times increased after it first implemented TRID, but that the delays subsequently declined. CFPB staff also said that they plan

---

[36] As part of the rulemaking process, CFPB conducted a cost-benefit analysis that indicated the rule would benefit consumers without imposing significant burdens on covered parties.

[37] The Federal Housing Finance Administration and CFPB conduct the survey every 2 years. CFPB officials said that the most recent survey for which complete data are available was conducted in 2015, and therefore did not reflect the impact of TRID implementation.

to analyze closing times using HMDA data now that they are collecting these data, and that they expect that delays that community banks and credit unions may have experienced so far would decrease as institutions adjusted to the new requirements.

Based on our review of TRID's requirements and discussions with community banks and credit unions, some of the burden related to TRID that community banks and credit unions described appeared to result from institutions taking actions not required by regulations, and community banks and credit unions told us they still were confused about TRID requirements. For example, representatives of some institutions we interviewed said that they believed TRID requires the entire closing disclosure process to be restarted any time any changes were made to a loan's amount. CFPB staff told us that this is not the case, and that revised loan estimates can be made in such cases without additional waiting periods. Representatives of several other community banks and credit unions cited 5- and 10-day waiting periods not in TRID requirements, or believed that the 7-day waiting period begins after the closing disclosure is received by the applicant, rather than when the loan estimate is provided. Participants in one focus group discussed that they were confused about when to provide disclosures and what needs to be provided. Representatives of one credit union said that if they did not understand a requirement, it was in their best interest to delay closing to ensure they were in compliance.

CFPB staff said that they have taken several steps to help lenders understand TRID requirements. CFPB has published a Small Entity Compliance Guide and a Guide to the Loan Estimate and Closing Disclosure Forms.[38] As of December 2017, these guides were accessible on a TRID implementation website that has links to other information about the rule, as well as blank forms and completed samples.[39] CFPB staff told

---

[38] Consumer Financial Protection Bureau, *TILA-RESPA Integrated Disclosure Rule, Small Entity Compliance Guide* (Washington, D.C.: October 2016), accessed on December 14, 2017, at https://www.consumerfinance.gov/policy-compliance/guidance/implementation-guidance/tila-respa-disclosure-rule/.

[39] See https://www.consumerfinance.gov/policy-compliance/guidance/implementationguidance/tila-respa-disclosure-rule/.

us that the bureau conducted several well-attended, in-depth webinars to explain different aspects of TRID, including one with more than 20,000 participants, and that recordings of the presentations remained available on the bureau's TRID website. CFPB also encourages institutions to submit questions about TRID through the website, and the staff said that they review submitted questions for any patterns that may indicate that an aspect of the regulation is overly burdensome.

However, the Mortgage Bankers Association reported that CFPB's guidance for TRID had not met the needs of mortgage lenders.[40] In a 2017 report on reforming CFPB, this association stated that timely and accessible answers to frequently asked questions about TRID were still needed, noting that while CFPB had assigned staff to answer questions, these answers were not widely circulated.[41] The association also reported that it had made repeated requests for additional guidance related to TRID, but the agency largely did not respond with additional materials in response to these requests.

Although we found that misunderstandings of TRID requirements could be creating unnecessary compliance burdens for some small institutions, CFPB had not assessed the effectiveness of the guidance it provided to community banks and credit unions. Under the Dodd-Frank Act, CFPB has a general responsibility to ensure its regulations are not unduly burdensome, and internal control standards direct federal agencies to analyze and respond to risks related to achieving their defined objectives. However, CFPB staff said that they have not directly assessed how well community banks and credit unions have understood TRID requirements and acknowledged that some of these institutions may be applying the regulations improperly. They said that CFPB intends to review the effectiveness of its guidance, but did not indicate when this review would be completed. Until the agency assesses how well community banks and credit unions understand TRID requirements, CFPB

---

[40] Mortgage Bankers Association, CFPB 2.0: Advancing Consumer Protection (Washington, D.C.: August 2017), accessed on December 14, 2017, at: https://www.mba.org/issues/residential-issues/cfpb-20-advancing-consumer-protection.

[41] CFPB made an audio recording of answers to frequently asked questions available on its website, but as of December 2017 had not published a document with these answers.

may not be able to effectively respond to the risk that some smaller institutions have implemented TRID incorrectly, unnecessarily burdening their staff and delaying consumers' home purchases.

Community Banks and Credit Unions Appeared to Be Receiving Applicable Regulatory Exemptions, but Expressed Concerns about Examiner Expectations

We did not find that regulators directed institutions to comply with regulations from which they were exempt, although institutions were concerned about the appropriateness of examiner expectations. To provide regulatory relief to community banks and credit unions, Congress and regulators have sometimes exempted smaller institutions from the need to comply with all or part of some regulations. Such exemptions are often based on the size of the financial institution or the level of particular activities. For example, CFPB exempted institutions with less than $45 million in assets and fewer than 25 closed-end mortgage loans or 500 open-end lines of credit from the expanded HMDA reporting requirements. In January 2013, CFPB also included exemptions for some institutions in a rule related to originating loans that meet certain characteristics—known as qualified mortgages—in order for the institutions to receive certain liability protections if the loans later go into default. To qualify for this treatment, the lenders must make a good faith effort to determine a borrower's ability to repay a loan and the loan must not include certain risky features (such as interest-only or balloon payments). In its final rule, CFPB included exemptions that allow small creditors to originate loans with certain otherwise restricted features (such as balloon payments) and still be considered qualified mortgage loans.[42]

---

[42] A small creditor, under CFPB's current rules, is a creditor that 1) together with its affiliates, must not have extended more than 2,000 covered transactions secured by first liens (excluding loans held in portfolio) in the preceding calendar year (with certain exceptions); and (2) together, with its affiliates that regularly extended covered transactions, must have had less than $2 billion in in total assets (adjusted annually) as of the end of the preceding calendar years (with certain exceptions).

Concerns expressed to legislators about exemptions not being applied appeared to be based on misunderstandings of certain regulations. For example, in June 2016, a bank official testified that he thought his bank would be exempt from all of CFPB's requirements. However, CFPB's rules applicable to banks apply generally to all depository institutions, although CFPB only conducts compliance examinations for institutions with assets exceeding $10 billion. The depository institution regulators continue to examine institutions with assets below this amount (the overwhelming majority of banks and credit unions) for compliance with regulations enacted by CFPB.

Although not generalizable, our analysis of select examinations did not find that regulators directed institutions to comply with requirements from which they were exempt. In our interviews with representatives from 17 community banks and credit unions, none of the institutions' representatives identified any cases in which regulators required their institution to comply with a regulatory requirement from which they should have been exempt. We also randomly selected and reviewed examination reports and supporting material for 28 examinations conducted by the regulators to identify any instances in which the regulators had not applied exemptions.[43] From our review of the 28

---

[43] For this analysis, we identified eight exemptions in regulations, resulting from the Dodd-Frank Act that apply to banks and credit unions with less than $1 billion in assets. Under the CFPB's current rules, these exemptions included (1) a special category of qualified mortgage, which applies to creditors that, together with their affiliates, did not originate more than 2,000 first-lien covered transactions (excluding loans held in portfolio) in the preceding calendar year; had, with their affiliates that regularly extended covered transactions, less than $2 billion in assets at the end of the proceeding calendar year; and, for an exemption allowing the origination of balloon payment qualified mortgages, originated a first-lien covered transaction on a property located in a rural or underserved area in the proceeding calendar year; (2) escrow account exemption—which applies to creditors that meet both the same small creditor, and small creditor operating in a rural or underserved area, requirements specified above for the qualified mortgage exemption; (3) TRID exemption—which applies to lenders that normally do not extend consumer credit; (4) appraisals for higher-priced mortgages exemption—which applies to creditors of mortgage transactions of $25,000 or less and creditors of certain manufactured home loans; (5) mortgage servicing exemption—which applies to servicers that service 5,000 and less mortgage loans; (6) international remittances exemption—which applies to companies that consistently provide 100 or fewer remittance transfers per year; (7) debit interchanges fee cap exemption—which applies to issuers, together with their affiliates, that have less than $10 billion in assets; and (8) regulatory capital rule stress test exemption—which applies to

examinations, we found no instances in the examination reports or the scoping memorandums indicating that examiners had required these institutions to comply with the regulations covered by the eight selected exemptions. Because of the limited number of the examinations we reviewed, we cannot generalize our findings to the regulatory treatment of all institutions qualifying for exemptions.

Although not identifying issues relating to exemptions, representatives of community banks and credit unions in about half of our interviews and focus groups expressed concerns that their regulators expected them to follow practices they did not feel corresponded to the size or risks posed by their institutions. For example, representatives from one institution we interviewed said that examiners directed them to increase BSA/AML activities or staff, whereas they did not see such expectations as appropriate for institutions of their size. Similarly, in public forums held by regulators as part of their EGRPRA reviews (discussed in the next section) a few bank representatives stated that regulators sometimes considered compliance activities by large banks to be best practices, and then expected smaller banks to follow such practices. However, institution representatives in the public forums and in our interviews and focus groups that said sometimes regulators' expectations for their institutions were not appropriate, but did not identify specific regulations or practices they had been asked to consider following when citing these concerns.

To help ensure that applicable exemptions and regulatory expectations are appropriately applied, federal depository institution regulators told us they train their staff in applicable requirements and conduct senior-level reviews of examinations to help ensure that examiners only apply appropriate requirements and expectations on banks and credit unions. Regulators said that they do not conduct examinations in a one-size-fits-all manner, and aim to ensure that community banks and credit unions are held to standards appropriate to their size and business model. To achieve this, they said that examiners undergo rigorous training. For example, FDIC staff said that its examiners have to complete four core trainings and

---

banks with less than $10 billion in total assets (they are not required or expected to conduct institution-wide stress testing).

then receive ongoing on-the-job instruction. Each of the four regulators also said they have established quality assurance programs to review and assess their examination programs periodically. For example, each Federal Reserve Bank reviews its programs for examination inconsistency and the Federal Reserve Board staff conducts continuous and point-in-time oversight reviews of Reserve Banks' examination programs to identify issues or problems, such as examination inconsistency.

The depository institution regulators also said that they have processes for depository institutions to appeal examination findings if they feel they were held to inappropriate standards. In addition to less formal steps, such as contacting a regional office, each of the four regulators have an ombudsman office to which institutions can submit complaints or concerns about examination findings. Staffs of the various offices are independent from the regulators' management and work with the depository institutions to resolve examination issues and concerns. If the ombudsman is unable to resolve the complaints, then the institutions can further appeal their complaints through established processes.

REVIEWS OF REGULATIONS RESULTED IN SOME REDUCTION IN BURDEN, BUT THE REVIEWS HAVE LIMITATIONS

Federal depository institution regulators address regulatory burden of their regulated institutions through the rulemaking process and also through retrospective reviews that may provide some regulatory relief to community banks. However, the retrospective review process has some limitations that limit its effectiveness in assessing and addressing regulatory burden on community banks and credit unions.

Mechanisms for Regulators to Address Regulatory Burden Include Mandated Decennial Reviews

Federal depository institution regulators can address the regulatory burden of their regulated institutions throughout the rulemaking process and through mandated, retrospective or "look back" reviews. According to the regulators, attempts to reduce regulatory burden start during the initial rulemaking process. Staff from FDIC, Federal Reserve, NCUA, and OCC all noted that when promulgating rules, their staff seek input from institutions and others throughout the process to design requirements that achieve the goals of the regulation at the most reasonable cost and effort for regulated entities.[44] Once a rule has been drafted, the regulators publish it in the *Federal Register* for public comment. The staff noted that regulators often make revisions in response to the comments received to try to reduce compliance burdens in the final regulation.

After regulations are implemented, banking regulators also address regulatory burdens by periodically conducting mandated reviews of their regulations. The Economic Growth and Regulatory Paperwork Reduction Act of 1996 (EGRPRA) directs three regulators (Federal Reserve, FDIC, and OCC, as agencies represented on the Federal Financial Institutions Examination Council) to review at least every 10 years all of their regulations and through public comment identify areas of the regulations that are outdated, unnecessary or unduly burdensome on insured depository institutions.[45] Under the act, the regulators are to categorize their regulations and provide notice and solicit public comment on all the regulations for which they have regulatory authority. The act also includes a number of requirements on how the regulators should conduct the review, including reporting results to Congress. The first EGRPRA review was completed in 2007. The second EGRPRA review began in 2014 and

---

[44] As part of its rulemaking process CFPB is required to convene small business review panels for rulemaking efforts that are expected to have a significant economic impact on a substantial number of small entities (this requirement does not apply to the depository institution regulators). *See* 5 U.S.C. § 609. These panels are intended to seek direct input early in the rulemaking process from small entities.

[45] *See* 12 U.S.C. § 3311.

the report summarizing its results was submitted to Congress in March 2017.

While NCUA is not required to participate in the EGRPRA review (because EGRPRA did not include the agency in the list of agencies that must conduct the reviews), NCUA has been participating voluntarily. NCUA's assessment of its regulations appears in separate sections of the reports provided to Congress for each of the 2007 and 2017 reviews.

Bank Regulators' 2017 EGRPRA Review Process and Results

Regulators began the most recent EGRPRA review by providing notice and soliciting comments in 2014–2016. The Federal Reserve, FDIC, and OCC issued four public notices in the Federal Register seeking comments from regulated institutions and interested parties on 12 categories of regulations they promulgated. The regulators published a list of all the regulations they administer in the notices and asked for comments, including comments on the extent to which regulations were burdensome.[46] Although not specifically required under EGRPRA, the regulators also held six public meetings across the country with several panels of banks and community groups. At each public meeting, at least three panels of bank officials represented banks with assets of generally less than $5 billion and a large number of the panels included banks with less than $2 billion in assets. Panels were dedicated to specific regulations or sets of regulations. For example, one panel covered capital-related rules, consumer protection, and director-related rules, and another addressed BSA/AML requirements. Although panels were dedicated to specific regulations or sets of regulations, the regulators invited comment on all of their regulations at all public meetings.

---

[46] The categories were (1) applications and reporting; (2) powers and activities; (3) international operations; (4) banking operations; (5) capital; (6) Community Reinvestment Act; (7) consumer protection; (8) directors, officers, and employees; (9) money laundering; (10) rules and procedures; (11) safety and soundness; and (12) securities. Regulatory Publication and Review Under the Economic Growth and Regulatory Paperwork Reduction Act of 1996, 79 Fed. Reg. 32172 (June 4, 2014); 80 Fed. Reg. 7980 (Feb. 13, 2015); 80 Fed. Reg. 32046 (June 5, 2015); and 80 Fed. Reg. 79724 (Dec. 23, 2015). The EGRPRA review process commences with the publication of the first *Federal Register* notice.

The regulators then assessed the public comments they received and described actions they intended to take in response. EGRPRA requires that the regulators identify the significant issues raised by the comments. The regulators generally deemed the issues that received the most public comments as significant. For the 2017 report, representatives at the Federal Reserve, FDIC, and OCC reviewed, evaluated, and summarized more than 200 comment letters and numerous oral comments they received.[47] For interagency regulations that received numerous comments, such as those relating to capital and BSA/AML requirements, the comment letters for each were provided to staff of one of the three regulators or to previously established interagency working groups to conduct the initial assessments.

The regulators' comment assessments also included reviews by each agency's subject-matter experts, who prepared draft summaries of the concerns and proposed agency responses for each of the rules that received comments. According to one bank regulator, the subject-matter experts assessed the comments across three aspects: (1) whether a suggested change to the regulation would reduce bank burdens; (2) how the change to the regulation would affect the safety and soundness of the banking system; and (3) whether a statutory change would be required to address the comment. The summaries drafted by the subject-matter experts then were shared with staff representing all three regulators and further revised. The staff of the three regulators said they then met jointly to analyze the merits of the comments and finalize the comment responses and the proposed actions for approval by senior management at all three regulators.

In the 2017 report summarizing their assessment of the comments received, the regulators identified six significant areas in which commenters raised concerns: (1) capital rules, (2) financial condition reporting (Call Reports), (3) appraisal requirements, (4) examination frequency, (5) Community Reinvestment Act, and (6) BSA/AML. Based on our analysis of the 2017 report, the Federal Reserve, FDIC, and OCC had taken or pledged to take actions to address 11 of the 28 specific concerns commenters had raised across these six areas. We focused our

---

[47] Of the more than 150 regulations for which they sought comments, the regulators received comments on almost 50 interagency regulations.

analysis on issues within the six significant issues that affected the smaller institution and defined an action taken by the regulators as a change or revision to a regulation or the issuance of guidance.

Capital Rules

The regulators noted in the 2017 EGRPRA report that they received comment letters from more than 30 commenters on the recently revised capital requirements. Although some of the concerns commenters expressed related to issues affecting large institutions, some commenters sought to have regulators completely exempt smaller institutions from the requirements. Others objected to the amounts of capital that had to be held for loans made involving more volatile commercial real estate.

In response, the regulators stated that the more than 500 failures of banks in the recent crisis, most of which were community banks, justified requiring all banks to meet the new capital requirements. However, they pledged in the report to make some changes, and have recently proposed rules that would alter some of the requirements. For example, on September 27, 2017, the regulators proposed several revisions to the capital requirements that would apply to banks not subject to the advanced approach requirements under the capital rules (generally, banks with less than $250 billion in assets and less than $10 billion in total foreign exposure).[48] For example, the proposed rule simplifies the capital treatment for certain commercial acquisition, development, and construction loans, and would change the treatment of mortgage servicing assets.[49]

Call Reports

The regulators also received more than 30 comments relating to the reports—known as Call Reports—that banks file with the regulators

---

[48] *See* Simplifications to the Capital Rule Pursuant to the Economic Growth and Regulatory Paperwork Reduction Act of 1996, 82 Fed. Reg. 49984 (Oct. 27, 2017). Generally, advanced approaches banks are those with consolidated total assets of $250 billion or more or with consolidated total on-balance sheet foreign exposure of $10 billion or more.

[49] A mortgage servicing right is created only when the act of servicing a mortgage loan is contractually separated from the underlying loan. A firm, for example, that originates a mortgage, sells it to a third party, and retains the servicing would report a mortgage servicing asset on its balance sheet, if certain conditions are met.

outlining their financial condition and performance. Generally, the commenters requested relief (reducing the number of items required to be reported) for smaller banks and also asked that the frequency of reporting for some items be reduced.

In response to these concerns, the regulators described a review of the Call Report requirements intended to reduce the number of items to be reported to the regulators. The regulators had started this effort to address Call Report issues soon after the most recent EGRPRA process had begun in June 2014. In the 2017 EGRPRA report, the regulators noted that they developed a new Call Report form for banks with assets of less than $1 billion and domestic offices only. For instance, according to the regulators, the new form reduced the number of items such banks had to report by 40 percent. Staff from the regulators told us that about 3,500 banks used the new small-bank reporting form in March 2017, which represented about 68 percent of the banks eligible to use the new form. OCC officials told us that an additional 100 federally chartered banks submitted the form for the 2017 second quarter reporting period. After the issuance of the 2017 EGRPRA report, in June 2017 the regulators issued additional proposed revisions to the three Call Report forms that banks are required to complete. These proposed changes are to become effective in June 2018.[50] For example, one of the proposed changes to the new community bank Call Report form would change the frequency of reporting certain data on non-accrual assets— nonperforming loans that are not generating their stated interest rate— from quarterly to semi-annually. In November 2017, the agencies issued further proposed revision to the community bank Call Report that would delete or consolidate a number of items and add a new, or raise certain existing, reporting thresholds. The proposed revision would take effect as of June 2018.[51]

---

[50] *See* Proposed Agency Information Collection Activities; Comment Request, 82 Fed. Reg. 29147 (June 27, 2017).

[51] *See* Proposed Agency Information Collection Activities; Comment Request, 82 Fed. Reg. 51908 (Nov. 8, 2017).

Appraisals

The three bank regulators and NCUA received more than 160 comments during the 2017 EGRPRA process related to appraisal requirements. The commenters included banks and others that sought to raise the size of the loans that require appraisals, and a large number of appraisers that objected to any changes in the requirements According to the EGRPRA report, several professional appraiser associations argued that raising the threshold could undermine the safety and soundness of lenders and diminish consumer protection for mortgage financing. These commenters argued that increasing the thresholds could encourage banks to neglect collateral risk-management responsibilities.

In response, in July 2017, the regulators proposed raising the threshold for when an appraisal is required from $250,000 to $400,000 for commercial real estate loans.[52] The regulators indicated that the appraisal requirements for 1-4 family residential mortgage loans above the current $250,000 would not be appropriate at the this time because they believed having such appraisals for loans above that level increased the safety of those loans and better protected consumers and because other participants in the housing market, such as the Department of Housing and Urban Development and the government-sponsored enterprises, also required appraisals for loans above that amount. However, the depository institution regulators included in the proposal a request for comment about the appraisal requirements for residential real estate and what banks think are other factors that should be included when considering the threshold for these loans. As part of the 2017 EGRPRA process, the regulators also received comments indicating that banks in rural areas were having difficulty securing appraisers. In the EGRPRA report, the regulators acknowledged this difficulty and in May 2017, the bank regulators and NCUA issued agency guidance on how institutions could obtain temporary waivers and use other means to expand the pool of persons eligible to prepare appraisals in cases in which suitable appraiser staff were unavailable. The agencies also responded to commenters who found the

---

[52] *See* Real Estate Appraisals, 82 Fed. Reg. 35478 (July 31, 2017).

evaluation process confusing by issuing an interagency advisory on the process in March 2016.[53] Evaluations may be used instead of an appraisal for certain transactions including those under the threshold.

Frequency of Safety and Soundness Examinations

As part of the 2017 EGRPRA process, the agencies also received comments requesting that they raise the total asset threshold for an insured depository institution to qualify for the extended 18-month examination cycle from $1 billion to $2 billion and to further extend the examinations cycle from 18 months to 36 months.

During the EGRPRA process, Congress took legislative action to reduce examination frequency for smaller, well-capitalized banks. In 2015, the FAST Act raised the threshold for the 18-month examination cycle from less than $500 million to less than $1 billion for certain well-capitalized and well-managed depository institutions with an "outstanding" composite rating and gave the agencies discretion to similarly raise this threshold for certain depository institutions with an "outstanding" or "good" composite rating.[54] The agencies exercised this discretion and issued a final rule in 2016 making qualifying depository institutions with less than $1 billion in total assets eligible for an 18-month (rather than a 12-month) examination cycle.[55] According to the EGRPRA report, agency staff estimated that the final rules allowed approximately 600 more institutions to qualify for an extended 18-month examination cycle, bringing the total number of qualifying institutions to 4,793.

---

[53] Board of Governors of the Federal Reserve System, Federal Deposit Insurance Corporation, and Office of the Comptroller of the Currency, *Interagency Advisory on the Use of Evaluations in Real-Estate Related Transactions* (Washington, D.C.: Mar. 4, 2016).

[54] *See* Pub. L. No. 114-94, Div. G, tit. LXXXIII, § 83001, 129 Stat. 1312, 1796 (2015) (amending 12 U.S.C. § 1820(d)); 12 U.S.C. § 1820(d)(4). Each financial institution is assigned a composite rating based on an evaluation of six financial and operational components, which are also rated. The component ratings reflect an institution's capital adequacy, asset quality, management capabilities, earnings sufficiency, liquidity position, and sensitivity to market risk (commonly referred to as CAMELS ratings).

[55] *See* Expanded Examination Cycle for Certain Small Insured Depository Institutions and U.S. Branches and Agencies of Foreign Banks, 81 Fed. Reg. 10063 (Feb. 29, 2016) (interim final rule) and 81 Fed. Reg. 90949 (Dec. 16, 2016) (final rule).

Community Reinvestment Act

The commenters in the 2017 EGRPRA process also raised various issues relating to the Community Reinvestment Act, including the geographic areas in which institutions were expected to provide loans to low- and moderate-income borrowers and whether credit unions should be required to comply with the act's requirements.[56]

The regulators noted that they were not intending to take any actions to revise regulations relating to this act because many of the revisions the commenters suggested would require changes to the statute (that is, legislative action). The regulators also noted that they had addressed some of the concerns by revising the Interagency Questions and Answers relating to this act in 2016. Furthermore, the agencies noted that they have been reviewing their existing examination procedures and practices to identify policy and process improvements.

BSA/AML

The regulators also received a number of comments as part of the 2017 EGRPRA process on the burden institutions encounter in complying with BSA/AML requirements. These included the threshold for reporting currency transactions and suspicious activities. The regulators also received comments on both BSA/AML examination frequency and the frequency of safety and soundness examinations generally.

Agencies typically review BSA/AML compliance programs during safety and soundness examinations. As discussed previously, regulators allowed more institutions of outstanding or good composite condition to be examined every 18 months instead of every 12 months.[57] Institutions that qualify for less frequent safety-and-soundness examinations also will be eligible for less frequent BSA/AML examinations. For the remainder of the issues raised by commenters, the regulators noted they do not have the

---

[56] Credit unions are not included under the definition of depository institutions under the purpose of the Community Reinvestment Act.

[57] BSA/AML is examined as part of the bank's safety and soundness examination. Therefore, institutions with assets between $500 million and less than $1 billion that are now eligible for safety-and-soundness examinations every 18 months generally also will be subject to less frequent BSA reviews.

regulatory authority to revise the requirements but provided the comments to FinCEN, which has authority for these regulations. A letter with FinCEN's response to the comments was included as an appendix of the EGRPRA report. In the letter, the FinCEN Acting Director stated that FinCEN would work through the issues raised by the comments with its advisory group consisting of regulators, law enforcement staff, and representatives of financial institutions.

Additional Burden Reduction Actions

In addition to describing some changes in response to the comments deemed significant, the regulators' 2017 report also includes descriptions of additional actions the individual agencies have taken or planned to take to reduce the regulatory burden for banks, including community banks.

- The Federal Reserve Board noted that it changed its Small Bank Holding Company Policy Statement that allows small bank holding companies to hold more debt than permitted for larger bank holding companies.[58] In addition, the Federal Reserve noted that it had made changes to certain supervisory policies, such as issuing guidance on assessing risk management for banks with less than $50 billion in assets and launching an electronic application filing system for banks and bank holding companies.
- OCC noted that it had issued two final rules amending its regulations for licensing/chartering and securities-related filings, among other things. According to OCC staff, the agency conducted an internal review of its agency-specific regulations and many of the changes to these regulations came from the internal review. The agency also noted that it integrated its rules for national banks and federal savings associations where possible. In addition, OCC noted that it removed redundant and unnecessary

---

[58] The Federal Reserve Board's Small Bank Holding Company Policy Statement permits the formation and expansion of small bank holding companies with debt levels that are higher than typically permitted for larger bank holding companies. The policy excludes small bank holding companies, which own community banks, from certain consolidated capital requirements.

information requests from those made to banks before examinations.

- FDIC noted that it had rescinded enhanced supervisory procedures for newly insured banks and reduced the consumer examination frequency for small and newly insured banks. Similarly to OCC, FDIC is integrating its rules for both non-state member banks and state-chartered savings and loans associations. In addition, FDIC noted it had issued new guidance on banks' deposit insurance filings and reduced paperwork for new bank applications.

NCUA 2017 EGRPRA Process and Results

The 2017 report also presents the results of NCUA's concurrent efforts to obtain and respond to comments as part of the EGRPRA process. NCUA conducts its review separately from the bank regulators' review. In four *Federal Register* notices in 2015, NCUA sought comments on 76 regulations that it administers. NCUA received about 25 comments raising concerns about 29 of its regulations, most of which were submitted by credit union associations. NCUA received no comments on 47 regulations.

NCUA's methodology for its regulatory review was similar to the bank regulators' methodology. According to NCUA, all comment letters responding to a particular notice were collected and reviewed by NCUA's Special Counsel to the General Counsel, an experienced, senior-level attorney with overall responsibility for EGRPRA compliance. NCUA staff told us that criteria applied by the Special Counsel in his review included relevance, depth of understanding and analysis exhibited by the comment, and degree to which multiple commenters expressed the same or similar views on an issue. The Special Counsel prepared a report summarizing the substance of each comment. The comment summary was reviewed by the General Counsel and circulated to the NCUA Board and reviewed by the Board members and staff.

NCUA identified in its report the following as significant issues relating to credit union regulation: (1) field of membership and chartering; (2) member business lending; (3) federal credit union ownership of fixed assets; (4) expansion of national credit union share insurance coverage; and

(5) expanded powers for credit unions. For these, NCUA took various actions to address the issues raised in the comments. For example, NCUA modified and updated its field of credit union membership by revising the definition of a local community, rural district and underserved area, which provided greater flexibility to federal credit unions seeking to add a rural district to their field of membership. NCUA also lessened some of the restrictions on member lending to small business; and raised some of the asset thresholds for what would be defined as a small credit union so that fewer requirements would apply to these credit unions. Also, in April 2016, the NCUA Board issued a proposed rule that would eliminate the requirement that federal credit unions must have a plan by which they will achieve full occupancy of premises within an explicit time frame.[59] The proposal would allow for federal credit unions to plan for and manage their use of office space and related premises in accordance with their own strategic plans and risk-management policies.

Bank Regulators and NCUA 2007 EGRPRA Review Process and Results

The bank and credit union regulators' process for the 2007 EGRPRA review also began with *Federal Register* notices that requested comments on regulations. The regulators then reviewed and assessed the comments and issued a report in 2007 to Congress in which they noted actions they took in some of the areas raised by commenters.

Our analysis of the regulators' responses indicated that the regulators took responsive actions in a few areas. The regulators noted they already had taken action in some cases (including after completion of a pending study and as a result of efforts to work with Congress to obtain statutory changes). However, for the remaining specific concerns, the four regulators indicated that they would not be taking actions.

Similar to its response in 2017, NCUA discussed its responses to the significant issues raised about regulations in a separate section of the 2007 report. Our analysis indicated that NCUA took responsive actions in about

---

[59] *See* Federal Credit Union Occupancy, Planning, and Disposal of Acquired and Abandoned Premises; Incidental Powers, 81 Fed. Reg. 24738 (Apr. 27, 2016).

half of the areas. For example, NCUA adjusted regulations in one case and in another case noted previously taken actions. For comments related to three other areas, NCUA took actions not reflected in the 2007 report because the actions were taken over a longer time frame (in some cases, after 8 years). In the remaining areas, NCUA deemed actions as not being desirable in four cases and outside of its authority in two other cases.

Other Retrospective Reviews

The bank regulators do not conduct other retrospective reviews of regulations outside of the EGRPRA process. We requested information from the Federal Reserve, FDIC, and OCC about any discretionary regulatory retrospective reviews that they performed in addition to the EGRPRA review during 2012–2016. All three regulators reported to us they have not conducted any retrospective regulatory reviews outside of EGRPRA since 2012. However, under the Regulatory Flexibility Act (RFA), federal agencies are required to conduct what are referred to as section 610 reviews. The purpose of these reviews is to determine whether certain rules should be continued without change, amended, or rescinded consistent with the objectives of applicable statutes, to minimize any significant economic impact of the rules upon a substantial number of small entities.[60] Section 610 reviews are to be conducted within 10 years of an applicable rule's publication. As part of other work, we assessed the bank regulators' section 610 reviews and found that the Federal Reserve, FDIC, and OCC conducted retrospective reviews that did not fully align with the Regulatory Flexibility Act's requirements.[61] Officials at each of the agencies stated that they satisfy the requirements to perform section 610 reviews through the EGRPRA review process. However, we found that the requirements of the EGRPRA reviews differ from those of the RFA-required section 610 reviews, and we made recommendations to these regulators to help ensure their compliance with this act in a separate report issued in January 2018.

---

[60] *See* 5 U.S.C. § 610(a).
[61] GAO, *Financial Services Regulations: Procedures for Reviews under Regulatory Flexibility Act Need to Be Enhanced,* GAO-18-256 (Washington, D.C.: Jan. 30, 2018).

In addition to participating in the EGRPRA review, NCUA also reviews one-third of its regulations every year (each regulation is reviewed every 3 years). NCUA's "one-third" review employs a public notice and comment process similar to the EGRPRA review. If a specific regulation does not receive any comments, NCUA does not review the regulation. For the 2016 one-third review, NCUA did not receive comments on 5 of 16 regulations and thus these regulations were not reviewed. NCUA made technical changes to 4 of the 11 regulations that received comments.

In August 2017, NCUA staff announced they developed a task force for conducting additional regulatory reviews, including developing a 4-year agenda for reviewing and revising NCUA's regulations.[62] The primary factors they said they intend to use to evaluate their regulations will be the magnitude of the benefit and the degree of effort that credit unions must expend to comply with the regulations. Because the 4-year reviews will be conducted on all of NCUA's regulations, staff noted that the annual one-third regulatory review process will not be conducted again until 2020.

Limitations of Reviews of Burden Include CFPB Exclusion and Lack of Quantitative Analysis

Our analysis of the EGRPRA review found three limitations to the current process.

CFPB Not Included and Significant Mortgage Regulations Not Assessed

First, the EGRPRA statute does not include CFPB and thus the significant mortgage-related regulations and other regulations that it administers— regulations that banks and credit unions must follow—were not included in the EGRPRA review. Under the Dodd-Frank Act, CFPB was given financial regulatory authority, including for regulations

---

[62] *See* Regulatory Reform Agenda, 82 Fed. Reg. 39702 (Aug. 22, 2017).

implementing the Home Mortgage Disclosure Act (Regulation C); the Truth-in-Lending Act (Regulation Z); and the Truth-in-Savings Act (Regulation DD). These regulations apply to many of the activities that banks and credit unions conduct; the four depository institution regulators conduct the large majority of examinations of these institutions' compliance with these CFPB-administered regulations.[63] However, EGRPRA was not amended after the Dodd-Frank Act to include CFPB as one of the agencies that must conduct the EGRPRA review.

During the 2017 EGRPRA review, the bank regulators only requested public comments on consumer protection regulations for which they have regulatory authority. But the banking regulators still received some comments on the key mortgage regulations and the other regulations that CFPB now administers. Our review of 2017 forum transcripts identified almost 60 comments on mortgage regulations, such as HMDA and TRID.[64]

The bank regulators could not address these mortgage regulation-related comments because they no longer had regulatory authority over these regulations; instead, they forwarded these comment letters to CFPB staff. According to CFPB staff, their role in the most recent EGRPRA process was very limited. CFPB staff told us they had no role in assessing the public comments received for purposes of the final 2017 EGRPRA report. According to one bank regulator, the bank regulators did not share non-mortgage regulation-related letters with CFPB staff because those comment letters did not involve CFPB regulations. Another bank regulator told us that CFPB was offered the opportunity to participate in the outreach meetings and were kept informed of the EGRPRA review during the quarterly FFIEC meetings that occurred during the review. Before the report was sent to Congress, CFPB staff said that they

---

[63] CFPB has primary supervisory and enforcement authority for federal consumer protection laws for depository institutions with more than $10 billion in assets and for their affiliates. See 12 U.S.C. § 5515. The Federal Reserve, OCC, FDIC, and NCUA—which previously supervised and examined all depository institutions and credit unions for consumer protection—share with CFPB supervisory and enforcement authority for certain consumer protection laws for those depository institutions with more than $10 billion in assets and for their affiliates. In addition, they continue to supervise for consumer protection institutions n that have $10 billion or less in assets.

[64] A number of comments included statements on the Home Mortgage Disclosure Act, TRID, and Qualified Mortgage/Ability-to-Repay regulations.

reviewed several late-stage drafts, but generally limited their review to ensuring that references to CFPB's authority and regulations and its role in the EGRPRA process were properly characterized and explained. As a member of FFIEC, which issued the final report, CFPB's Director was given an opportunity to review the report again just prior to its approval by FFIEC.

CFPB must conduct its own reviews of regulations after they are implemented. Section 1022(d) of the Dodd-Frank Act requires CFPB to conduct an assessment of each significant rule or order adopted by the bureau under federal consumer financial law.[65] CFPB must publish a report of the assessment not later than 5 years after the effective date of such rule or order. The assessment must address, among other relevant factors, the rule's effectiveness in meeting the purposes and objectives of title X of the Dodd-Frank Act and specific goals stated by CFPB. The assessment also must reflect available evidence and any data that CFPB reasonably may collect. Before publishing a report of its assessment, CFPB must invite public comment on recommendations for modifying, expanding, or eliminating the significant rule or order.

CFPB announced in *Federal Register* notices in spring 2017 that it was commencing assessments of rules related to Qualified Mortgage/Ability-to-Repay requirements, remittances, and mortgage servicing regulations.[66] The notices described how CFPB planned to assess the regulations. In each notice, CFPB requested comment from the public on the feasibility and effectiveness of the assessment plan, data, and other factual information that may be useful for executing the plan; recommendations to improve the plan and relevant data; and data and other factual information about the benefits, costs, impacts, and effectiveness of the significant rule. Reports of these assessments are due in late 2018 and early 2019. According to CFPB staff, the requests for

---

[65] *See* Pub. L. No. 111-203, § 1022(d), 124 Stat. 1376, 1984 (2010) (codified at 12 U.S.C. § 5512(d)).

[66] *See* Request for Information Regarding Remittance Rule Assessment, 82 Fed. Reg. 15009 (March 24, 2017); Request for Information Regarding 2013 Real Estate Settlement Procedures Act Servicing Rule Assessment, 82 Fed. Reg. 21952 (May 11, 2017); and Request for Information Regarding Ability-to-Repay/Qualified Mortgage Rule Assessment, 82 Fed. Reg. 25246 (June 1, 2017).

data and other factual information are consistent with the statutory requirement that the assessment must reflect available evidence and any data that CFPB reasonably may collect. The *Federal Register* notices also describe other data sources that CFPB has in-house or has been collecting pursuant to this requirement.

CFPB staff told us that they have not yet determined whether certain other regulations that apply to banks and credit unions, such as the revisions to TRID and HMDA requirements, will be designated as significant and thus subjected to the one-time assessments. CFPB staff also told us they anticipate that within approximately 3 years after the effective date of a rule, it generally will have determined whether the rule is a significant rule for section 1022(d) assessment purposes.

In tasking the bank regulators with conducting the EGRPRA reviews, Congress indicated its intent was to require these regulators to review all regulations that could be creating undue burden on regulated institutions.

According to a Senate committee report relating to EGRPRA, the purpose of the legislation was to minimize unnecessary regulatory impediments for lenders, in a manner consistent with safety and soundness, consumer protection, and other public policy goals, so as to produce greater operational efficiency.[67] Some in Congress have recognized that the omission of CFPB in the EGRPRA process is problematic, and in 2015 legislation was introduced to require that CFPB—and NCUA—formally participate in the EGRPRA review.[68]

Currently, without CFPB's participation, key regulations that affect banks and credit unions may not be subject to the review process. In addition, these regulations may not be reviewed if CFPB does not deem them significant. Further, if reviewed, CFPB's mandate is for a one-time, not recurring, review. CFPB staff told us that they have two additional initiatives designed to review its regulations, both of which have been announced in CFPB's spring and fall 2017 Semiannual Regulatory Agendas. First, CFPB launched a program to periodically review individual

---

[67] Committee on Banking, Housing, and Urban Affairs, Economic Growth and Regulatory Paperwork Reduction Act of 1995, S. Rep. No. 104-185 (1995).
[68] *See* Financial Regulatory Improvement Act of 2015, S. 1484, § 125, 114th Cong.

existing regulations—or portions of large regulations—to identify opportunities to clarify ambiguities, address developments in the marketplace, or modernize or streamline provisions.[69] Second, CFPB launched an internal task force to coordinate and bolster their continuing efforts to identify and relieve regulatory burdens, including with regard to small businesses such as community banks that potentially will address any regulation the agency has under its jurisdiction. Staff told us the agency has been considering suggestions it received from community banks and others on ways to reduce regulatory burden. However, CFPB has not provided public information specifically on the extent to which it intends to review regulations applicable to community banks and credit unions and other institutions or provided information on the timing and frequency of the reviews. In addition, it has not indicated the extent to which it will coordinate the reviews with the federal depository institution regulators as part of the EGRPRA reviews. Until CFPB publicly provides additional information indicating its commitment to periodically review the burden of all its regulations, community banks, credit unions, and other depository institutions may face diminished opportunities for relief from regulatory burden.

Regulators Have Not Conducted or Reported Quantitative Analyses

Second, the federal depository institution regulators have not conducted or reported on quantitative analyses during the EGRPRA process to help them determine if changes to regulations would be warranted. Our analysis of the 2017 report indicated that in responses to comments in which the regulators did not take any actions, the regulators generally only provided their arguments against taking actions and did not cite analysis or data to support their narrative. In contrast, other federal agencies that are similarly tasked with conducting retrospective regulatory reviews are required to follow certain practices for such reviews that could

---

[69] CFPB announced in its fall 2017 Semiannual Regulatory Agenda that for its first review, the CFPB expects to focus primarily on subparts B and G of Regulation Z, which implement the Truth-in-Lending Act with respect to open-end credit generally and credit cards in particular.

serve as best practices for the depository institution regulators. For example, the Office of Management and Budget's Circular A-4 guidance on regulatory analysis notes that a good analysis is transparent and should allow qualified third parties reviewing such analyses to clearly see how estimates and conclusions were determined.[70] In addition, executive branch agencies that are tasked under executive orders to conduct retrospective reviews of regulations they issue generally are required under these orders to collect and analyze quantitative data as part of assessing the costs and benefits of changing existing regulations.[71]

However, EGRPRA does not require the regulators to collect and report on any quantitative data they collected or analyzed as part of assessing the potential burden of regulations. Conducting and reporting on how they analyzed the impact of potential regulatory changes to address burden could assist the depository institution regulators in conducting their EGRPRA reviews. For example, as discussed previously, Community Reinvestment Act regulations were deemed a significant issue, with commenters questioning the relevance of requiring small banks to make community development loans and suggesting that the asset threshold for this requirement be raised from $1 billion to $5 billion. The regulators told us that if the thresholds were raised, then community development loans would decline, particularly in underserved communities. However, regulators did not collect and analyze data for the EGRPRA review to determine the amount of community development loans provided by banks with assets of less than $1 billion; including a discussion of quantitative analysis might have helped show that community development loans from smaller community banks provided additional credit in communities—and

---

[70] Office of Management and Budget, *Regulatory Analysis*, Circular A-4 (Washington, D.C.: Sept. 17, 2003). As independent agencies, the depository institution regulators that conduct the EGRPRA review are not required to follow Circular A-4.

[71] GAO, *Reexamining Regulations Agencies Often Made Regulatory Changes, but Could Strengthen Linkages to Performance Goals*, GAO-14-268 (Washington D.C.: Apr. 11, 2014). In this report, we reviewed executive orders, including Executive Order 13563, "Improving Regulation and Regulatory Review," and Executive Order 13610, "Identifying and Reducing Regulatory Burdens." We found that the orders included eight primary requirements for executive branch agencies to follow when conducting retrospective reviews of regulations, including the need to conduct a quantifiable assessment of current costs and benefits of changing regulations.

thus helped to demonstrate the benefits of not changing the requirement as commenters requested.

By not performing and reporting quantitative analyses where appropriate in the EGRPRA review, the regulators may be missing opportunities to better assess regulatory impacts after a regulation has been implemented, including identifying the need for any changes or benefits from the regulations and making their analyses more transparent to stakeholders. As the Office of Management and Budget's Circular A-4 guidance on the development of regulatory analysis noted, sound quantitative estimates of costs and benefits, where feasible, are preferable to qualitative descriptions of benefits and costs because they help decision makers understand the magnitudes of the effects of alternative actions.[72] By not fully describing their rationale for the analyses that supported their decisions, regulators may be missing opportunities to better communicate their decisions to stakeholders and the public.

Reviews Have Not Considered Cumulative Effects of Regulations

Lastly, in the EGRPRA process, the federal depository institution regulators have not assessed the ways that the cumulative burden of the regulations they administer may have created overlapping or duplicative requirements. Under the current process, the regulators have responded to issues raised about individual regulations based on comments they have received, not on bodies of regulations. However, congressional intent in tasking the depository institution regulators with the EGRPRA reviews was to ensure that they considered the cumulative effect of financial regulations. A 1995 Senate Committee on Banking, Housing, and Urban Affairs report stated while no one regulation can be singled out as being the most burdensome, and most have meritorious goals, the aggregate burden of banking regulations ultimately affects a bank's operations, its profitability, and the cost of credit to customers.[73] For example, financial

---

[72] Office of Management and Budget, *Regulatory Analysis*, Circular A-4 (Washington, D.C.: Sept. 17, 2003).

[73] Committee on Banking, Housing, and Urban Affairs, Economic Growth and Regulatory Paperwork Reduction Act of 1995, S. Rep. No 104-185 (1995).

regulations may have created overlapping or duplicative regulations in the areas of safety and soundness. One primary concern noted in the EGRPRA 2017 report was the amount of information or data banks are required to provide to regulators. For example, the cumulative burden of information collection was raised by commenters in relation to Call Reports, Community Reinvestment Act, and BSA/AML requirements. But in the EGRPRA report, the regulators did not examine how the various reporting requirements might relate to each other or how they might collectively affect institutions.

In contrast, the executive branch agencies that conduct retrospective regulatory reviews must consider the cumulative effects of their own regulations, including cumulative burdens.[74] For example, Executive Order 13563 directs agencies, to the extent practicable, to consider the costs of cumulative regulations.[75] Executive Order 13563 does not apply to independent regulatory agencies such as the Federal Reserve, FDIC, OCC, NCUA, or CFPB. A memorandum from the Office of Management and Budget provided guidance to the agencies required to follow this order for assessing the cumulative burden and costs of regulations.[76] The actions suggested for careful consideration include conducting early consultations with affected stakeholders to discuss potential interactions between rulemaking under consideration and existing regulations as well as other anticipated regulatory requirements. The executive order also directs agencies to consider regulations that appear to be attempting to achieve the same goal. However, other researchers often acknowledge that cumulative assessments of burden are difficult. Nevertheless, until the Federal Reserve, FDIC, OCC, and NCUA identify ways to consider the cumulative burden of regulations, they may miss opportunities to streamline bodies of regulations to reduce the overall compliance burden among financial institutions, including community banks and credit unions. For example, regulations applicable to specific activities of banks, such as lending or

---

[74] See GAO-14-268 for additional information.
[75] *See* Exec. Order No. 13563, Improving Regulation and Regulatory Review, 76 Fed. Reg. 3821 (Jan. 21, 2011).
[76] The Office of Management and Budget additional guidance about Executive Order 13563 was issued on March 20, 2012.

capital, could be assessed to determine if they have overlapping or duplicative requirements that could be revised without materially reducing the benefits sought by the regulations.

CONCLUSION

New regulations for financial institutions enacted in recent years have helped protect mortgage borrowers, increase the safety and soundness of the financial system, and facilitate anti-terrorism and anti-money laundering efforts. But the regulations also entail compliance burdens, particularly for smaller institutions such as community banks and credit unions, and the cumulative burden on these institutions can be significant. Representatives from the institutions with which we spoke cited three sets of regulations—HMDA, BSA/AML, and TRID—as most burdensome for reasons that included their complexity. In particular, the complexity of TRID regulations appears to have contributed to misunderstandings that in turn caused institutions to take unnecessary actions. While regulators have acted to reduce burdens associated with the regulations, CFPB has not assessed the effectiveness of its TRID guidance. Federal internal control standards require agencies to analyze and respond to risks to achieving their objectives, and CFPB's objectives include addressing regulations that are unduly burdensome. Assessing the effectiveness of TRID guidance represents an opportunity to reduce misunderstandings that create additional burden for institutions and also affect individual consumers (for instance, by delaying mortgage closings).

The federal depository institution regulators (FDIC, Federal Reserve, OCC, as well as NCUA) also have opportunities to enhance the activities they undertake during EGRPRA reviews. Congress intended that the burden of all regulations applicable to depository institutions would be periodically assessed and reduced through the EGRPRA process. But because CFPB has not been included in this process, the regulations for which it is responsible were not assessed, and CFPB has not yet provided public information about what regulations it will review, and when, and whether it will coordinate with other regulators during EGPRA reviews. Until such information is publicly available, the extent to which the regulatory burden of CFPB regulation will be periodically addressed remains unclear. The effectiveness of the EGRPRA process also has been hampered by other limitations, including not conducting and reporting on depository institution regulators' analysis of quantitative data and assessing the cumulative effect of regulations on institutions. Addressing these limitations in their EGRPRA processes likely would make the analyses the regulators perform more transparent, and potentially result in additional burden reduction.

RECOMMENDATIONS FOR EXECUTIVE ACTION

We make a total of 10 recommendations, which consist of 2 recommendations to CFPB, 2 to FDIC, 2 to the Federal Reserve, 2 to OCC, and 2 to NCUA.

- The Director of CFPB should assess the effectiveness of TRID guidance to determine the extent to which TRID's requirements are accurately understood and take steps to address any issues as necessary. (Recommendation 1)
- The Director of CFPB should issue public information on its plans for reviewing regulations applicable to banks and credit unions, including information describing the scope of regulations the timing and frequency of the reviews, and the extent to which the reviews will be coordinated with the federal depository institution regulators as part of their periodic EGRPRA reviews. (Recommendation 2)
- The Chairman, FDIC, should, as part of the EGRPRA process, develop plans for their regulatory analyses describing how they will conduct and report on quantitative analysis whenever feasible to strengthen the rigor and transparency of the EGRPRA process. (Recommendation 3)

- The Chairman, FDIC, should, as part of the EGRPRA process, develop plans for conducting evaluations that would identify opportunities for streamlining bodies of regulation. (Recommendation 4)
- The Chair, Board of Governors of the Federal Reserve System, should, as part of the EGRPRA process develop plans for their regulatory analyses describing how they will conduct and report on quantitative analysis whenever feasible to strengthen the rigor and transparency of the EGRPRA process. (Recommendation 5)
- The Chair, Board of Governors of the Federal Reserve System, should, as part of the EGRPRA process, develop plans for conducting evaluations that would identify opportunities to streamline bodies of regulation. (Recommendation 6)
- The Comptroller of the Currency should, as part of the EGRPRA process, develop plans for their regulatory analyses describing how they will conduct and report on quantitative analysis whenever feasible to strengthen the rigor and transparency of the EGRPRA process. (Recommendation 7)
- The Comptroller of the Currency should, as part of the EGRPRA process, develop plans for conducting evaluations that would identify opportunities to streamline bodies of regulation. (Recommendation 8)
- The Chair of NCUA should, as part of the EGRPRA process, develop plans for their regulatory analyses describing how they will conduct and report on quantitative analysis whenever feasible to strengthen the rigor and transparency of the EGRPRA process. (Recommendation 9)
- The Chair of NCUA should, as part of the EGRPRA process, develop plans for conducting evaluations that would identify opportunities to streamline bodies of regulation. (Recommendation 10)

AGENCY COMMENTS AND OUR EVALUATION

We provided a draft of this chapter to CFPB, FDIC, FinCEN, the Federal Reserve, NCUA, and OCC. We received written comments from CFPB, FDIC, the Federal Reserve, NCUA, and OCC that we have reprinted in appendixes II through VI, respectively. CFPB, FDIC, FinCEN, the Federal Reserve, NCUA, and OCC also provided technical comments, which we incorporated as appropriate.

In its written comments, CFPB agreed with the recommendation to assess its TRID guidance to determine the extent to which it is understood. CFPB stated it intends to solicit public input on how it can improve its regulatory guidance and implementation support. In addition, CFPB agreed with the recommendation on issuing public information on its plan for reviewing regulations. CFPB committed to developing additional plans with respect to their reviews of key regulations and to publicly releasing such information and in the interim, CFPB stated it intends to solicit public input on how it should approach reviewing regulations.

FDIC stated that it appreciated the two recommendations and stated that it would work with the Federal Reserve and OCC to find the most appropriate ways to ensure that the three regulators continue to enhance their rulemaking analyses as part of the EGRPRA process. In addition, FDIC stated that as part of the EGRPRA review process, it would continue to monitor the cumulative effects of regulation through for example, a review of the community and quarterly banking studies and community bank Call Report data.

The Federal Reserve agreed with the two recommendations pertaining to the EGRPRA process. Regarding the need conduct and report on quantitative analysis whenever feasible to strengthen and to increase the transparency of the EGRPRA process, the Federal Reserve plans to coordinate with FDIC and OCC to identify opportunities to conduct quantitative analyses where feasible during future EGRPRA reviews. With respect to the second recommendation, the Federal Reserve agreed that the cumulative impact of regulations on depository institutions is important and plans to coordinate with FDIC and OCC to identify further opportunities to seek comment on bodies of regulations and how they could be streamlined.

NCUA acknowledged the report's conclusions as part of their voluntary compliance with the EGRPRA process; NCUA should improve its qualitative analysis and develop plans for continued reductions to regulatory burden within the credit union industry. In its letter, NCUA noted it has appointed a regulatory review task force charged with reviewing and developing a four-year plan for revising their regulations and the review will consider the benefits of NCUA's regulations as well as the burden they have on credit unions.

In its written comments, OCC stated that it understood the importance of GAO's recommendations. They stated they OCC will consult and coordinate with the Federal Reserve and FDIC to develop plans for regulatory analysis, including how the regulators should conduct and report on quantitative analysis and also, will work with these regulators to increase the transparency of the EGRPRA process. OCC also stated it will consult with these regulators to develop plans, as part of the EGRPRA process, to conduct evaluations that identify ways to decrease the regulatory burden created by bodies of regulations.

As agreed with your office, unless you publicly announce the contents of this chapter earlier, we plan no further distribution until 30 days from the report date. At that time, we will send copies to CFPB, FDIC, FinCEN, the Federal Reserve, NCUA, and OCC.

Sincerely yours,

Lawrance L. Evans, Jr.
Managing Director,
Financial Markets and Community Investment

APPENDIX I: OBJECTIVES, SCOPE, AND METHODOLOGY

This chapter examines the burdens that regulatory compliance places on community banks and credit unions and actions that federal regulators have taken to reduce these burdens; specifically: (1) the financial regulations that community banks and credit unions reported viewing as the most burdensome, the characteristics of those regulations that make them burdensome, and the benefits are associated with those regulations and (2) federal financial regulators' efforts to reduce any existing regulatory burden on community banks and credit unions.

To identify the regulations that community banks and credit unions viewed as the most burdensome, we first constructed a sample frame of financial institutions that met certain criteria for being classified as community banks or community-focused credit unions for the purposes of this review. These sample frames were then used as the basis for drawing our non-probability samples of institutions for purposes of interviews, focus group participation, and document review. Defining a community bank is important because, as we have reported, regulatory compliance may be more burdensome for community banks and credit unions than for larger banks because they are not able to benefit from economies of scale in compliance resources.[77] While there is no single consensus definition for what constitutes a community bank, we reviewed criteria for defining community banks developed by the Federal Deposit Insurance Corporation (FDIC), officials from the Independent Community Bankers Association, the Office of the Comptroller of the Currency (OCC).[78] Based on this review, we determined that institutions that had the following characteristics would be the most appropriate to include in our universe of institutions, (1) fewer total assets, (2) engage in traditional lending and deposit taking activities, have limited geographic scope, and (3) did not have complex operating structures.

To identify banks that met these characteristics, we began with all banks that filed a Consolidated Reports of Condition and Income (Call Report) for the first quarter of 2016 (March 31, 2016) and are not

---

[77] GAO, *Community Banks and Credit Unions: Impact of the Dodd-Frank Act Depends Largely on Future Rule Makings*. GAO-12-881 (Washington, D.C.: Sep. 13, 2012).

[78] See Federal Deposit Insurance Corporation, *Community Banking Study*, December 2012.

themselves subsidiaries of another bank that filed a Call Report.[79] We then excluded banks using an asset-size threshold, to ensure we are including only small institutions. Based on interviews with regulators and our review of the FDIC's community bank study, we targeted institutions around the $1 billion in assets as the group that could be relatively representative of the experiences of many community banks in complying with regulations. Upon review of the Call Reports data, we found that the banks in the 90th percentile by asset size were had about $1.2 billion, and we selected this to be an appropriate cutoff for our sample frame. In addition we excluded institutions with characteristics suggesting they do not engage in typical community banking activities like such as deposit-taking and lending; and those with characteristics suggesting they conduct more specialized operations not typical of community banking, such as credit card banks.[80] In addition to ensure that we excluded banks whose views of regulatory compliance might be influenced by being part of a large and/or complex organization, we also excluded banks with foreign offices and banks that are subsidiaries of either foreign banks or of holding companies with $50 billion or more in consolidated assets. Finally, as a practical matter, we excluded banks for which we could not obtain data on one or more of the characteristics listed below.

We also relied on a similar framework to construct a sample frame for credit unions. We sought to identify credit unions that were relatively small, engaged in traditional lending and deposit taking activities, and had limited geographic scope. To do this, we began with all insured credit unions that filed a Call Report for the first quarter of 2016 (March 31, 2016). We then excluded credit unions using an asset-size threshold of $860 million, which is the 95th percentile of credit unions, to ensure we are including only smaller institutions. The percentile of credit unions was higher than the percentile of banks because there are more large banks than there are credit unions. We then excluded credit unions that did not engage in activities that are typical of community lending, such as taking

---

[79] Every national bank, state member bank, insured state nonmember bank, and savings association is required to file a consolidated Call Report normally as of the close of business on the last calendar day of each calendar quarter.

[80] For example, we excluded banks that were considered credit card banks.

deposits, making loans and leases, and providing consumer checking accounts, as well as those credit unions with headquarters outside of the United States.

We assessed the reliability of data from FFIEC, FDIC, the Federal Reserve Bank of Chicago, and NCUA by reviewing relevant documentation and electronically testing the data for missing values or obvious errors, and we found the data from these sources to be sufficiently reliable for the purpose of creating sample frames of community banks and credit unions. The sample frames were then used as the basis for drawing our nonprobability samples of institutions for purposes of interviews and focus groups.

To identify regulations that community banks and credit unions viewed as among the most burdensome, we conducted structured interviews and focus groups with a sample of a total of 64 community banks and credit unions. To reduce the possibility of bias, we selected the institutions to ensure that banks and credit unions with different asset sizes and from different regions of the country were included. We also included at least one bank overseen by each of the three primary federal depository institution regulators, Federal Reserve, FDIC, NCUA, and OCC in the sample. We interviewed 17 institutions (10 banks and 7 credit unions) about which regulations their institutions experienced the most compliance burden. On the basis of the results of these interviews, we determined that considerable consensus existed among these institutions as to which regulations were seen as most burdensome, including those relating to mortgage fees and terms disclosures to consumers, mortgage borrower and loan characteristics reporting, and anti-money laundering activities.[81]

---

[81] Home Mortgage Disclosure Act and its implementing regulation, Regulation C (codified at 12 C.F.R. pt. 1003); BSA/AML statutes include the Currency and Foreign Transactions Reporting Act, commonly known as the Bank Secrecy Act (BSA), and the 2001 USA PATRIOT Act; Integrated Mortgage Disclosure Rule Under the Real Estate Settlement Procedures Act (Regulation X) and the Truth-in-Lending Act (Regulation Z) (codified at 12 C.F.R. pt. 1024 and 12 C.F.R. pt. 1026).

As a result, we determined to conduct focus groups with institutions to identify the characteristics of the regulations identified in our interviews that made these regulations burdensome. To identify the burdensome characteristics of the regulations identified in our preliminary interviews, we selected institutions to participate in three focus groups of community banks and three focus groups of credit unions.

- For the first focus group of community banks, we randomly selected 20 banks among 647 banks between $500 million and $1 billion located in nine U.S. census geographical areas using the sample frame of community banks we developed, and contacted them asking for their participation. Seven of the 20 banks agreed to participate in the first focus group. However, mortgages represented a low percentage of the assets of two participants in the first focus group, so we revised our selection criteria because two of the regulations identified as burdensome were related to mortgages.
- For the remaining two focus groups with community banks, we randomly selected institutions with more than $45 million and no more than $1.2 billion in assets to ensure that they would be required to comply with the mortgage characteristics reporting and with at least a 10 percent mortgage to asset ratio to better ensure that they would be sufficiently experienced with mortgage regulations. After identifying the large percentage of FDIC regulated banks in the first 20 banks we contacted, we decided to prioritize contact with banks regulated by OCC and the Federal Reserve for the institutions on our list. When banks declined or when we determined an institution merged or was acquired, we selected a new institution from that state and preferenced institutions regulated by OCC and the Federal Reserve.

The three focus groups totaled 23 community banks with a range of assets. We used a similar selection process for three focus groups of credit unions consisting of 23 credit unions. We selected credit unions with at least $45 million in assets so that they would be required to comply with the mortgage regulations and with at least a 10 percent mortgage-to-asset ratio.

During each of the focus groups, we asked the representatives from participating institutions what characteristics of the relevant regulations made them burdensome with which to comply. We also polled them about the extent to which they had to take various actions to comply with regulations, including hiring or expanding staff resources, investing in additional information technology resources, or conducting staff training. During the focus groups, we also confirmed with the participants that the three sets of regulations (on mortgage fee and other disclosures to consumers, reporting of mortgage borrower and loan characteristics, and anti-money laundering activities) were generally the ones they found most burdensome.

To identify in more detail the steps a community bank or credit union may take to comply with the regulations identified as among the most burdensome, we also conducted an in-depth on-site interview with one community bank. We selected this institution by limiting the community bank sample to only those banks in the middle 80 percent of the distribution in terms of assets, mortgage lending, small business lending, and lending in general that were no more than 70 miles from Washington, D.C. We limited the sample in this way to ensure that the institution was not an outlier in terms of activities or size, and to limit the travel resources needed to conduct the site visit.

We also interviewed associations representing consumers to understand the benefits of these regulations. These groups were selected using professional judgement of their knowledge of relevant banking regulations. We interviewed associations representing banks and credit unions.

To identify the requirements of the regulations identified as among the most burdensome, we reviewed the Home Mortgage Disclosure Act (HMDA) and its implementing regulation, Regulation C; Bank Secrecy Act and anti-money laundering (BSA/AML) regulations, including those deriving from the Currency and Foreign Transactions Reporting Act, commonly known as the Bank Secrecy Act (BSA), and the 2001 USA PATRIOT Act; and the Integrated Mortgage Disclosure Rule Under the Real Estate Settlement Procedures Act (RESPA) with the implementing Regulation X; and the Truth-in-Lending Act (TILA) with implementing Regulation Z. We reviewed the Consumer Financial Protection Bureau's (CFPB) small entity guidance and supporting materials on the TILA-RESPA Integrated Disclosure (TRID) regulation and HMDA to clarify the specific requirements of each rule and to analyze the information included in the CFPB guidance.

We interviewed staff from each of the federal regulators responsible for implementing the regulations, as well as from the federal regulators responsible for examining community banks and credit unions. To identify the potential benefits of the regulations that were considered burdensome by community banks and credit unions, we interviewed representatives from four community groups to document their perspectives on the benefits provided by the identified regulations.

To determine whether the bank regulators had required banks to comply with certain provisions from which the institutions might be exempt, we identified eight exemptions from the Dodd-Frank Wall Street Reform and Consumer Protection Act of 2010 from which community banks and credit unions should be exempt and reviewed a small group of the most recent examinations to identify instances in which a regulator may not have applied an exemption for which a bank was eligible.[82]

---

[82] Under CFPB's current rules, these exemptions included (1) a special category of qualified mortgage, which applies to creditors that, together with their affiliates, did not originate more than 2,000 first-lien covered transactions (excluding loans held in portfolio) in the preceding calendar year; had, with their affiliates that regularly extended covered transactions, less than $2 billion in assets at the end of the proceeding calendar year; and, for an exemption allowing the origination of balloon payment qualified mortgages, originated a first-lien covered transaction on a property located in a rural or underserved area in the proceeding calendar year; (2) escrow account exemption—which applies to

We reviewed 20 safety and soundness and consumer compliance examination reports of community banks and eight safety and soundness examination reports of credit unions. The bank examination reports we reviewed were for the first 20 community banks we contacted requesting participation in the first focus group. The bank examination reports included examinations from all three bank regulators (FDIC, Federal Reserve, and OCC). The NCUA examination reports we reviewed were for the eight credit unions that participated in the second focus group of credit unions. Because of the limited number of the examinations we reviewed, we cannot generalize whether regulators extended the exemptions to all qualifying institutions.

To assess the federal financial regulators' efforts to reduce the existing regulatory burden on community banks and credit unions, we identified the mechanisms the regulators used to identify burdensome regulations and actions to reduce potential burden. We reviewed laws and congressional and agency documentation. More specifically, we reviewed the Economic Growth and Regulatory Paperwork Reduction Act of 1996 (EGRPRA) that requires the Federal Reserve, FDIC, and OCC to review all their regulations every 10 years and identify areas of the regulations that are outdated, unnecessary, or unduly burdensome and reviewed the 1995 Senate Banking Committee report, which described the intent of the legislation.[83] We reviewed the *Federal Register* notices that bank regulators and NCUA published requesting comments on their regulations.

---

creditors that meet both the same small creditor, and small creditor operating in a rural or underserved area, requirements specified above for the qualified mortgage exemption; (3) TRID exemption—which applies to lenders that normally do not extend consumer credit; (4) appraisals for higher-priced mortgage exemption—which applies to creditors of mortgage transactions of $25,000 or less and creditors of certain manufactured home loans; (5) mortgage servicing exemption—which applies to servicers that service 5,000 and less mortgage loans; (6) international remittances exemption—which applies to companies that consistently provide 100 or fewer remittance transfers per year; (7) debit interchanges fee cap exemption—which applies to issuers, together with their affiliates, that have less than $10 billion in assets; and (8) regulatory capital rule stress test exemption—which applies to banks with less than $10 billion in total assets (they are not required or expected to conduct institution-wide stress testing).

[83] 12 U.S.C. § 3311; Committee on Banking, Housing, and Urban Affairs, Economic Growth and Regulatory Paperwork Reduction Act of 1995, S. Rep. No 104-185 (1995).

We also reviewed over 200 comment letters that the regulators had received through the EGRPRA process from community banks, credit unions, their trade associations, and others, as well as the transcripts of all six public forums regulators held as part the 2017 EGRPRA regulatory review efforts they conducted.

We analyzed the extent to which the depository institutions regulators addressed the issues raised in comments received for the review. In assessing the 2017 and 2007 EGRPRA reports sent to Congress, we reviewed the significant issues identified by the regulators and determined the extent to which the regulators proposed or took actions in response to the comments relating to burden on small entities.

We compared the requirements of Executive Orders 12866, 13563, and 13610 issued by Office of Management and Budget with the actions taken by the regulators in implementing their 10-year regulatory retrospective review. The executive orders included requirements on how executive branch agencies should conduct retrospective reviews of their regulations.

For both objectives, we interviewed representatives from CFPB, FDIC, Federal Reserve, Financial Crimes Enforcement Network, NCUA, and OCC to identify any steps that regulators took to reduce the compliance burden associated with each of the identified regulations and to understand how they conduct retrospective reviews. We also interviewed representatives of the Small Business Administration's Office of Advocacy, which reviews and comments on the burdens of regulations affecting small businesses, including community banks.

We conducted this performance audit from March 2016 to February 2018 in accordance with generally accepted government auditing standards. Those standards require that we plan and perform the audit to obtain sufficient, appropriate evidence to provide a reasonable basis for our findings and conclusions based on our audit objectives. We believe that the evidence obtained provides a reasonable basis for our findings and conclusions based on our audit objectives.

APPENDIX II: COMMENTS FROM THE CONSUMER FINANCIAL PROTECTION BUREAU

1700 G Street, N.W., Washington, DC 20552

January 18, 2018

Lawrence L. Evans, Jr.,
Managing Director, Financial Markets and Community Investment
Government Accountability Office
441 G Street, NW
Washington DC, 20548

Dear Mr. Evans:

Thank you for the opportunity to comment on the Government Accountability Office's (GAO) draft report, titled *Community Banks and Credit Unions: Regulators Could Take Additional Steps to Address Compliance Burdens (GAO-18-213)*. We greatly appreciate GAO's work over the course of this engagement and believe the report provides valuable insights regarding (1) the regulations that community banks and credit unions identified as being the most burdensome and (2) the efficacy of federal financial regulators' regulatory review programs.

The Bureau is committed to fulfilling its statutory objective of ensuring that outdated, unnecessary, or unduly burdensome regulations are regularly identified and addressed in order to reduce unwarranted regulatory burdens.[1] The Bureau recognizes the critical role community banks and credit unions play in the financial marketplace, and the unique challenges that regulatory compliance can pose for them. GAO's work in this report, including interviewing and conducting focus groups with representatives of over 60 community banks and credit unions, provides valuable information that will further inform the Bureau's work.

After identifying the regulations that community banks and credit unions stated were most burdensome, the report found that some of the burden affecting community banks and credit unions stemmed from misunderstandings of regulatory requirements, leading institutions to take actions not actually required. Specifically, GAO found that community banks and credit unions were confused about the Bureau's TILA-RESPA Integrated Disclosure rule (TRID). Therefore, GAO recommended that the Bureau "assess the effectiveness of TRID guidance to determine the extent to which TRID's requirements are accurately understood and take steps to address any issues as necessary."

The Bureau agrees with this recommendation and commits to evaluating the effectiveness of its guidance and updating it as appropriate. As such, the Bureau intends to solicit public input on how the Bureau can improve its regulatory guidance and implementation support.

---

[1] 12 U.S.C. 5511(b)(3).

GAO also examined how federal financial regulators addressed regulatory burden through regulatory review. With respect to the Bureau, GAO found that because the Bureau is not required to participate in the Economic Growth and Regulatory Paperwork Reduction Act of 1996 (EGRPRA) review process, key regulations that affect banks and credit unions may not be subject to review. Therefore, GAO recommended that the Bureau "issue public information on its plans for reviewing regulations applicable to banks and credit unions, including information describing the scope of regulations the timing and frequency of the reviews, and the extent to they will be coordinated with the federal depository institution regulators as part of their periodic EGRPRA reviews."

The Bureau agrees with this recommendation and commits to developing additional plans with respect to the review of key regulations and to publicly releasing such information. In the interim, the Bureau intends to solicit public input on how it should approach reviewing regulations.

The Bureau looks forward to continuing to work with GAO as it monitors the Bureau's progress in implementing these recommendations.

Sincerely,

David Silberman
Associate Director for Research, Markets, and Regulations

APPENDIX III: COMMENTS FROM THE BOARD OF GOVERNORS OF THE FEDERAL RESERVE SYSTEM

BOARD OF GOVERNORS OF THE FEDERAL RESERVE SYSTEM
WASHINGTON, D. C. 20551

MARK E. VAN DER WEIDE
GENERAL COUNSEL

January 11, 2018

Mr. Lawrance Evans, Jr.
Managing Director
Financial Markets and Community Investment
United States Government Accountability Office
441 G Street, N.W.
Washington, D.C. 20548

Dear Mr. Evans:

Thank you for providing the Board of Governors of the Federal Reserve System ("Federal Reserve" or "Board") with an opportunity to review the final draft of the Government Accountability Office ("GAO") report titled: *Community Banks and Credit Unions: Regulators Could Take Additional Steps to Address Compliance Burdens*.

(GAO-18-213). The draft report reviews compliance burdens reported by community banks and credit unions and the actions taken by depository institution regulators to address such burdens. We appreciate the report's recognition of the Federal Reserve's extensive efforts, in conjunction with the Office of the Comptroller of the Currency ("OCC") and the Federal Deposit Insurance Corporation ("FDIC"), to solicit and review public comments as part of the Economic Growth and Regulatory Paperwork Reduction Act of 1996 ("EGRPRA") process to identify and address significant areas of concern related to regulatory burden imposed on depository institutions.

The GAO's report makes two recommendations to the Federal Reserve regarding the EGRPRA process:

1. [D]evelop plans for the Federal Reserve's regulatory analyses describing how it will conduct and report on quantitative analysis whenever feasible to strengthen the rigor and transparency of the EGRPRA process[; and,]

2. [D]evelop plans for conducting evaluations that would identify opportunities to streamline bodies of regulation.

With respect to the GAO's first recommendation regarding plans to conduct and report on quantitative analysis in the EGRPRA process, when feasible, in order to increase transparency and rigor in the EGRPRA review, we agree that transparency and a rigorous review of the banking agencies' regulations are important aspects of the EGRPRA process. Of course, not every regulation lends itself to quantitative analysis, and certain regulations that the Federal Reserve is tasked with administering are required by law, which limits our discretion in their implementation. Notwithstanding these constraints, the Federal Reserve recently has conducted significant quantitative impact analyses in connection with some rule makings,[1] and we plan to continue to improve the quantitative and qualitative impact analysis we do of our regulations.

As you know, the EGRPRA review is conducted through an interagency process that requires the Federal Reserve, FDIC, and the OCC to jointly review their regulations. Consequently, the Federal Reserve plans to coordinate with the FDIC and the OCC to identify opportunities to conduct quantitative analyses, where feasible, during future EGRPRA reviews.

With respect to the GAO's second recommendation regarding identifying opportunities to streamline not only individual regulations but also bodies of regulation, we agree that the cumulative impact of our regulations on depository institutions is worthy of further review. We are mindful of the cumulative burden on depository institutions that all the regulations of the banking agencies may impose. Accordingly, the Federal Reserve plans to coordinate with the FDIC and the OCC to identify further opportunities to seek comment on bodies of regulation and how they could be streamlined.

We appreciate the GAO's review of the Federal Reserve's oversight of community banks, for its professional approach to the review, and for the opportunity to comment.

Sincerely,

Mark Van Der Weide

---

[1] See, for example, the final rules regarding (1) risk-based capital surcharges for global systemically important bank holding companies (GSIBs), and (2) total loss-absorbing capacity requirements, for GSIBs and U.S. intermediate holding companies of certain foreign banking organizations. 80 Fed. Reg. 49082 (August 14, 2015) and 82 Fed. Reg. 8266 (January 24, 2017), respectively.

APPENDIX IV: COMMENTS FROM THE FEDERAL DEPOSIT INSURANCE CORPORATION

Federal Deposit Insurance Corporation
550 17th Street NW, Washington, D.C. 20429-9990

Legal Division

January 19, 2018

Mr. Lawrance L. Evans, Jr., Managing Director
Financial Markets and Community Investment
U.S. Government Accountability Office
441 G Street, NW
Washington, D.C. 20548

Dear Mr. Evans:

Thank you for the opportunity to review and comment on the Government Accountability Office's (GAO) draft report entitled *COMMUNITY BANKS AND CREDIT UNIONS: Regulators Could Take Additional Steps to Address Compliance Burdens (GAO-18-213)* ("Report"). The Report reviews (1) the regulations community banks and credit unions viewed as most burdensome and why, and (2) the efforts taken by the depository institution regulators to reduce any regulatory burden.

The Report contains two recommendations to assist the FDIC, along with the Office of the Comptroller of the Currency ("OCC") and the Board of Governors of the Federal Reserve System ("FRB") (together the "agencies"), to further enhance the Economic Growth and Regulatory Paperwork Reduction Act of 1996 ("EGRPRA") review process. Specifically, the Report recommends that the FDIC, as part of the EGRPRA process, develop:

1. Plans for conducting and reporting quantitative analysis whenever feasible.
2. Plans that would identify opportunities for streamlining bodies of regulation.

We appreciate the two recommendations and will work with the OCC and the FRB to find the most appropriate ways to ensure that we continue to enhance our rulemaking analyses as part of the EGRPRA process. In particular, as the primary federal regulator of the majority of community banks in the United States, we are keenly aware that they are concerned about the burden of complying with regulations.

As noted in the Report, during the latest EGRPRA review process the agencies focused, consistent with the statute, on the significant issues raised by commenters. Comments were provided in writing in response to notices of regulatory review in the *Federal Register* as well as in person at outreach events, which focused on hearing the views of community bank panelists and other local stakeholders. This approach allowed the agencies to prioritize areas that were viewed by commenters as the most burdensome. As a result, the agencies have taken or are in the process of taking key initiatives – identified by commenters – to reduce burden. For example, the agencies (1) proposed increasing the appraisal threshold for commercial real estate transactions, (2) proposed amending the regulatory capital rules, particularly for community banks, and (3) are continuing the process of simplification of call reports, including the introduction of a streamlined call report (thus far removing 40 percent of the data items previously included in the report with about an additional 11 percent of data items expected to be removed effective June 30, 2018) available to the vast majority of community banks. Where possible and appropriate, the agencies gathered additional quantitative data through the notice and comment process to enable more in-depth analysis and review.

It is important to note, however, the difficulty and costs associated with quantifying regulatory costs, as described in Appendix B of the 2012 *FDIC Community Banking Study*. Community bankers interviewed in that study noted that it is difficult to separate regulatory costs from non-regulatory costs and any regulatory requirement for them to specifically identify regulatory costs would be, in itself, "very costly."[1] We note that in this Report the GAO also relied on structured interviews with focus groups of bankers to assess regulatory efforts to reduce existing regulatory burden. Moreover, the two cited studies published by the Credit Union National Association and the Mercatus Center also relied exclusively on non-quantitative survey results in assessing changes in regulatory costs. The choice of methodologies by the GAO and outside researchers cited in this Report reflects the difficulties in precisely quantifying the costs and benefits of specific regulations.

In addition, we note that the aggregate post-crisis performance of community banks has been a recurring area of research and analysis for the FDIC. Our analysis indicates that the post-crisis performance of community banks in terms of profitability and loan growth has been relatively strong in spite of the headwinds associated with relatively slow rates of economic growth and historically low levels of interest rates. This is a reliable and highly relevant measure of the cumulative effects of post-crisis regulatory reform that can help to inform policymakers. These results should not be ignored when assessing the cumulative effects of post-crisis regulation in the context of overall economic conditions.

Going forward, and as part of the EGRPRA review process, the FDIC will continue to monitor the cumulative effects of regulations through, for example, review of the community and quarterly banking studies and community bank call report data. And as noted earlier, we will work with the OCC and FRB to further enhance our EGRPRA processes and analyses where feasible and consistent with the statute.

Thank you for your efforts and if you have any questions or need additional follow-up information, please do not hesitate to contact us.

Sincerely,

Charles Yi
General Counsel

---

[1] FDIC Community Banking Study, at B-3, available at: https://www.fdic.gov/regulations/resources/cbi/report/cbsi-b.pdf.

Appendix V: Comments from the National Credit Union Administration

 National Credit Union Administration
Office of the Executive Director

January 16, 2018

SENT BY E-MAIL

Mr. Lawrence L. Evans, Jr.
Managing Director, Financial Markets and Community Investment
U.S. Government Accountability Office
441 G Street, NW
Washington, DC 20548
evansl@gao.gov

Dear Managing Director Evans:

We reviewed the GAO report, *Community Banks and Credit Unions – Regulators Could Take Additional Steps to Address Compliance Burdens*, which identifies regulations community banks and credit unions view as the most burdensome and discusses what regulators are doing to reduce regulatory burden.

We acknowledge the report's conclusions that, as part of the NCUA's continued voluntary compliance with the EGRPRA process, we should improve our quantitative analysis and develop plans for continued reductions to regulatory burden within the credit union industry. NCUA appointed a regulatory review task force charged with reviewing and developing a four-year plan for revising NCUA's regulations. This review will consider the benefit of our regulations as well as the burden they have on the credit unions we regulate.

Thank you for the opportunity to comment.

Sincerely,

Mark Treichel
Executive Director

Appendix VI: Comments from the Office of the Comptroller of the Currency

Office of the Comptroller of the Currency

Washington, DC 20219

February 01, 2018

Mr. Lawrance L. Evans, Jr.
Managing Director, Financial Markets and Community Investment
U. S. Government Accountability Office
Washington, DC 20548

Dear Mr. Evans:

The Office of the Comptroller of the Currency (OCC) has reviewed the Government Accountability Office's (GAO) draft report titled "Community Banks and Credit Unions Regulators Could Take Additional Steps to Address Compliance Burdens." The report examined (1) the regulations community banks and credit unions viewed as most burdensome and why, and (2) efforts by depository institution regulators to reduce any regulatory burden.

As part of this review, the GAO makes two recommendations to the OCC. The GAO recommends that the OCC should, as part of the Economic Growth and Regulatory Paperwork Reduction Act (EGRPRA) process, develop plans for regulatory analyses describing how the agency will conduct and report on quantitative analysis whenever feasible to strengthen the rigor and transparency of the EGRPRA process. The GAO also recommends that the OCC should, as part of the EGRPRA process, develop plans for conducting evaluations that would identify opportunities to streamline bodies of regulation.

The OCC appreciates the GAO's recommendations and understands their importance. As a result, the OCC will consult and coordinate with the Federal Reserve Board (Board) and the Federal Deposit Insurance Corporation (FDIC) to develop plans for the agencies' regulatory analyses, including how the agencies will conduct and report on quantitative analysis.

We note that the OCC already conducts impact assessments for proposed and final rules. These impact assessments inform the OCC about opportunities to reduce regulatory burden on national banks and Federal savings associations, including community banks. In addition, the OCC will work with the Board and the FDIC to increase the transparency of the EGRPRA process, while also considering the availability of data and legal constraints on the ability to disclose certain information. To supplement the OCC's ongoing efforts to review and streamline regulations while preserving the safety and soundness of the Federal banking system, the OCC will consult with the Board and the FDIC to develop, as part of the EGRPRA process, plans for conducting evaluations for identifying opportunities to decrease regulatory burden created by bodies of regulation.

Sincerely,

Karen Solomon
Acting Senior Deputy Comptroller and Chief Counsel

INDEX

A

advocacy, viii, 2, 9, 35, 40, 68, 83, 193
agencies, 11, 12, 15, 26, 39, 53, 82, 96, 97, 180, 186, 187, 193, 194, 203, 204, 212, 217, 218, 221, 222, 223, 224, 225, 228, 230, 233, 234, 236, 237, 249
amortization, 60, 61, 88
anti-money laundering efforts, viii, 178, 237
authority, 11, 14, 184, 186, 188, 193, 217, 225, 228, 229, 230
average costs, 47

B

balance sheet, 55, 74, 127, 220
bank holding companies, 12, 15, 187, 189, 225
bank populations, vii, viii, 2, 31, 110
Bank Secrecy Act, 12, 13, 17, 39, 53, 83, 177, 187, 188, 192, 200, 203, 244, 247
bankers, 26, 68
banking, viii, 2, 3, 9, 10, 15, 16, 43, 47, 55, 58, 65, 68, 73, 76, 96, 97, 98, 99, 110, 138, 161, 179, 180, 182, 184, 185, 186, 191, 217, 218, 219, 230, 235, 240, 243, 246
banking industry, 76
banking sector, 16
benefits, 16, 47, 59, 60, 65, 184, 193, 197, 201, 231, 234, 235, 237, 241, 242, 246, 247
bias, 23, 79, 80, 87, 102, 116, 244
board members, 9, 184
borrowers, 4, 18, 35, 38, 41, 65, 82, 94, 131, 132, 145, 146, 154, 155, 168, 169, 193, 195, 205, 209, 210, 224, 237
Bureau of Labor Statistics, 32, 48, 50, 64, 86, 107, 108, 111, 112, 116, 119, 121
business model, 119, 215
businesses, 3, 4, 6, 9, 14, 15, 18, 19, 23, 25, 27, 30, 31, 40, 65, 66, 70, 78, 80, 84, 85, 102, 201

C

cash, 12, 16, 187, 200, 202, 203
Census, 6, 32, 48, 50, 64, 84, 87, 89, 90, 107, 108, 111, 112, 116, 119, 121
central bank, 15, 189

commercial, 7, 10, 18, 19, 23, 27, 33, 37, 39, 78, 80, 101, 119, 127, 150, 185, 190, 194, 220, 222
commercial bank, 27, 190
community banks, v, vii, viii, 1, 2, 3, 4, 6, 7, 8, 9, 10, 11, 14, 15, 17, 18, 19, 20, 21, 22, 23, 24, 25, 26, 27, 29, 30, 31, 32, 34, 35, 36, 37, 38, 39, 40, 42, 43, 44, 45, 46, 47, 48, 49, 50, 51, 52, 53, 54, 55, 56, 57, 58, 59, 60, 61, 62, 63, 64, 65, 66, 67, 68, 70, 72, 73, 74, 75, 76, 77, 78, 79, 80, 81, 82, 83, 84, 85, 86, 87, 88, 89, 90, 92, 93, 94, 95, 96, 97, 100, 101, 102, 103, 106, 107, 108, 109, 110, 111, 112, 113, 116, 117, 119, 120, 121, 122, 123, 125, 127, 128, 129, 130, 131, 132, 133, 134, 135, 136, 137, 138, 139, 140, 141, 142, 143, 144, 145, 146, 147, 177, 178, 179, 180, 181, 182, 183, 184, 185, 186, 188, 189, 192, 193, 194, 195, 196, 197, 198, 201, 202, 205, 206, 207, 208, 210, 211, 212, 213, 214, 215, 216, 220, 225, 233, 234, 236, 237, 241, 242, 243, 244, 245, 246, 247, 248, 249
competition, 28, 82, 97, 98, 99, 101, 103, 105, 110, 116, 119, 126, 149
complement, 66, 86, 95, 203
complexity, 68, 237
compliance, viii, 4, 11, 13, 14, 15, 38, 42, 53, 60, 67, 68, 74, 83, 97, 99, 106, 141, 164, 178, 179, 182, 184, 186, 188, 189, 190, 191, 194, 195, 196, 199, 200, 201, 202, 205, 208, 211, 212, 214, 215, 217, 224, 226, 228, 230, 236, 237, 241, 242, 243, 244, 248, 249
computer software, 196
computer systems, 202
congressional hearings, 92
consumer advocates, 197
consumer protection, viii, 2, 6, 11, 14, 96, 177, 178, 181, 186, 188, 196, 212, 218, 222, 230, 232, 247

consumers, vii, 2, 14, 28, 40, 179, 184, 192, 205, 209, 210, 213, 222, 237, 244, 246
cost, 27, 47, 66, 68, 82, 83, 88, 97, 191, 197, 205, 206, 210, 217, 235
cost-benefit analysis, 210
costs of compliance, 68
credit market, 66
credit unions, v, vii, viii, 6, 7, 8, 10, 11, 12, 14, 17, 21, 28, 33, 34, 38, 41, 42, 43, 44, 46, 47, 49, 51, 54, 56, 57, 58, 59, 60, 61, 63, 65, 69, 70, 72, 76, 77, 80, 81, 82, 83, 84, 85, 86, 87, 88, 89, 90, 91, 92, 93, 94, 95, 97, 104, 114, 115, 121, 148, 149, 150, 151, 152, 153, 154, 155, 156, 157, 158, 159, 160, 161, 162, 163, 164, 165, 166, 167, 168, 169, 170, 177, 178, 179, 180, 181, 182, 183, 185, 186, 187, 188, 190, 192, 193, 194, 195, 196, 197, 198, 199, 201, 202, 205, 206, 207, 208, 210, 211, 212, 213, 214, 215, 216, 224, 227, 229, 230, 232, 236, 237, 238, 241, 242, 243, 244, 245, 246, 247, 248, 249
creditors, 15, 206, 213, 214, 247
creditworthiness, 35
criminal activity, 200
customer service, 5
customers, 6, 10, 12, 39, 53, 58, 70, 72, 82, 95, 139, 162, 181, 182, 185, 187, 200, 201, 204, 205, 208, 235

D

data analysis, 66, 93
data collection, 93, 94, 193, 194, 198
data set, 75, 107, 108
database, 93
demographic characteristics, 16
demographic factors, 53
Department of Agriculture, 53, 55, 86
Department of the Treasury, 12, 201
dependent variable, 99

Index

depository institution regulators, vii, viii, 11, 12, 15, 178, 179, 180, 181, 183, 187, 189, 214, 215, 216, 217, 222, 230, 233, 234, 235, 237, 238, 244
depository institutions, 6, 11, 12, 16, 18, 25, 120, 127, 186, 187, 198, 214, 216, 217, 223, 224, 230, 233, 237, 240, 249
deposits, 10, 12, 16, 50, 51, 52, 55, 56, 73, 74, 75, 77, 88, 101, 104, 114, 115, 117, 118, 120, 185, 187, 203, 244
direct cost, 190
disbursement, 128, 142, 151, 165
disclosure, 179, 193, 205, 206, 208, 209, 211
discrimination, 179, 197
distribution, 53, 71, 241, 246
diversification, 27, 105, 115, 118

E

economic downturn, 13
economic growth, 117, 120
economic indicator, 13
economic well-being, 6
economies of scale, 8, 45, 47, 48, 242
employees, 6, 57, 88, 132, 146, 155, 169, 218
employment, 6, 13, 57, 74, 77, 88
employment levels, 57
endogeneity, 100, 101, 102
enforcement, 11, 15, 16, 70, 96, 127, 150, 186, 195, 196, 203, 204, 230
environment, vii, 2, 3, 4, 6, 8, 9, 13, 17, 27, 28, 29, 32, 33, 34, 35, 36, 38, 39, 41, 42, 45, 46, 47, 48, 50, 51, 52, 53, 56, 57, 58, 60, 61, 62, 64, 65, 66, 67, 68, 69, 72, 81, 82, 83, 84, 88, 92, 93, 94, 95, 96, 97, 98, 99, 102, 105, 106, 107, 108, 109, 110, 111,112, 113, 126, 128, 129, 130, 131, 132, 133, 134, 135, 136, 137, 138, 139, 140, 142, 143, 144, 145, 146, 147, 150, 151, 152, 153, 154, 155, 156, 157, 158, 159, 160, 161, 162, 163, 165, 166, 167, 168, 169, 170
equity, 13, 28, 104, 113, 117, 120, 148, 171
ethnicity, 16, 193, 195
evidence, 9, 19, 26, 95, 184, 231, 232, 249
examinations, 11, 13, 17, 39, 68, 109, 183, 186, 194, 196, 197, 198, 200, 214, 215, 223, 224, 226, 230, 247
executive branch, 180, 234, 236, 249
executive orders, 234, 249

F

federal agency, 82
federal banking regulators, 16, 18, 127
Federal Bureau of Investigation, 204
federal funds, 103, 121
Federal Government, 27, 93
Federal Housing Finance Agency, 32, 48, 50, 64, 107, 108, 111, 112, 116, 119, 121
federal law, 200
Federal Register, 217, 218, 226, 227, 231, 248
federal regulations, 148, 171
Federal Reserve, 1, 5, 9, 11, 12, 13, 25, 26, 27, 32, 46, 47, 48, 49, 50, 52, 55, 64, 65, 66, 67, 68, 71, 75, 77, 78, 82, 83, 94, 95, 107, 108, 111, 112, 116, 119, 120, 121, 122, 123, 124, 125, 171, 178, 180, 183, 186, 187, 189, 193, 216, 217, 218, 219, 223, 225, 228, 230, 236, 237, 238, 239, 240, 241, 244, 245, 248, 249, 251
Federal Reserve Board, 123, 124, 125, 216, 225
financial, vii, viii, 2, 3, 5, 6, 7, 9, 10, 11, 12, 13, 14, 15, 16, 17, 18, 21, 24, 30, 35, 39, 42, 43, 44, 45, 46, 52, 53, 55, 57, 61, 62, 65, 66, 68, 69, 70, 72, 74, 77, 81, 83, 84, 85, 86, 87, 88, 89, 92, 93, 94, 95, 96, 97, 110, 122, 126, 127, 132, 141, 146, 149,

260 Index

150, 155, 164, 169, 178, 180, 181, 182, 184, 186, 187, 188, 191, 194, 196, 197, 200, 201, 202, 203, 204, 210, 213, 219, 221, 223, 225, 229, 231, 235, 236, 237, 242, 248
financial activities, vii, viii, 178
financial condition, 43, 46, 65, 69, 86, 184, 219, 221
Financial Crimes Enforcement Network, 2, 12, 178, 184, 204, 249
financial crisis, vii, 2, 3, 5, 13, 14, 17, 18, 21, 24, 30, 35, 44, 45, 52, 55, 61, 62, 65, 66, 89, 96, 110, 122, 126, 149, 181, 188, 197
financial data, viii, 2, 68, 74, 127
financial institutions, viii, 6, 10, 12, 14, 15, 17, 39, 53, 65, 83, 85, 92, 97, 121, 126, 127, 149, 150, 178, 181, 182, 185, 186, 187, 188, 190, 196, 198, 200, 202, 203, 204, 217, 225, 236, 237, 242
financial markets, 11, 186
financial performance, vii, viii, 2, 4, 6, 7, 42, 56, 57, 61, 65, 72, 77, 81, 83, 84, 85, 87, 88, 93, 94, 95
financial regulation, 141, 164, 180, 182, 191, 235, 242
financial reports, 18, 127
financial sector, 13, 16, 126, 149, 203
financial soundness, viii, 178
financial system, 65, 70, 204, 237
focus groups, 83, 92, 179, 183, 192, 193, 194, 195, 196, 199, 200, 201, 202, 205, 206, 208, 215, 244, 245, 246
foreign banks, 12, 120, 187, 243
funding, 114
fundraising, 201
funds, 11, 28, 128, 142, 151, 165, 186

G

growth, 6, 17, 28, 33, 53, 66, 76, 85, 101, 103, 114, 115, 117, 120
growth rate, 17, 76, 103, 114, 115, 117
guidance, 70, 179, 180, 204, 211, 212, 220, 222, 225, 226, 234, 235, 236, 237, 238, 240, 247
guidelines, 68, 194, 198, 199

H

holding company, 43, 46, 49, 51, 73, 85, 101
House of Representatives, 1, 72, 177, 181

I

income, 10, 18, 40, 60, 61, 63, 69, 74, 88, 102, 103, 117, 120, 127, 132, 146, 155, 169, 186, 193, 224
income tax, 61, 63
increased competition, 113
individuals, 26, 28, 76, 188
industry, vii, viii, 14, 15, 65, 69, 82, 92, 94, 97, 178, 180, 182, 188, 203, 210, 241
inflation, 3, 19, 20, 23, 25, 26, 76, 77, 78, 84, 85, 101, 202
information technology, 191, 246
institutions, vii, viii, 2, 4, 6, 7, 10, 11, 12, 14, 15, 16, 17, 18, 21, 22, 23, 24, 28, 32, 36, 37, 38, 39, 42, 43, 44, 45, 46, 47, 48, 49, 50, 51, 53, 54, 55, 56, 57, 58, 59, 60, 61, 63, 64, 65, 68, 69, 70, 72, 74, 77, 78, 79, 81, 82, 83, 84, 85, 86, 87, 88, 90, 92, 93, 94, 95, 96, 107, 108, 109, 111, 112, 116, 119, 120, 121, 125, 126, 127, 149, 178, 179, 181, 182, 183, 184, 185, 186, 187, 188, 189, 190, 191, 192, 193, 195, 196, 197, 198, 199, 200, 201, 202,

204, 208, 211, 212, 213, 214, 215, 216, 217, 218, 220, 222, 223, 224, 230, 232, 233, 236, 237, 238, 242, 243, 244, 245, 246, 247
intelligence, 12, 187, 203
interest rates, 28, 38, 41, 67, 114, 117, 120, 126, 149, 151, 152, 153, 154, 155, 156, 157, 158, 159, 160, 161, 162, 163, 165, 166, 167, 168, 169, 170, 197
issues, 9, 12, 35, 42, 66, 183, 187, 196, 212, 215, 216, 219, 220, 221, 224, 226, 227, 235, 238, 249

L

law enforcement, 200, 203, 204, 225
laws, 6, 11, 15, 16, 28, 96, 186, 192, 196, 230, 248
laws and regulations, 6, 16, 28, 192, 196
lending, vii, viii, 2, 3, 4, 5, 6, 7, 8, 9, 10, 15, 16, 17, 18, 19, 20, 21, 22, 23, 24, 25, 26, 27, 28, 29, 30, 31, 32, 33, 34, 35, 37, 38, 39, 40, 41, 42, 47, 57, 65, 66, 67, 68, 69, 70, 71, 72, 73, 77, 78, 79, 80, 81, 82, 83, 84, 85, 88, 89, 90, 91, 92, 93, 94, 95, 96, 98, 101, 102, 103, 104, 105, 110, 111, 117, 118, 119, 126, 127, 129, 143, 148, 149, 150, 152, 166, 171, 179, 181, 182, 183, 185, 186, 193, 195, 196, 197, 205, 206, 210, 226, 236, 242, 243, 246
lending process, vii, viii, 2, 4, 6, 34, 35, 38, 39, 40, 41, 42, 72, 210
loans, vii, 2, 3, 4, 7, 8, 10, 13, 17, 18, 19, 22, 23, 24, 25, 26, 27, 28, 29, 30, 31, 32, 33, 35, 36, 37, 38, 39, 40, 41, 42, 55, 56, 65, 66, 69, 70, 73, 74, 77, 78, 79, 80, 81, 82, 84, 85, 87, 88, 90, 94, 99, 101, 102, 104, 109, 110, 111, 117, 118, 119, 120, 127, 128, 130, 131, 132, 133, 142, 144, 145, 146, 147, 148, 150, 151, 153, 154, 155, 156, 165, 167, 168, 169, 170, 171,

185, 186, 195, 196, 198, 199, 205, 207, 208, 210, 213, 214, 220, 221, 222, 224, 226, 234, 244, 247
local community, 184, 227

M

majority, 4, 12, 29, 34, 39, 41, 43, 44, 45, 52, 53, 67, 68, 109, 187, 191, 196, 201, 214, 230
management, 8, 9, 52, 57, 68, 89, 91, 92, 94, 126, 127, 149, 150, 184, 216, 219, 222, 223, 227
market concentration, 104
market share, 7, 42, 55, 56, 88
marketplace, 99, 233
materials, 212, 247
mergers, 3, 4, 7, 8, 43, 44, 45, 47, 48, 49, 64, 75, 77, 85, 96, 98, 105, 106, 107, 110, 116, 120
methodology, 9, 18, 35, 42, 46, 52, 53, 57, 62, 67, 76, 78, 83, 100, 125, 148, 184, 226
models, viii, 2, 4, 8, 28, 29, 31, 81, 84, 88, 97, 98, 99, 100, 102, 103, 104, 105, 106, 110, 111, 113, 116, 119, 185
money laundering, viii, 12, 17, 39, 53, 83, 177, 178, 181, 184, 187, 192, 200, 218, 237, 244, 246, 247
multiple factors, 36, 37, 52
multiple-choice questions, 126, 149

O

officials, 9, 15, 18, 19, 23, 25, 26, 27, 37, 40, 46, 55, 65, 66, 67, 68, 69, 70, 74, 75, 77, 79, 81, 83, 85, 87, 95, 97, 189, 197, 199, 203, 204, 209, 210, 218, 221, 242
operating costs, 68
operating revenue, 60, 61

operations, 8, 61, 67, 73, 113, 191, 218, 235, 243
opportunities, 15, 53, 69, 70, 233, 235, 236, 237, 239, 240
outreach, 26, 93, 94, 180, 230
oversight, 6, 14, 65, 106, 181, 188, 216
overtime, 132, 146, 155, 169
ownership, 21, 121, 202, 204, 226

P

participants, 68, 81, 83, 87, 94, 97, 99, 127, 148, 150, 171, 194, 196, 199, 200, 201, 202, 206, 208, 212, 222, 245, 246
policy, 27, 65, 68, 95, 197, 211, 224, 225
policy issues, 27
policymakers, 3, 27, 71, 196, 197
population, 4, 7, 19, 20, 21, 22, 23, 24, 28, 30, 31, 36, 37, 38, 43, 44, 53, 55, 61, 62, 68, 76, 79, 87, 89, 90, 92, 102, 103, 109, 114, 119, 120, 121, 125, 148, 191
population density, 28, 53, 55, 87
population growth, 114, 120
price index, 103, 121
private investment, 197
probability, 92, 182, 242
profitability, 4, 7, 47, 53, 54, 57, 61, 62, 63, 67, 88, 97, 102, 191, 235

R

real estate, 19, 37, 40, 78, 80, 101, 104, 118, 119, 120, 127, 220, 222
recommendations, iv, 3, 5, 179, 203, 228, 231, 238, 240, 241
reforms, 6, 14, 15, 97, 181, 188, 189
regression, 29, 98, 100, 101, 102, 105, 106, 107, 108, 111, 112, 113, 114, 117, 120
regression model, 29, 98, 102, 105, 107, 108, 111, 112

regulations, vii, viii, 2, 5, 7, 11, 12, 14, 15, 16, 26, 28, 39, 53, 57, 69, 83, 96, 97, 98, 103, 106, 122, 126, 150, 178, 179, 180, 181, 182, 183, 184, 187, 188, 189, 190, 192, 193, 200, 201, 205, 206, 207, 211, 212, 213, 214, 215, 217, 218, 219, 224, 225, 226, 227,228, 229, 230, 231, 232, 233, 234, 235, 236, 237, 238, 240, 241, 242, 243, 244, 245, 246, 247, 248, 249
regulatory agencies, 14, 188, 236
regulatory changes, vii, viii, 2, 4, 5, 9, 28, 31, 40, 42, 67, 68, 69, 70, 99, 105, 106, 107, 108, 109, 110, 111, 112, 113, 116, 119, 189, 234
regulatory requirements, 6, 11, 96, 97, 181, 186, 191, 236
researchers, 9, 49, 67, 81, 87, 190, 191, 197, 236
response, 6, 14, 26, 27, 42, 47, 55, 56, 65, 68, 88, 89, 91, 95, 127, 128, 129, 130, 131, 132, 133, 134, 135, 136, 137, 138, 139, 140, 142, 143, 144, 145, 146, 147, 148, 150, 151, 152, 153, 154, 155, 156, 157, 158, 159, 160, 161, 162, 163, 165, 166, 167, 168, 169,170, 171, 188, 191, 193, 198, 203, 212, 217, 219, 220, 221, 222, 225, 227, 249
restrictions, 10, 14, 18, 49, 185, 188, 227
risk, 15, 68, 69, 96, 97, 189, 192, 200, 204, 213, 222, 223, 225, 227
risk aversion, 96
risk management, 225
risk profile, 68
rules, 11, 68, 69, 95, 97, 181, 182, 184, 186, 191, 195, 197, 201, 203, 213, 214, 217, 218, 219, 220, 223, 225, 226, 228, 231, 247

S

safety, 11, 16, 40, 65, 70, 186, 218, 219, 222, 223, 224, 232, 236, 237, 248
savings, 12, 27, 74, 187, 190, 225, 226, 243
savings account, 190
scale economies, 99, 106
semi-structured interviews, 83
services, iv, 9, 14, 38, 41, 59, 60, 82, 83, 94, 95, 97, 126, 129, 143, 149, 152, 166, 184, 188, 191, 205, 207, 208, 209
small business, vii, viii, 2, 3, 4, 5, 6, 7, 8, 10, 13, 15, 17, 18, 19, 20, 21, 22, 23, 24, 25, 26, 27, 28, 29, 31, 32, 33, 34, 35, 36, 37, 38, 39, 40, 41, 42, 57, 65, 66, 67, 68, 69, 70, 71, 72, 77, 78, 79, 80, 81, 83, 84, 85, 88, 89, 90, 91, 92, 93, 95, 96, 98, 99, 101, 105, 109, 110, 111, 117, 119, 127, 128, 129, 130, 131, 132, 133, 181, 185, 217, 227, 233, 246, 249
small business lending, v, vii, viii, 1, 2, 3, 4, 6, 7, 8, 10, 15, 17, 18, 19, 20, 21, 22, 23, 24, 25, 26, 27, 28, 29, 31, 32, 33, 34, 35, 38, 39, 40, 41, 42, 57, 65, 66, 67, 68, 69, 70, 72, 77, 78, 80, 81, 83, 84, 85, 88, 90, 91, 92, 93, 95, 96, 98, 101, 105, 109, 110, 111, 117, 118, 119, 124, 127, 129, 185, 246
sources of credit, vii, 2
statutes, 13, 188, 196, 200, 207, 228, 244

T

tax evasion, 200
technical assistance, 68
technical comments, 71, 240
technological advancement, 8
technological advances, 53, 58
technological change, 26, 28, 32, 70, 82, 88, 99, 110, 126, 149
technology, 53, 58, 97, 122, 138, 161, 191
terrorism, 17, 181, 201, 203, 237
terrorist attacks, 181
testing, 39, 74, 75, 77, 81, 86, 87, 194, 198, 244
time frame, 205, 209, 227, 228
transactions, 12, 17, 53, 179, 187, 194, 200, 201, 202, 209, 213, 214, 223, 224, 247
transcripts, viii, 94, 179, 183, 230, 249
transparency, 196, 197, 210, 238, 239, 240, 241
treatment, 69, 100, 101, 107, 108, 213, 215, 220

U

U.S. economy, 13
unemployment rate, 13, 28, 120, 121, 126, 149
union representatives, 42, 52, 54, 57, 69, 70, 81, 83, 93, 94, 95, 148, 192
unions, vii, viii, 6, 7, 8, 10, 11, 12, 14, 17, 21, 28, 33, 34, 41, 42, 43, 44, 46, 49, 51, 54, 56, 57, 58, 59, 60, 61, 63, 65, 69, 70, 72, 76, 77, 80, 81, 82, 83, 84, 85, 86, 87, 89, 90, 91, 92, 93, 94, 95, 104, 114, 115, 121, 148, 149, 150, 151, 152, 153, 154,155, 156, 157, 158, 159, 160, 161, 162, 163, 165, 166, 167, 168, 169, 170, 178, 179, 180, 181, 182, 183, 185, 186, 187, 188, 190, 192, 193, 194, 195, 196, 197, 198, 199, 201, 202, 205, 206, 208, 210, 211, 212, 213, 214, 215, 216, 224, 227, 229, 230, 232, 236, 237, 238, 241, 242, 243, 244, 246, 247, 248
urban, 8, 53, 55, 83, 86, 89, 90, 91, 95

V

variables, 8, 28, 99, 100, 101, 102, 103, 104, 114, 115, 116, 117, 118, 119

Related Nova Publications

Electronic Commerce: Technologies, Challenges and Future Prospects

Editor: Costanzo Mazzanti

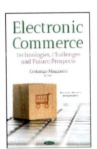

Series: Banks and Banking Developments

Book Description: In chapter one, Mark T. Leung, Shaotao Pan, and Minghe Sun introduce and evaluate a range of data analytic methods that are frequently implemented in e-commerce research, providing readers with important insight.

Hardcover ISBN: 978-1-53612-505-4
Retail Price: $160

U.S. Financial Regulatory Structure: Overview, Complexities, and the Effects of Fragmentation and Overlap

Editor: Laurence Watson

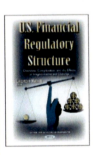

Series: Banks and Banking Developments

Book Description: This book provides an overview of the regulatory policies of the agencies that oversee banking and securities markets and explains which agencies are responsible for which institutions, activities, and markets.

Hardcover ISBN: 978-1-63485-636-2
Retail Price: $150

To see a complete list of Nova publications, please visit our website at www.novapublishers.com

Related Nova Publications

BANK REGULATION: PROPOSED RELIEF LEGISLATION AND BURDEN ON SMALL BANKS

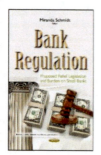

EDITOR: Miranda Schmidt

SERIES: Banks and Banking Developments

BOOK DESCRIPTION: This book assesses banking regulatory relief proposals contained in bills that have been marked up by committee or have seen floor action in the 114th Congress; explains the concept of regulatory burden and the different ways it can be manifested; and analyzes whether small banks are relatively more burdened by regulation than big banks.

HARDCOVER ISBN: 978-1-63485-520-4
RETAIL PRICE: $150

BANK FAILURES AND REGULATORY RESPONSES: LESSONS AND OVERSIGHT EFFORTS

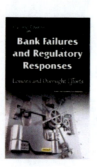

EDITOR: Pauline Owens

SERIES: Banks and Banking Developments

BOOK DESCRIPTION: This book discusses regulatory lessons learned from these past crises and offers a framework that the Government Accountability Office and other oversight bodies, such as inspectors general, can use to provide continuous future oversight of regulatory responses to emerging risks.

HARDCOVER ISBN: 978-1-63484-234-1
RETAIL PRICE: $140

To see a complete list of Nova publications, please visit our website at www.novapublishers.com